*Second Edition*

# Community Organizing in a Diverse Society

**Felix G. Rivera**
*San Francisco State University*

**John L. Erlich**
*California State University, Sacramento*

**Allyn & Bacon**
Boston • London • Toronto • Sydney • Tokyo • Singapore

*To Vicky,*
*Sophia and Olivia*

*To Kathleen*
*and*
*Lynn, Kathy, John and Megan*

*To people of color*
*struggling to achieve their rightful*
*share of the American dream*
*and*
*their own dreams*

Executive Editor: Karen Hanson
Managing Editor: Judy S. Fifer
Vice President and Publisher, Social Sciences: Susan Badger
Editorial Assistant: Sarah L. Dunbar
Production Editor: Catherine Hetmansky
Cover Administrator: Suzanne Harbison
Composition Buyer: Linda Cox
Manufacturing Buyer: Louise Richardson
Editorial-Production Service: Ruttle, Shaw & Wetherill, Inc.
Executive Marketing Manager: Joyce Nilsen

*Library of Congress Cataloging-in-Publication Data*

Community organizing in a diverse society / [edited by] Felix G.
Rivera, John L. Erlich.—2nd ed.
    p.  cm.
Includes bibliographical references and index.
ISBN 0205156207
1. Community development—United States. 2. Minorities—Housing—
United States, 3. Community organization—United States.
4. Neighborhood—United States. I. Rivera, Felix G. II. Erlich,
John.
HN90.C6C6633  1995
307.1'0973—dc20                                      94–26040
                                                        CIP

Printed in the United States of America

10  9  8  7  6  5  4  3  2  1      99  98  97  96  95  94

# Contents

**Contributors**     v

**Preface**     viii

**In Memoriam: Cesar Chavez**     x

1  **A Time of Fear; A Time of Hope**     1
by Felix G. Rivera and John L. Erlich

2  **Community Development with Native Americans**     25
by E. Daniel Edwards and Margie Egbert Edwards

3  **Chicanos, Communities, and Change**     43
by Miguel Montiel and Felipe Ortego y Gasca

4  **Organizing for Violence Prevention: An African-American Community Perspective**     61
by Wynetta Devore

5  **Community Social Work with Puerto Ricans in the United States**     77
by Julio Morales

6  **A Feminist Perspective on Organizing with Women of Color**     95
by Lorraine M. Gutierrez and Edith A. Lewis

7  **Organizing in the Chinese-American Community: Issues, Strategies, and Alternatives**    **113**
   by Peter Ching-Yung Lee

8  **Organizing in the Japanese-American Community**    **143**
   by Kenji Murase

9  **The Pilipino-American Community: Organizing for Change**    **161**
   by Royal F. Morales

10  **Organizing with Central-American Immigrants in the United States**    **177**
   by Carlos B. Córdoba

11  **Southeast Asians in the United States: A Strategy for Accelerated and Balanced Integration**    **197**
   by Vu-Duc Vuong

12  **Community Development and Community Restoration: A Perspective**    **217**
   by Antonia Pantoja and Wilhelmina Perry

13  **Epilogue: Reaching toward the Twenty-First Century—Fraud in the Inducement?**    **243**
   by Felix G. Rivera and John L. Erlich

**Appendix: Examples from Training Manual, Center for Third World Organizing**    **259**

**Glossary of Selected Organizing Terms**    **269**

**Index**    **271**

# Contributors

**Carlos B. Córdoba, Ed.D.,** is an associate professor in the School of Ethnic Studies, San Francisco State University, California, where he teaches in La Raza Studies. He has published numerous articles on refugee issues, including a portfolio of his photographs taken in El Salvador.

**Felipe Ortego y Gasca, Ph.D.,** is a professor of English at Arizona State University. He has taught English and Chicano literature at various universities. He is a long-time activist.

**Wynetta Devore, Ph.D.,** is a professor at the School of Social Work, Syracuse University, New York, where she teaches practice. Dr. Devore is co-author of *Ethnic-Sensitive Social Work Practice.*

**Daniel E. Edwards, D.S.W.,** is an associate professor at the Graduate School of Social Work, University of Utah. He is a member of the Yurok tribe, and a long-time director of the American Indian Social Work Program at the university. His varied publications reflect his broad concern for Native American cultures.

**Margie Egbert-Edwards, Ph.D.,** is a professor of social work at the Graduate School of Social Work, University of Utah; she is the former codirector of the American Indian Social Work Career Training Program.

**John L. Erlich, A.B.D.,** is a professor in the Division of Social Work at California State University, Sacramento, where he chairs the Child and Family Services Concentration and teaches child and family macro practice courses. He has worked as an organizer in New York City, Michigan, and Sacramento. Professor Erlich has served as a planning and organizing consultant to numerous community-based organizations. He has published extensively in the areas of community organization and planning, social change, emerging minority communities, and burnout. Among the books he has coauthored or edited are *Changing Organizations and Community Programs, Tactics and Techniques of Community Practice,* and *Strategies of Community Organization.*

**Lorraine M. Gutiérrez, Ph.D.,** is an assistant professor, School of Social Work, University of Washington. She teaches courses in Community and Organizational Services and in the Concentration on Women and Minorities. Her publications have added to the theories about empowerment and women of color. Dr. Gutiérrez has extensive experience organizing against violence against women, particularly within urban, multiethnic communities.

**Peter C. Y. Lee, Ph.D.,** is a professor at the College of Social Work and director of the Center for Human Service. He has worked with numerous community organizations such as the Asian Americans for Community Involvement, vice president of the American Cancer Society, president of Chinese American Economic and Technology Development Association, and currently serves as president of South Bay Charity Cultural Service Center. Dr. Lee has written or edited several books, including *Social Policy Analysis: Theory and Practice* (1994) and *Dimensions of Social Welfare Transition* (1988). He is also on the editorial board of the *Journal of Social Development Issues* and now serves as secretary-general of the Inter-University Consortium for International Social Development.

**Edith A. Lewis, Ph.D.,** is an assistant professor at the School of Social Work, University of Michigan, where she teaches practice. She has done research on social support systems and low-income mothers, and role strain in African-American women. Her publications cover such diverse topics as students of color, socialization, and social supports as a prevention strategy.

**Miguel Montiel, Ph.D.,** is a professor in the School of Public Affairs at Arizona State University. He has served as assistant vice president for academic affairs at A.S.U. and has taught social research, policy, and Chicano issues in social work at the University of California, Berkeley, and at Arizona State University.

**Julio Morales, Ph.D.,** is a Professor at the School of Social Work, University of Connecticut. A long-time activist, he has been instrumental in founding Puerto Rican Studies Projects and numerous social service agencies and programs in New York, Massachusetts, and Connecticut.

**Royal Morales, M.S.W.,** is a long-time community activist in the Los Angeles Pilipino community. He teaches field work at U.C.L.A. and the Pilipino Experience in Asian American Studies program. He has been the past director of NASW's Region I, as well as NASW's representative to the Committee to Rebuild Los Angeles. His organizing work has emphasized alcohol-related services for Pilipino and Tongan youth. Mr. Morales builds and demonstrates the art of Pilipino kites. His kites have been represented at cultural fairs, on television, and in museums.

**Kenji Murase, D.S.W.,** is a retired professor from the Department of Social Work Education, San Francisco State University. His areas of teaching and Community involvement are minority issues, research, and program planning and development, to mention a few. He is noted for his teaching, research, and grantsmanship skills, and many publications pertaining to Asian-American communities.

**Antonia Pantoja, Ph.D.,** has taught at the schools of social work at Columbia University and the University of Puerto Rico. She has also taught at the New School for Social Research, New York. She has been responsible for the development of such organizations as the Puerto Rican Association for Community Affairs, The Puerto Rican Forum, Aspira, and Boricua College. In 1984 she began to work with residents to organize Producir, Inc., a community economic development corporation in Canovanas, Puerto Rico. Dr. Pantoja's publications reflect a broad-based commitment to multicultural approaches to social change and community development. She is also a consulting editor to the *Journal of Progressive Human Services.*

**Wilhelmina Perry, Ph.D.,** was a faculty member at the School of Social Work, Stony Brook, N.Y. Dr. Perry has been adjunct faculty for students in alternative educational programs, such as the Union Graduate School, Rural Development Leadership Network and the Western Institute for Social Research. She, with Dr. Pantoja, resigned her tenured faculty position at the School of Social Work, San Diego State University, to organize, administer, and teach at the Graduate School for Community Development, a private alternative educational institution working with low-income and people of color learners from communities around the United States. She helped establish, with Dr. Pantoja, Producir, Inc. She is a consulting editor to the *Journal of Progressive Human Services.*

**Felix G. Rivera, Ph.D.,** is a professor in the Department of Social Work Education, San Francisco State University, where he chairs the Social Development Concentration. He also teaches social and evaluative research. Dr. Rivera has been a grass-roots organizer and has worked with numerous community-based organizations as a planner, program developer, and evaluator. His research and numerous publications range in subject from emerging and changing communities of color and social change, to the application of Bushido (martial arts) strategies to community organizing and decision-making. He is on the editorial boards of the *Journal of Community Practice, Journal of Progressive Human Services,* and the *Humboldt Journal of Social Relations.*

**Vu-Duc Vuong, M. A., M.S.W., J.D.,** is executive director and economic development specialist with the Southeast Asian Refugee Resettlement Center. He was born in Nam Dinh, Vietnam, and came to the United States in 1968. Mr. Vuong is highly visible throughout the refugee communities in the San Francisco Bay Area both as an economic developer and as a social activist. Mr. Vuong was the first Vietnamese American to run for political office in San Francisco, California. He is the president of the Southeast Asian Chamber of Commerce, another vehicle to promote trade and understanding between the United States and Southeast Asia.

# *Preface*

Maybe it was the smells.

Even more than the sights and sounds, the neighborhoods where we grew up were defined by smells. Aromas of frying pork and plantains, simmering pasta and sausage, boiling cabbage and chicken, announced a homecoming as we returned to our apartments after school or a game of stickball in the street.

The streets were alive with people and action—talking, walking, playing, or just "hanging out." Children were admonished from front windows by observing parents, grandparents, aunts, and uncles in Spanish, Italian, Yiddish, or variously accented English. While not always delivered with a full appreciation of who had done what to whom, the comments on youthful misbehavior were made with commanding vigor and directness. It was usually some variant of "Stop, or else!" (and the "or else" was likely to be embarrassing, to hurt, or both). We didn't have much privacy, but each of us felt a deep and abiding sense of belonging.

We were privileged to see all different ages and kinds of people: very old and very young; tradespeople, winos, and numbers runners; brown, black, and white. The city blocks of the easily identified geography of our youth had natural rhythms of time and place. It made sense to us, and there was a power to it that we somehow shared.

The idea for this book has been part of each of us since the 1950s. Growing up in New York City's Spanish Harlem and Upper West Side, we did not know what special communities we shared. Indeed, it was the resurgence of community organization in the 1960s and 1970s and our own involvement in it—as organizers, consultants, and teachers—that led us to take a careful look at our roots. We recognized that these roots, despite the problems of poverty, racial conflict, alcoholism, and drugs, had been a major source of nurturance, strength, and validation for us both.

In each of our neighborhoods, part of what made them places of identity and empowerment were elements of ethnic solidarity. Aspects of religion and language, similarity of economic status and life situation, contributed to this solidarity. The contempt of more affluent surrounding communities also contributed to defensive, but supportive efforts of mutual aid.

There was a sense of continuity and meaning in these communities—a sense perhaps only rivaled in recent years by what we saw in the 1960s and 1970s. But despite the lack of public recognition in the 1980s (more like a systematic disparaging of the validity of ethnic minority communities), the mid-1990s have again brought us face-to-face with the extraordinary influence of these areas. Gangs and drugs and drive-by shootings are one part of the story, a drama in which communities of color are waging an uphill struggle to protect their integrity and build their power. But it is also about two kids growing up with an immeasurable belief that people can come together to enrich their lives and increase their influence with the forces that control their destinies. Perhaps this is part of the promise of the twenty-first century.

We are pleased to present the second edition of our book. This revised edition includes an increased emphasis on skills and intervention strategies; coverage of the most recent social, cultural, political, and economic issues in the chapter discussions by experts from within these communities; and updated bibliographies. This edition also includes a new chapter about Pilipino Americans with information never before published.

We particularly wish to thank the reviewers of our text, who provided valuable suggestions: Wynne DuBray, California State University-Sacramento; Terry Mizrahi, Hunter College; Michael Reisch, San Francisco State University; and Robert F. Vernon, University of Indianapolis.

The enthusiastic support for our text reinforces our belief in the value of such a reader, and in the belief that there are many community workers committed to the challenge of what needs to be done to bring about lasting change in communities of color.

Felix G. Rivera
John L. Erlich

# In Memoriam:
# Cesar Chavez, 1927–1993

For 41 years, Cesar Chavez taught the poorest people in America to stand up for their rights—and to do it without violence. Against tremendous odds, he organized the first successful farm workers union in U.S. history. He turned compliant and submissive people into courageous champions of their families and communities.

Later, critics would sometimes say Cesar was out of fashion; that people in the 1990s are tired of social causes. But at a time when so few Americans seem willing to risk their careers—much less their lives—on behalf of a principle in which they believe, the life of Cesar Chavez shines through ever more brightly.

His formal education ended after the eighth grade. He never owned a home or earned more than $6,000 a year. He chose a life of self-imposed poverty, grueling hours, and the frequent threat of physical violence and death. Yet his deeds live on in the millions of people he inspired with an unshakable conviction that society can be transformed from within. "You have to convert one person at a time, time after time," he once said. "Progress only comes when people just plow ahead and do it. It takes patience. The concept is so simple that most of us miss it."

Arturo S. Rodrigues, President
United Farm Workers of America, AFL-CIO

# 1

# *A Time of Fear;*
# *A Time of Hope*

*FELIX G. RIVERA AND JOHN L. ERLICH*

> *What is to be done, and what remedy is to be applied? I
> will tell you, my friends. Hear what the Great Spirit has
> ordered me to tell you! You are to make sacrifices, in the
> manner that I shall direct; to put off entirely from
> yourselves the customs which you have adopted since the
> white people came among us; you are to return to that
> former happy state, in which we live in peace and plenty,
> before these strangers came to disturb us, and above all,
> you must abstain from drinking their deadly besonm
> [liquor] which they have forced upon us for the sake of
> increasing their gains and diminishing our numbers . . .
> Wherefore do you suffer the whites to dwell upon your
> lands? Drive them away; wage war against them.*[1]

Little did the Delaware leader know that his warning of the destruction of his people
would reflect many of the concerns of people of color in the 1990s. Indeed, the
media attention devoted to violence, gangs, and drug traffic has heightened the
popular view of ethnic minority communities (especially poor ethnic communities)
as devastated disaster areas that might best be dealt with by eradication. From the

1

perspective of those who reside in the communities, the feelings are often of being surrounded and embattled.

However, there is a strong undercurrent of renewed organizing activity in many of these communities—urban and rural, larger and smaller. But if the recent past is a reasonable predictor of the near future, these efforts will go largely unreported and unrewarded.

Moreover, very little written material is available to guide such efforts among people of color. Until the first edition of this book was published, a book on community organizing with people of color did not exist. The reasons for this deficiency are multiple, complex, and interwoven. Racism—political, economic, and social—is at the core of the problem. At the same time, societal interest in the problems of the poor has sharply declined, especially in early 1990s.

Despite all the research evidence to the contrary, the disenfranchised are again being forced to bear the major burden for their oppression. The problems of drug abuse, crime, inadequate housing, alcoholism, AIDS, teen pregnancy, underemployment, and the like have had their most devastating impact on poor communities of color. The lack of resources to combat these problems, likewise, falls most heavily on the same people. The growing national debt has served conservative forces well as an excuse for not meeting the urgent need to expand services in these areas.

As if their many problems and needs were not enough, the incredibly dramatic population increases bear sobering witness to the daunting challenges ahead for us all. Preliminary Census Bureau reports show an increase in all populations of color. Out of a total of over 248 million people in the United States, almost 30 million are African American, representing 23 percent of the total population and an increase of 64.6 percent over the 1980 census figures; Native Americans, Eskimos, and Aleuts comprise .08 percent of the population, almost two million people, representing an increase of 33.7 percent over the last census; Asian or Pacific Islanders, about 2.9 percent of the total at over seven million strong, show an increase of 144.9 percent over the 1980 count; Latinos represent 8.9 percent of the population with over 22 million people, an increase of 87.3 percent over the 1980 census.

These figures are far from fixed. A heated debate is going on about the problems of undercounting, especially in communities of color. The Census Oversight Committee claims that over two million African Americans have not been counted. They state that the undercount is between 5.5 percent and 6.5 percent, compared with an undercount of 5.2 percent in 1980. Other critics of the census claim that as many as nine million people were not counted. Whatever the final count, these statistics are a reminder of the awesome amount of work that needs to be done by agents of social change. The challenge is unparalleled in this nation's history.

The government's pro-contra and anti-Salvadoran rebel role in Central America, as well as the invasions of Grenada and Panama—and the vast commitment to the Persian Gulf—however justified they may have been have contributed to a decline in our commitment to racial equality.

Our priorities in foreign affairs, along with a realignment of domestic preferences, have sharply reduced support for community-based human services as well as the resources necessary to provide training for people to work in these services. One result is decreased interest in and demand for training in community organization and community development. In many cases, the rhetoric of working along multicultural lines has been a smokescreen to avoid funding programs for desperately underserved ethnic enclaves. All too many joint police–community antidrug efforts, for example, make good copy for the six o'clock news while deflecting public attention away from underlying problems of poverty and racism.

The fact that of all social work methods community organization has been the most resistant to consistent definition has further exacerbated this situation. As Erlich and Rivera have noted, community organization has evolved from being the general rubric under which all social work practice beyond the level of individual, family, and small group was subsumed—including grassroots organizing, community development, planning, administration and policymaking—to being the smallest subsegment of macro-level practice (where it exists at all). Perhaps this definitional difficulty is well illustrated by what the editors believe is one of the better contemporary definitions of community organization.

> *Community Development refers to efforts to mobilize people who are directly affected by a community condition (that is, the "victims," the unaffiliated, the unorganized, and the nonparticipating) into groups and organizations to enable them to take action on the social problems and issues that concern them. A typical feature of these efforts is the concern with building new organizations among people who have not been previously organized to take social action on a problem.*[2]

However, by any definition, it was not until the 1960s that large numbers of schools of social work were willing to regard it as a legitimate concentration. Majors in community organization in graduate schools increased from 85 in 1960 to 1,125 in 1969, or from 1.5 percent to over 9 percent of full-time enrollments.[3]

By 1990, the number of students nationwide training to work as organizers had declined significantly. The Council on Social Work Education's most recent statistics demonstrate that there were 154 master's degree students (1.8 percent) in Community Organization and Planning, 417 (4.9 percent) in Administration and Management, and 101 (1.2 percent) in a combination of CO and Planning with Administration or Management. Despite growing acceptance as a legitimate area of study in social work, urban planning and labor studies, community organization and planning has been held hostage by the political and social vagaries of a society that has never accepted its strategies and tactics, especially if methods like public demonstrations and boycotts caused disruptive embarrassment to those in positions of political authority and power.

From an educational standpoint, the result has been a diminished community organization curriculum—few field placement opportunities, few courses, and a sparse literature. This is particularly surprising in light of the important, documented successes of community organization and development during the 1960s and early 1970s.[4]

Community organizing and community development by people of color have been virtually ignored. Isolated electives and rare articles in the professional journals have done little to fill this void. Work of a multicultural nature has received only slightly more attention. No book is available that addresses a broad range of the organizing efforts currently proceeding in diverse minority communities. This book is an effort to remedy that situation.

What is the status of community organization practice that this book is attempting to address? The civil rights gains of the 1960s in voting rights, public accommodations, and job opportunities, for example, were tempered by the belief that the African-American community had gone too far, that its gains were based on unacceptable levels of violence. Quickly forgotten by the white community was the continuing history of violence experienced by African Americans and other communities of color. "What more do they want?" was more than mere inflammatory rhetoric. These gains seemed to threaten white job security, community housing patterns, and long-cherished social interaction networks. The bitter residue of racism remains, and the resentment experienced throughout much of the United States has been part of the conservative backlash we are witnessing (as everything from skinheads and antiminority high school violence to "English-only" public school curricula poignantly illustrates).

Similarly, efforts toward enfranchisement of new voters, changes in immigration laws, and women's and gay rights have also suffered from the limits imposed by methods deemed acceptable and resulting in "reasonable" benefits. As long as "someone else" did the social protesting—and as long as it was far enough away from their homes and places of work—most white people did not complain actively or publicly resist slow, nondisruptive changes.

A concomitant shift has marked the reluctant acceptance of the "worthy" among each ethnic minority (largely dependent on whose economic interests are being threatened), while at the same time rejecting those without education or job skills or at high risk for drug problems and sexually transmitted diseases.

Not surprisingly, with the emergence of reverse discrimination as a legitimate response to the enfranchisement of people of color, a new consciousness permeated schools of social work whose espoused philosophy was that of commitment to aiding poor and oppressed populations. It was no longer fashionable to invite a Black Panther as a speaker for a seminar on social action, or a Young Lord from New York's Puerto-Rican community to discuss how they initiated the movement against lead poisoning in New York's slum tenements, or have Angela Davis address the systematic exclusion of women of color by the women's movement in key policy and strategy sessions. Instead, the invited ethnic "leaders" focused on issues like creatively funded drug education programs, multicultural day care and pre-school efforts, and the demographics of rapidly expanding minority populations around the country.

As funding sources evaporated, we saw people of color being relegated to the not-so-symbolic back of the bus once again. The ferocity with which affirmative action was attacked became trendy. Ethnic studies programs were closed or cut back at alarming rates throughout the country, and many community-based agencies in ethnic areas were forced to close their doors. The Supreme Court's chipping away at civil rights legislation seemed to be a culmination of much of the backlash being experienced.

## *People of Color and Organizing: A Troubled Alliance*

Why has community organization not been more successful in working with people of color? What happened to some of the cross-cultural efforts that appeared to be so productive in the 1960s and early 1970s? Traditionally, much of the writing on community organization attempts to be color-blind. It has been the experience of the editors and many of our authors that organizers work with specific strategies and tactics applied to different situations, but the methods that combine them rarely—if ever—change.[5]

Alinsky's mobilization model is a good case in point.[6] Too often the level of analysis of a community's problems has been determined by an organizing strategy that identifies a particular strata of people or social problem for intervention, and by doing so, ignores the racial and cultural uniqueness of the community. We are not writing about conservative or even liberal community organizers but well-intentioned, progressive-thinking organizers who have been victimized by what may be termed "organizers' myopia" because of their single-minded organizing ideology or preordained methodology.[7]

One thing that becomes readily apparent in the chapters in this book is the absence of an easily identified "radical" or "progressive" ideology along class lines. That does not mean the authors are apolitical; far from it. What it does indicate, however, is the fact that issues surrounding race, culture, and their attendant problems are often more urgent concerns than social class, which historically has often been conceptualized by white theoreticians apart from the dynamics deemed more critical to the self-determination of communities of color by communities of color. Middle-class Asians, Latinos, or African Americans are still viewed as minorities because of a most easily identifiable characteristic: skin color. Good clothes and an elegant briefcase are not much help when you need a cab in the middle of the night in Chicago or Washington, D.C.

People of color have traditionally been caught between the polarized struggles of conservative and liberal theoretical forces. Too many liberal community organizers have emphasized class issues at the expense of racism and cultural chauvinism, relegating them to "logical" extensions of the political and economic structure. Much of the neo-Marxist literature has treated race from a reductive, negative posture: "superexploitation" and the "divide and conquer" strategies of individual capitalist employers. On the other hand, many conservative thinkers have emphasized a kind of uniqueness of each community, which divides it from other communities of color, as well as separating those who can "make it" from those who cannot.[8]

These perspectives largely disregarded many questions, including the fact that racism existed long before monopoly capitalism was institutionalized. Racial harmony does not necessarily follow the passing of capitalism, as the persistence of racial antagonism in postcapitalist societies (like Sweden) demonstrates. The structural analysis that leads to a unified ideological interpretation of racism is thus deficient.

What too many organizers fail to consider is that there appears to be little or no history or contemporary evidence to substantiate that relations established and legitimated on the basis of race were or are identical to those established and legitimated on the basis of class. For example, the increasing violence against students of color on college campuses cannot be explained primarily as a class phenomenon, especially when one recognizes that many of these students of color are economically similar to the white students attacking them. By continuing to look at racism mostly as a broad structural issue, organizers are underestimating the roles played by schools, churches, social welfare agencies, and other institutions in negatively influencing and changing race relations.

How might we best define the equality and liberation struggles being waged by the African-American communities? The Native-American communities? The Chinese-American and Vietnamese-American communities? The communities of women of color? The immediate reaction of most oppressors is based on skin color and other physical characteristics, language, and culture, then class. The oversimplification of the struggles of people of color has led to unwarranted generalizations about their economic, social, political, and cultural behaviors and attitudes as groups.

Writers criticize the tendency of mainstream and radical theorists to divide society into separate domains culturally and structurally. They argue that this arbitrary distinction promotes essentialism (single-cause explanations) in contemporary thinking about race. Race and culture cannot be separated as "things in themselves." They have to be linked to other social processes and dynamics operating in a society that continues oppressing communities because of skin tone. We hold that at least three dynamics—race, class, and gender—are significant in understanding oppression and the roles played by social welfare institutions in that process. None are reducible to the others, and class is not necessarily paramount.[9]

The phenomenological day-to-day realities of race, language, class, gender, and age help to shape ideological perspectives and give force to the hostilities with which one lives (as well as the strengths that make survival possible). The resulting process is difficult to analyze because it manifests itself differently from one community to another across the country, thereby making the task of organizing against these attacks that much more difficult a challenge. These realities do not lend themselves easily to simple categorizations by agents of social change or schools teaching community organization practice. The need for a more integrated and receptive social change paradigm in working with communities of color must be a main goal of organizers.

The conservative tradition in community organizing—especially within social work education—has also had an impact on the way organizers of color and their communities view the political implications of the social change efforts in which they have been involved. The conventional perspective that education should be ideologically value-free and politically nonpartisan has been especially evident in community organizing. Typical textbooks on organizing have avoided clear political and moral positions on issues.[10] These books were guided by a "professional" and largely mechanistic value base.

Fisher notes:

> *The social work tradition views the community essentially as a social organism; it focuses on social issues such as building a sense of community gathering together social service organizations or lobbying for and delivering social resources. It assumes that basically the community's problem is social disorganization. The organizer functions either as an "enabler" to help the community gather itself together or as an advocate to secure additional services for the community. The strategy is gradualist and consensual, which means that organizers assume a unity of interest between the power structure and the neighborhood and assume a willingness of at least some in power to meet community needs.*[11]

In contrast, Freire proposes:

> *. . . one cannot be a social worker and be like the educator who's a coldly neutral technician. To keep our options secret, to conceal them in the cobwebs of technique, or to disguise them by claiming neutrality does not constitute neutrality; quite the contrary, it helps maintain the status quo.*

Many professors of macro practice still resist the systematic inclusion of discussions on analyzing power and confrontational empowerment, the development of critical consciousness, and racism as fundamental components of community organization. The lack of attention to critical consciousness—that is, how personal and political factors interact with each other and one's work, as well as how values, ideas, and practice skills are influenced by social forces and, in turn, influence them—is both particularly noteworthy and undermining. This neoconservative stance has had the net effect of leaving students of color (as well as white students) confused about their potential roles in their communities and how far they might go in fighting racism and social injustices.

While the rhetoric of self-determination implies that students are intended to be agents of social change, the reality clearly calls for modest improvements that do not seriously upset the status quo. The tools that might help lead to more fundamental change through a thorough questioning of what is happening and what it means to a community and a person working there are largely absent from the curriculum. Indeed, as a totality, the picture is not very promising.[12]

## *A Paradigm for Organizing with People of Color*

The different racial and cultural characteristics present in oppressed and disadvantaged communities represent an unprecedented challenge to organizers of the 1990s. We are defining culture as a collection of behaviors and beliefs that constitute "standards for deciding what is, standards for deciding what can be, standards for deciding how one feels about it, standards for deciding what to do about it, and standards for deciding how to go about doing it." A recent history of benign or belligerent neglect has required people of color to mobilize their skills and limited resources in creative ways that challenge prevailing community programs. Although they get little attention or help from mainstream society—indeed, in some areas, overt opposition is more typical—many of those communities are trying to tackle their problems with strategies unique to their situations.

For example, the African-American community of West Oakland, California, has attacked the drug problem head-on, with many community leaders making themselves visible enemies of major dealers. Also, nearby, an African-American first-grade teacher has promised to pay for the college education of her entire first-grade class if they maintain a "C" average and go on to college. The teacher annually saves $10,000 from her modest salary for this fund. In the rural mountains of eastern Puerto Rico there is an exciting revitalization of the community through an energetic community development program. Southeast-Asian communities in Boston, New York, Houston, and San Francisco have organized legal immigration and refugee task forces to help fight the arbitrary deportation of undocumented workers. Derelict neighborhoods in New York, Chicago, and Philadelphia are being revitalized through cooperatives and community development activities. Native-American tribes are attacking problems of alcoholism through indigenous healing rituals that utilize the sweat lodge ceremony. Success rates are often dramatic. In the village of Akhiok, Alaska, 90 percent of its adults were chronically drunk. After Native treatments, at least 80 percent were able to sustain sobriety. The Latino community in Boston has a very successful grassroots health program called Mujeres Latina en Action, which has successfully integrated third world health models that include the concept of the extended family in health care delivery systems. A culture and gender-sensitive model of community organization is used to reach women in the barrios.

Traditionally, communities of color have not been involved in issues related to ecology and the protection of the environment. For many neighborhoods, these are among the last priorities listed of the many problems people face. However, one example deserves special attention, for it may well be a model for similar actions across the country. In California's East Los Angeles, which is predominantly Mexican American/Chicano, a group of Latina mothers was organized by a parish priest in the mid 1980s into militant urban ecologists. They call themselves Mothers of East Los Angeles. They have successfully mobilized against threats to their community, such as (1) the construction of a state prison in a residential area near neighborhood schools, (2) an above-ground oil pipeline that would have cut through their middle- to low-income barrio while avoiding much more affluent coastal towns, (3) the local use of dangerous and potentially polluting pesticides, and (4) local construction of a large incinerator. They believe in peaceful tactics and wear white kerchiefs as a symbol of their nonviolent philosophy. They are often seen pushing strollers during demonstrations, and they lobby the state capitol, engage in letter writing, and serve as pacesetters of a growing environmental movement in the Los Angeles area among people of color.

From an ethnically sensitive practice perspective, organizing strategies in the Vietnamese or Laotian communities (and with different ethnic groups within these communities) cannot be the same as in Puerto-Rican, African-American, Native-American, or Japanese-American enclaves. The experience of one of the editors illustrates this point. In the early 1970s he was organizing in a Mexican-American barrio. One of the outcomes of the struggle was the establishment of a storefront information and referral center. In furnishing and decorating the center, several political and cultural posters were displayed, much to the anger of some of the *viejitos* (elders) in the neighborhood. One particular poster featured Emiliano Zapata, and the staff was told in no uncertain terms that the poster had to come down because Zapata was still perceived as an enemy. Several fathers of the *viejitos* had fought against Zapata during the Mexican Revolution. Although the editor is a Latino, he is not of Mexican decent. However, he does know the conflicting loyalties of Mexico's revolutionary history and should have checked with the community to be sure none of the posters would be offensive. This apparently innocuous mistake set the organizing effort back many months and required the staff to work doubly hard to regain the community's confidence.

Unfortunately, the history of organizing is replete with such examples. Certainly organizers of color must accept a share of the blame. However, the overwhelming majority of organizing writers and practitioners are white males, many of whom come from liberal or radical traditions and most often got their theoretical and practice feet wet in the social upheavals of the 1960s. Their apparent successes seemed destined to be color blind. From a community perspective, white radical groups were often more enamored of their political ideologies than they were committed to the needs of minority neighborhoods. The editors experienced many situations where communities of color were waging various struggles. The Detroit-based battles of African Americans within the United Auto Workers are a prime example. Frequently hovering on the fringes were white radical groups looking to make the struggle their own. They were very critical of the efforts of people of color, accusing them of being culturally nationalistic and methodically not progressive enough. Too often we forget that experiencing racism, economic deprivation, and social injustice are the key relevant politicizing forces in most urban areas. Indeed, it was this kind of elitist attitude that caused many minority organizers to shy away from predetermined ideological postures that seemed to define peoples for them. Even many liberal white groups seemed to disdain poor whites in favor of more visible organizing efforts in communities of color.

Thus, it is not sufficient to identify the three classic (and presumably "color-blind") models of community practice—locality development, social planning, and social action—as the foundation within which community organizing with people of color takes place. Factors that must be addressed are (1) the racial, ethnic, and cultural uniqueness of people of color; (2) the implications of these unique qualities in relation to such variables as the roles played by kinship patterns, social systems, power, leadership networks, religion, the role of language (especially among subgroups), and the economic and political configuration within each community; and (3) the process of empowerment and the development of critical consciousness. (This contrasts with what Freire has called "naive consciousness," or a tendency to romanticize intense, satisfying past events and force the same experiences into the future without fully taking into account such multidimensional elements as those noted above.) In addition, the physical setting within which the community finds itself is an essential component for consideration as it plays a significant part in the way people view their situation. The need for a new, revised paradigm is clear and urgent.[13]

One of the most critical factors affecting organizing outcomes hinges on determining how strategies and tactics are played out based on the nature and intensity of contact and influence that will help to determine the constraints placed on the organizers' (whether indigenous or not) knowledge and identification with the community, and when and how technical skills may be brought into play. This "meta approach" will help organizers arrange their strategies and tactics within parameters that are goal, task, skill, and process specific. We suggest that the degree and nature of contacts is a three-tier process that—for the sake of simplicity—may be conceptualized as contact intensity and influence at the primary, secondary, and tertiary levels of community development (see Figure 1.1).

The primary level of involvement is most immediate and personal with the community. It is that level that requires racial, cultural, and linguistic identity. The

Community Levels

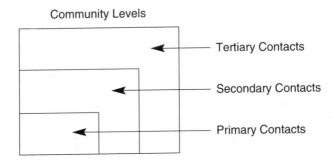

**FIGURE 1.1  Organizer's Contact Intensity and Influence**

primary level of contact intensity and influence is the most intimate level of community involvement where the only way of gaining entré into the community is to have full ethnic solidarity with the community. For example, this would not be possible for a Chinese-American in a Vietnamese- or African-American area.

The secondary level consists of contact and influence that is one step removed from personal identification with the community and its problems. Language—although a benefit and help—is not absolutely mandatory. Many of the functions are those of liaison with the outside community and institutions, and service as a resource with technical expertise based on the culturally unique situations experienced by the community. Examples of persons able to work at this level include a Puerto Rican in a Mexican-American neighborhood or a person who identifies her/himself as Haitian in an African-American area.

The tertiary level is that of the outsider working for the common interests and concerns of the community. Cultural or racial similarity is not a requirement. The responsibilities of these organizers will see them involved primarily with the outside infrastructures as an advocate and broker for communities of color. However, their tasks are less that of liaison than of a helpful technician approaching or confronting outside systems and structures. Clearly, whites and nonsimilar people of color may be particularly effective at this level.

Devore, in chapter 4, has applied our contact model in conceptualizing the strategies and tactics necessary in organizing in the struggle against violence in African-American communities. This approach helps to put the organizing tasks within a context similar to an approach used in public health.

The issue over whether or not organizers should be part of the racial and cultural group with whom they work has been given much attention within and outside communities of color. Alinsky and his Industrial Area Foundation organizers were often caught in the middle of this question. However, a careful review of these efforts suggests that in most cases, indigenous organizers played key roles in the success of their organizations. Thus, it seems imperative that if communities of color are to empower themselves by giving more than symbolic recognition to the ideal of self-determination and community control, then we must search hard for the successful roles played by people within their own communities and the lessons they can teach outside organizers. Furthermore, many emerging communities of color are underrepresented in the society's infrastructure because their languages and customs make them especially difficult to approach. In the emerging Southeast-Asian communities, there are nationalities, ethnic and subethnic groups whose cultures are quite different from one another and where there exists an assortment of languages, dialects, and idioms. An outside organizer simply does not stand a chance of gaining rapid access to such unique and insular community groups. Even the Native-American nations, it should be remembered, speak over 200 different languages. Clearly, special care must be taken in recruiting people to work in widely varied Indian communities—on reservations and rancherias, in both rural and urban areas.[14]

The knowledge necessary to understand and appreciate customs and traditions in all communities presents an incredible challenge. Organizing and social change strategies are complex and stress-inducing enough without further exacerbating the community's problems by having organizers who have very limited (or no) aware-ness of the customs, traditions, and languages of these communities. We are not saying that persons without some of this knowledge cannot fulfill certain important functions; for indeed, they have served and should continue to serve effectively in secondary and tertiary roles. But we must emphasize that the most successful organizers are those who know their culture intimately: its subtleties of language, mores, and folkways. A white outsider, however sensitive and knowledgeable, simply cannot appreciate all that needs to be considered about a fundamentally different nonwhite culture or subculture. Some newly emerging communities are so well defended that there would be little chance for an outsider to gain meaningful admission to them, not to mention becoming a successful organizer. However, it must be made very clear that cultural and racial similarity—by themselves—are no guarantor of organizer effectiveness or community acceptance. Indeed, an arrogant, know-it-all insider may be viewed with more suspicion than a similarly styled outsider.[15]

Despite these difficulties, there are common practice elements that may be identified as prerequisite to successful organizing. These principles are not exhaus-tive, but if organizers take command of these elements, they can increase the likelihood of being effective change agents in their communities. Knowing when and how to mix and phase these strategies and skill areas is critical to the successful outcome of a struggle. Organizing has to be conceptualized as a process that is educational both for the community and the organizers.

## *Organizer's Profile*

What follows is a summary of those qualities—knowledge, skill, attributes, and values—that we believe are most important for the success of organizers. We recognize that the list is an idealized one in the sense that those few who have already fully attained the lofty heights described can probably also walk on water. Realistically, it is more a set of goals to be used by organizers and communities together to help achieve desired changes. The careful reader will also note that many of these qualities are addressed by each contributor in describing a particular community. Illustrations and examples of parts of this "model-in-progress" may be found throughout the chapters that follow.

**1.** *Similar cultural and racial identification.* The most successful organizers are those activists who can identify with their communities, culturally, racially, and linguistically. There is no stronger identification with a community than truly being a part of it.

**2.** *Familiarity with customs and traditions, social networks, and values.* This dimension of organizing stresses the importance of having a thorough grounding in the customs and traditions of the community being organized. This is especially critical for those people who have cultural, racial, and linguistic identification, but who, for a variety of reasons, have been away from that community and are returning as organizers.

For example, how have the dynamics between organized religion and the community changed throughout the years? Ignored, its effect may imperil a whole organizing effort. Both the definition of the problems and the setting of goals to address them are involved. A number of Latino mental health and advocacy programs regularly consult with priests, ministers, and folk healers about the roles they all play (or might play) in advocating mental health needs. These mental health activities are very clear about the importance of these other systems—formal and informal—in the community's spiritual life. The superstitions and religious archetypes are addressed by a variety of representatives, thereby making the advocacy work that much more relevant and effective. The Native-American nations give deference to their medicine man, with no actions being taken until he has given approval. Similarly, the Vietnamese, Cambodian, and Laotian communities have strong religious leaders who help to define community commitments and directions.

All too often there exists a cultural gap, as typified by younger, formally educated organizers working with community elders. The elders may be too conservative for the young organizers, or they may disagree about tactics. Knowledge of and appreciation for the culture and traditions will help close the gap among key actors, or at least reduce the likelihood of unnecessary antagonisms.

**3.** *An intimate knowledge of language and subgroup slang.* We separate this dimension from the one just mentioned so as to emphasize its importance. Knowledge of a group's language style is indispensable when working with communities that are bi- or monolingual. Many embarrassing situations have arisen because of the organizer's ignorance of a community's language style. Approved idiomatic expressions in one area of the community may be totally unacceptable in another. Some expressions have sexual overtones in one community while being inoffensive to other communities. Certain expressions may denote a class bias that may be offensive to one group of people or another. The literature on sociolinguistics has done an excellent job of alerting us to the importance of language subtleties and nuances. For a discussion of the role played by similar language in culturally different populations see a special issue of *Harvard Educational Review*.[16]

**4.** *Leadership styles and development.* Organizers must be leaders and lead organizers, but they must also work with existing community leaders and help in training emerging leadership. We recognize that there are significant differences in leadership styles from one community of color to another. The contributors have addressed many of these issues in their chapters throughout the book. Indispensable to the composition of a successful leader are the individual's personality, how she or he fits her or his roles within the organizing task, and how personal values help to shape a world view. However achieved, a leader should have a sense of power that may be used in a respectful manner within the community.

**5.** *An analytical framework for political and economic analysis.* This is one dimension where an understanding of the dynamics of oppression through class analysis is paramount. A sophisticated knowledge of political systems with their access and leverage points is very important. It must include an appraisal of who has authority within the ethnic community as well as who in it has power (often less formally acknowledged). The sources of mediating influence between the ethnic community and wider communities also must be understood. This knowledge fulfills two needs: (1) It helps to give the organizer the necessary analytical perspective in judging where the community fits in the hierarchy of economic analysis; and (2) It serves as a tool for educating the community, thereby increasing the community's consciousness of the roles and functions of the organizer within broader economic and social systems.[17]

**6.** *Knowledge of past organizing strategies, their strengths, and limitations.* It is imperative that organizers learn how to structure their organizing activities within a historical framework. This framework helps them to look at those strategies and tactics that have succeeded and failed in each community in the past. Since so little knowledge-building is evident in the field, it is critical that organizers develop and share a historical knowledge base that helps identify the many mistakes made so as to illuminate those techniques that appear to have worked best in recent similar situations.

**7.** *Skills in conscientization and empowerment.* A major task of the organizer in disenfranchised communities is to empower people through the process of developing critical consciousness. How the personal and political influence each other, and the local environment in which they are played out, is a key to this process. It is not enough to succeed in ameliorating or even solving community problems if there is little or no empowerment of the community.

At the same time, power must be understood as both a tool and part of a process by the organizer. As Rubin and Rubin write, "community organizations need not focus exclusively on campaigns to achieve specific goals; they can make building their own power a long-term effort."[18] Power may be destructive or productive in the sense of germinating ideas and concerns, and being integrative, or community-building. Of course, power is typically experienced in poor communities as both a negative and positive. The kind of power that is based on threats is often the most common in disenfranchised areas. When Organizer A makes Target B act in ways it does not wish to act solely because of the sanctions A can levy against B, typically this becomes an imposed "win-lose" situation. A limited special hiring program usually takes this form.[19]

Power may also be a form of exchange, when Organizer A and Target B involve themselves in a reciprocal relationship or exchange because both parties have something to win from the process. Exchange is an integrative component of power because it involves some degree or trust, where the final outcome may be "win-win." Coalition building often takes this form. Power may also be defined as love—love of community, lifestyle, or family—that which should motivate an organizer and the community.

Organizer and community need to view each other as subject rather than object, as learners and as equals. No organizer should enter a community with a sense that she or he has "the" answers for it. The development of critical consciousness through the process of conscientization may be visualized as a double spiraling helix, where both the organizer and community learn from each other, the problems at hand and the strategies and tactics employed (Figure 1.2).[20]

The phenomenology of the experience is based on praxis, the melding of theory and experience, for both parties, which in turn makes them stronger actors because

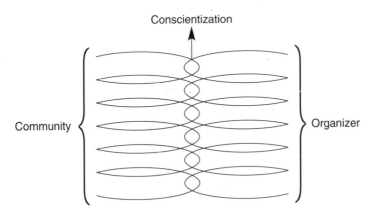

**FIGURE 1.2  Development of Critical Consciousness**

their learning is mutual, supportive, and liberating of any preconceived notions one had about the other.

**8.** *Skills in assessing community psychology.* Organizers need to learn about the psychological makeup of their communities free of stereotypes. Scant attention has been paid to this knowledge area by most community organizers. Creating a methodology without understanding the motivations of the community is a risky undertaking.

Organizers also need to understand what keeps a community allied and synergized. What is the life cycle of the community? Is it growing, mature, or declining? Are there new arrivals? Have they been in the community for generations? Does their language work as a cohesive force or, because of the multigenerational patterns, serve as a problem in getting people together? If the community has experienced a failure recently (like the loss of a valued school), what has it done to the shared psychological identification of the community? Does it feel frustrated and powerless? Or has it served to focus anger? If the latter is the case, what strategies may be employed to mobilize the community to action?

**9.** *Knowledge of organizational behavior and decision-making.* Knowledge about organizational behavior and decision-making are critical to the success of an organizer. The work of Bachrach and Baratz around decisionless decisions and nondecisions as decisions has demonstrated its worth in the field. Decisionless decisions are those decision-making strategies that "just happen" and "take on a life of their own." Nondecisions as decisions are defined as:

> *a means by which demands for change in the existing allocation of benefits and privileges in the community can be suffocated before they are even voiced or kept covert; or killed before they gain access to the relevant decision-making arena; or, fail all these things, maimed or destroyed in decision-implementing stage of the policy process.*[21]

An awareness of these dynamics is necessary both to be able to ascertain strategies being employed by the institutions targeted for change and as a tactic that may also be employed by the community in its organizing.

**10.** *Skills in evaluative and participatory research.* One of the reasons that communities of color have lost some of their political, economic, and legal battles is the increasing vacuum created by the lack of supportive information that has kept up with growing social problems experienced by most communities. Many communities are being victimized by data and demographics that have redefined their situations in manageable terms as far as the traditional systems are concerned. There needs to be an expanded role for organizers to include developing skills in demographic and population projections and in social problem analysis. More organizers should develop theories about the declining social, economic, and political base of communities of color, and how people are still managing to survive in times of open hostility and encroachment on their civil rights and liberties. Crime, including that related to drugs, is a major arena for these pressures.

Research continues to be an indispensable and powerful tool for social change. Organizers should pay special attention to the use of participatory approaches, where both researchers and community people are involved as equal participants in securing knowledge to empower the community.[22]

Skill in evaluation research is another indispensable tool for organizers. We are suggesting that evaluative research not be used only to assess program outcomes but that it be used to analyze the success and value of different organizing strategies and their relevance in disparate situations.

**11.** *Skills in program planning and development and administration management.* One of the bitter lessons learned from the War on Poverty had to do with the "set-up for failure" nature of the administrative jobs offered to many people of color. Most had little or no administrative or managerial experience. One of the editors, then little-experienced, was offered a position that required him to administer a four-county migrant education and employment training program. With crash courses on organizational behavior, information processing and budgeting, the challenge was met, but many mistakes were made along the way. Needless to say, the mistakes were widely reported by the program's detractors and administrator's enemies.

Many administrators of color have fallen by the wayside because they were not given the opportunity to sharpen their managerial skills, and thus, a self-fulfilling prophecy of incompetence was validated in the eyes of people who desired to see these programs fall. Organizers must be aggressive in seeking out this knowledge base and not be deterred by the institutional barriers—financial, political, or otherwise—to attaining it.

**12.** *An awareness of self and personal strengths and limitations.* Reading through the list above may raise the question "Does such a superorganizer possessing all the enumerated skills and knowledge exist?" The answer is both yes and no.

There are people throughout the country with these skills, and many who have most of them. We ask that organizers of color know their limitations and struggle to improve themselves. Organizers must know when to seek help, when to share responsibilities, and when to step aside to let others take over. Conversely, skilled and knowledgeable organizers must be open to sharing their expertise with communities and community leaders, especially when such sharing may mean their departure might come that much sooner.

A successful organizer is one who gains respect within the context of the actions being taken, not the individual who is (or appears to be) more knowledgeable than another. Honest intentions and abilities are worth more than degrees. Organizers also need to understand how to react to stress. We all have our ways of coping with conflict. We need to know when our coping is no longer working for us, thereby jeopardizing the community. The danger of burnout is too well documented to be ignored.

Finally, we would like to caution against "doing it *for* the community." Not only is this counterproductive, but it also increases the risk of feeling that one is being eaten alive by the people with whom one is working. And it all too often results in another abandonment of a community whose experiences with social services have been much more of good rhetoric than serious social change.

## *The Readings*

The next eleven chapters represent a wide panorama of history, oppression, social problems, organizing, and community development experienced by their respective communities. For the second edition we have added more case studies and have identified specific skill areas that must be present for working successfully with their respective communities. While some might be inclined to argue that this book would have been more coherent if each contributor had rigorously followed a standardized outline, we have taken a different view. Each contributor (or contributing team) was invited to direct attention to the following areas: (1) the historical context of social problems in the community about which they were writing—including their nature, magnitude and severity; (2) the current state of affairs in their communities—from a personal rather than "objective" point of view; (3) which skill areas are necessary to work successfully with their communities; and (4) whatever final conclusions the writer(s) might wish to offer.

Rather than creating a book weakened by a lack of parallel composition across chapters, we believe that the mosaic that follows is strengthened by the rich and unique approaches taken by the contributors. Unlike Oscar Lewis, who believed that poor people were largely the same through his misguided notion of the "culture of poverty," the contributors offer a diverse canvas of problems, hopes, dreams, and actions experienced by individual communities.

The contributors have placed each community's social problems within a historical context that is political, social, and economic. The structural, leadership, power, fiscal, and human issues that have been responsible for making their communities what they are today are analyzed. They address what they see as the strategies for change in the future: the most effective ways of dealing with their communities' problems and the implications these have for community organization practice and, where relevant, social work education.

Chapter 2, "Community Development with Native Americans," by E. Daniel Edwards and Margie Egbert Edwards, presents a paradigm for working with Native Americans, whose values reflect a cultural sensitivity that is necessary for effective organizing with any Native-American tribe. They identify the many values shared by Native Americans, which helps in defining their extensive communities and the compatibility of locality development with tribal work, and they identify process goals for such work. Special attention is given to enhancing community ownership and positive regard through cultural identification. Finally, the authors identify important skills for successful community organization with native people.

Edwards and Egbert Edwards develop a cultural enhancement/community development model for community organizing with special emphasis on identification with the journey and visions of Native Americans. They discuss the dynamics of understanding and implementing the community development process with examples of successful programs in a variety of settings and tribes.

"Chicanos, Communities, and Change," chapter 3, was written by Miguel Montiel and Felipe Ortega y Gasca. The authors analyze the nature of change within the context of the Chicano experiences and communities. They put the Chicano experience within a historical perspective, discussing the roles played by community-based organizations in sustaining the Chicano ethos. They assess the movement away from community-based organizations to "profession-centered organizations" and the roles these emerging organizations will play in the Chicano communities in the 1990s and beyond.

They assess and reevaluate the continuity of change in Chicano communities by considering the contributions made to that assessment by the difficulties in sustaining meaningful organizations and change, the importance of dialogue in creating organizations, jobs, and the development of a courageous vision of action.

Wynetta Devore is author of chapter 4, "Organizing for Violence Prevention: An African-American Community Perspective." Devore sets the tone of the African-American experience with violence by putting it within both a historical and social context. Violence is seen as a public health issue. She analyzes the role public health must play in dealing with this problem. Devore discusses the efficacy of various organizing techniques, emphasizing the critical nature of making strategy choices. The author supports her theoretical framework with a variety of case studies. Devore concludes her chapter by laying out an integrated model for practice, which involves social work and public health.

Chapter 5, "Community Social Work with Puerto Ricans in the United States," by Julio Morales, introduces the Puerto-Rican community's unique political situation, and its ongoing relationships with the United States government. He discusses the roles played by ideology, values, and social change within the Puerto-Rican community, along with the dynamics represented by culture and practice issues.

The significance of such attributes as respect, honor, dignity, and hospitality in the Puerto-Rican community are assessed. Similarly, the nature of the extended family, "personalismo," "confianza," and "espiritismo" are analyzed with their importance to organizers evaluated. The dynamics of self-oppression are explored with a discussion of their negative outcomes and their implications for change. "Machismo," "marianismo," and other "isms" are considered, as well as the strengths inherent in the Puerto-Rican community. Finally, Morales introduces the reader to the problems, programs, strategies, and tactics that should be employed by a successful agent for social change, strongly supported by case studies.

A critical look at the feminist movement and the reasons women of color have been systematically excluded from significant policymaking arenas is taken up by chapter 6, "A Feminist Perspective on Organizing with Women of Color," by Lorraine Gutierrez and Edith A. Lewis. They define what they mean by women of color, looking at ethnic, racial, social, political, and economic factors that have helped shape that definition. A distinction is made between the interests of women of color and men of color. Additionally, a feminist perspective is introduced, emphasizing power and powerlessness as an integral part of their perspective, and as a way for women of color to begin assessing their situation in the United States.

The authors define feminist organizing, introducing a model delineating its dynamics. Issues for feminists organizing with women of color are discussed, as is community organizing by women of color, richly illustrated by case examples. Finally, the authors discuss future directions for feminist organizing with women of color, listing practice principles that should be addressed.

Chapter 7, "Organizing in the Chinese-American Community: Issues, Strategies, and Alternatives," by Peter C. Y. Lee portrays the complex, multigenerational world of the Chinese in the United States. Lee profiles Chinese-American sociodemographic characteristics, their changing values and behaviors, and the implication of these dynamics in the changing nature of their social, economic, and political problems.

The author develops a theoretical framework that looks at classic organizing theories and assesses their relevance or lack thereof for Chinese Americans. Emphasizing the unique cultural experiences of the community, Lee discusses and assesses community organizing strategies through case studies. In conclusion Lee looks at the efficacy of the social development perspective, assessing its value while also emphasizing an integrated sociocultural approach.

Kenji Murase introduces the reader to the sociodemographics of the Japanese in chapter 8, "Organizing in the Japanese-American Community." A brief history follows the Japanese immigrants from 1880 to the present. The author points out that historically the Japanese in America had a tradition of establishing formal organizations for the purpose of taking action to advocate their interests. The exclusion and internment period is presented and analyzed, including the rebuilding of the community at the end of World War II with emphasis on the role of community organizations. The redress and reparations movement is also reviewed. Murase introduces some key theoretical perspectives in assessing the Japanese-American organizing experience. The roles played by such dynamics as accommodation, exceptionalism (the "model minority" syndrome), racial subordination, and political economy are presented, interwoven with themes of loyalty and patriotism.

The author analyzes and assesses the role of community organizing in the Japanese-American community, within a generational context. The chapter closes with a discussion of needed skills and practice knowledge for successful organizing. These skills are critical as they are exercised within trends identified by the author: accelerating dispersal, and structural assimilation.

Royal F. Morales is the author of a new ninth chapter, "The Pilipino-American Community: Organizing for Change." Morales profiles the Pilipino-American community's social, cultural, and sociopolitical history. The community is identified as one of the largest-growing Asian communities. The author identifies unique cultural dynamics and the barriers these pose to organizing. An organizer profile is introduced that encompasses cultural sensitivities. Finally, Morales looks at future challenges for schools of social work, social workers, and community activists.

Chapter 10, "Organizing with Central-American Immigrants in the United States," by Carlos B. Córdoba, looks at the complex history of the Salvadoran, Guatemalan, Nicaraguan, and Honduran communities in the United States. Córdoba analyzes those economic and political issues that have forced so many of these people to flee their homelands, and the role played by United States politics and the Immigration and Naturalization Service. Córdoba looks at the structure of Central-American communities in the United States, how they function and survive. He analyzes the political power and influence in these communities and the reactions to threats by homeland opponents.

Córdoba develops a model of empowerment using Paulo Friere's concept of critical consciousness. The author looks at what needs to be done in the future in the areas of research, immigration reform, counseling services, education, and medical and mental health needs, especially addressing the problems associated with Post-traumatic Stress Syndrome. Finally, Córdoba addresses the limits of the literature on community organization with Central-American refugees and the need to develop new models of practice in these areas, while organizers change and adapt existing models of community and economic development.

Vu-Duc Vuong presents a demographic profile of the Southeast-Asian communities and the complexities that exist in working with them—both culturally and linguistically—in chapter 11, "Southeast Asians in the United States: A Strategy for Accelerated and Balanced Integration." Migration patterns are traced and analyzed, beginning with the wealthy elites that left Vietnam in the mid 1970s to the boat people of more recent times.

The author addresses critical issues for these communities, dividing them into two main concerns: adaptation and maintenance issues. The importance of community building is addressed, and the author presents a strategy for accelerated and balanced integration into the mainstream of society. Examples of the kind of work being done with the diverse communities is also presented.

Chapter 12 is included as a special chapter that—although it does not address a particular community of color—is placed, nevertheless, within a poor Puerto-Rican community. The intent of the chapter is to demonstrate a broad community development and restoration approach that has wide applicability and relevance to all poor and disenfranchised communities of color. An innovative model of activist community development is presented by Antonia Pantoja and Wilhelmina Perry in "Community Development/Community Restoration: A Perspective." They begin by defining what they mean by "community" and introduce a model of analysis that expedites the development process. The nature of dysfunctional communities and the implications this has for the community developer are explored. The authors identify the prerequisites for being a successful community development worker and define their approach to community development/restoration. The major processes of community development are identified, supported by case studies. Inherent throughout these processes, the authors make clear, is the development of political awareness at the same time they are working in the organizing process. One cannot exist without the other.

The authors were not available to rewrite their chapter for the second edition. But, because the chapter has been well received, we have included it in the second edition without changes.

In a brief epilogue, we offer our perspectives on the patterns, trends, and possibilities that have been illuminated by all the contributors. The diverse and unique histories, racial and ethnic differences, language and cultural patterns are synthesized into a model that addresses the similarities and differences experienced by the communities addressed by the contributors, and the implications these have for successful organizing outcomes. We look at the need for coalition building, with its attendant challenges and rewards. In conclusion, the international implications of the struggles by communities of color in the United States are explored.

An appendix has been added to this edition of the book. We have introduced selected material from the Center for Third World Organizing, Oakland, California, to illustrate what a community-based social action organization's training material looks like. The material, while illustrative, gives the reader an excellent introduction to the quality and detail of such training materials.

## *Summary*

There is little doubt that the struggle to bring about significant social change at the community level is a Herculean task. Despite widely heard political rhetoric to the contrary, the gates to social justice are sliding further shut, not open. Increasing numbers of people of color continue to be thrown into disadvantage and poverty—homeless, drug addicted, alcoholic, imprisoned, AIDS-infected, unemployed and underemployed, without regular health care, and pushed out of deteriorating schools with no marketable skills.

Community organization and development with people of color offers one small vehicle for battling to reverse this trend. The editors join the authors in the belief that organizers can make a difference. Though it is never lucrative and rarely romantic, the work can be critical in helping to meet people's needs. It can also be a way of enabling people to connect their own histories with the future. Perhaps above all it is about empowerment, an empowerment that community and organizer can share.

As Zimmerman and Rappaport note:

*Empowerment is a construct that links individual strengths and competencies, natural helping systems, and proactive behaviors to matters of social change. It is thought to be the process by which individuals gain mastery or control over their own lives and democratic participation in the life of their community.*[23]

## ENDNOTES

1. Delaware leader Neolin advising Indians in the 1760s to be prepared to fight back to protect their culture. Gary Nash, *Red, White and Black: People of Early America* (Englewood Cliffs, NJ: Prentice-Hall, 1974), pp. 302–303.
2. John L. Erlich and Felix G. Rivera, in N. Gilbert and H. Specht (ed.), *Handbook of Social Services* (Englewood Cliffs, NJ: Prentice-Hall, 1981); R. Kramer and H. Specht, *Readings in Community Organization Practice,* 3rd ed. (Englewood Cliffs, NJ: Prentice-Hall, 1983).
3. R. Fisher, "Community Organization in Historical Perspective: A Typology," *The Houston Review* (summer 1984): 75–87.
4. R. Fisher, *Let the People Decide: Neighborhood Organizing in America* (Boston: Twayne, 1984).
5. H. Boyte, *The Backyard Revolution: Understanding the New Citizen Movement* (Philadelphia: Temple University Press, 1980); G. Frederickson (ed.), *Neighborhood Control in the 1970s* (New York: Chandler, 1970).
6. Sanford Horwitt, *Let Them Call Me Rebel: Saul Alinsky—His Life and Legacy* (New York: Knopf, 1989).
7. Ibid.
8. R. Blauner, *Racial Oppression in America* (New York: Harper and Row, 1972); J. Roemer, "Divide and Conquer: Microfoundations of Marxian Theory of Wage Discrimination," *Bell Journal of Economics* vol. 10 (autumn 1979): 695–705.
9. E. P. Thompson, *The Making of the English Working Class* (New York: Vintage, 1966); *Harvard Educational Review* (August 1988), special issue on "Race and Racism in American Education."
10. A. Dunham, *The New Community Organization* (New York: Crowell, 1970).
11. Fisher, "Community Organization."
12. Paulo Freire, *Education for Critical Consciousness* (New York: Seabury, 1973).
13. *Los Angeles Times,* December 5, 1989.
14. S. Burghardt, *The Other Side of Organizing* (Cambridge, Mass.: Schenkman, 1982); Erlich and Rivera, "Community Organization and Community Development"; Fisher, *Let the People Decide;* Horwitt, *Let Them Call Me Rebel.*
15. J. Gibbs, L. Huang, and associates, *Children of Color* (San Francisco: Jossey-Bass, 1989).
16. *Harvard Educational Review* (August 1988).
17. H. J. Rubin and I. Rubin, *Community Organizing and Development* (Columbus, Ohio: Merrill, 1986).

18. Ibid., p. 2354.

19. Ibid.

20. Kenneth Boulding, *Three Faces of Power* (Beverly Hills: Sage, 1989).

21. P. Bachrach and M. S. Baratz, *Power and Poverty: Theory and Practice* (New York: Oxford University Press, 1970).

22. For example, an entire issue of *Community Development Journal* was devoted to participatory research and evaluation, thus stressing its international importance in working with disenfranchised and oppressed communities (vol. 23, no. 1 [January 1988]).

23. Marc A. Zimmerman and Julian Rappaport, "Citizen Participation, Perceived Control, and Psychological Empowerment" *American Journal of Community Psychology,* vol. 16, no. 5 (1988): 725–750.

# 2

# Community Development with Native Americans

## E. DANIEL EDWARDS AND MARGIE EGBERT EDWARDS

Community organization continues to offer direction to Native-American people as they seek to implement self-determination and self-governance programs in reservation, rural, and urban areas.* The numbers of Native Americans continue to grow as does their diversity. Factors such as mobility contribute to the diversification of urban Native-American populations. Whether residences are maintained in rural, reservation, or urban areas, Native Americans are influenced by strong cultural ties to their native identity. Professional people will find considerable challenge and stimulation in working with Native Americans and validating their cultural heritage and community development.

### Community Approaches: Compatibility with Native-American Values

A sense of "community" is traditionally an important part of the culture of the more than 500 American-Indian tribal groups in this country. Historically, many

*The terms "Native American" and "American Indian/Alaska Native" are used interchangeably to refer to the first "native" peoples of this country and their descendants.

American-Indian tribes and bands were relatively small in number and culturally bound together by strong community support networks. Daily living and decision-making were facilitated by considering the opinions of all tribal members according to well-developed tribal practices and customs.

A review of the community organization literature suggests that "communities provide meaning, a sense of belonging, and well-being" (Martinez-Brawley, 1990, p. 50). Fully functioning communities are those in which there is an appreciation for the capacity of the whole. These communities have a sense of the breadth and depth of members' capacities, their strengths as well as their weaknesses. This capacity promotes "shared responsibility"—shaped by the unique contributions of each member—and strives for equity through collective efforts (McKnight, 1987). Within these communities, members share a sense of solidarity, significance, and security. Solidarity is exemplified in feelings of cohesiveness. Significance is reflected in the contributions of individuals for the collective good. Security is reinforced through the mutuality of relationships and the sense of belonging (Martinez-Brawley, 1990, pp. 14–15).

The sense of community is an important part of traditional American-Indian culture. Decision-making is facilitated by considering the opinions of all tribal members through well-developed cultural values of individual and tribal acceptance. Positive interpersonal relationships (significance), individual and collective solidarity, and security are promoted through the many values shared by Native-American people, including the following:

1. *A belief in a Supreme Being,* which promotes community and individual responsibility for living in harmony with nature and Native-American religious beliefs.
2. *A belief in the continuity of life* beyond this "mother earth" experience.
3. *Appreciation, hospitality, and sharing,* which promote positive individual, group, and community interactions.
4. *Respect for autonomy and the worth of every individual.* In return, everyone is encouraged to contribute to the work and stability of the community.
5. *Responsibility and industriousness.* Each tribal member's contribution is important to the success and well-being of the community.
6. *Balance in life,* with opportunities for work, fun, and laughter.
7. *Honesty and integrity.* Tribal members are expected to act in accordance with cultural teachings and to avoid bringing shame on oneself, family, clan and tribe.
8. *Group consensus and decision-making.* Each person's opinions and contributions are important to the total group.
9. *Attainment of knowledge and wisdom* will perpetuate tribal well-being and native culture.
10. *Respect for "Elders"* as the "keepers" of the culture and the reservoirs of knowledge and wisdom.

Respect for and adherence to these values promote community solidarity, significance, and security. Validation of the strength of these relationships has been acknowledged by Martinez-Brawley (1990) in her observation "probably the best example of caring in the broad context of community is the collective responsibility assumed by Native American communities for their members" (p. 91).

## Native-American Community Organization: Compatibility with Locality Development and Community Development Models

The involvement of tribal members in the active work of Native-American communities closely resembles the "locality development" model as described by Rothman and Tropman (1987); and the community development model as explicated by Chavis, Florin, and Felix (1993).

An assumption underlying locality development theory is that "community change may be pursued optimally through broad participation of a wide spectrum of people at the local community level in goal determination and action" (Rothman and Tropman, 1987, p. 5). This assumption is compatible with Native-American values that advocate respect for the autonomy and worth of every individual, and the importance of each person's contribution to the well-being of the whole in the community decision-making process.

Community development, according to Khinduka (1987) enhances the locality development process by bringing people together, encouraging participatory democracy, and promoting local reasoning and decision-making processes (p. 360). Community development is strengthened through program development. "Community projects . . . strengthen the spirit of unity in a community through enhancement of community feelings, self-reliance and local leadership" (Khinduka, 1987, p. 36).

Chavis, Florin, and Felix (1993) identify three stages of community development capacity building. These are (1) expanding the base of citizen involvement; (2) enhancing the leadership pool and augmenting leadership skills; and (3) expanding the information and resource base. All these strategies are important to the community development and cultural enhancement model advocated for work with Native-American communities.

## Native-American Approaches to Community Problem Solving

In 1985 a national survey of minority people identified many problems affecting their health status. Subsequently, the United States Public Health Service and the National Academy of Health Science formed the "Healthy People 2000 Consortium." Their final report, published in 1990, identifies three goals: (1) to increase the span of healthy life for Americans; (2) to reduce health disparities among Americans; and (3) to achieve access to prevention services for all Americans. The American Indian Health Care Association drafted the publication *Promoting Healthy Traditions Workbook* (Scott, 1990) to serve as a guide to Indian communities seeking to address the goals of the Healthy People 2000 Campaign. This publication proposes to address Indian community health problems through a "Circle of Community Wellness" approach (p. 12). The steps to community intervention are outlined as follows:

1. Conduct assessments to answer questions related to the health status of communities;
2. Mobilize efforts to bring the community together;
3. Create a vision for the future;
4. Create a vision for change;
5. Nurture the vision through program development; and
6. Celebrate the vision and goal accomplishment.

The *Promoting Healthy Traditions Workbook* is a valuable resource, especially for American-Indian groups that are addressing the health problems of their communities. Many of their approaches and recommendations are appropriate for addressing a variety of other community problems as well.

Whatever approach or combination of approaches is utilized, consideration should be given to both process goals and outcome goals (See Table 2.1).

## *Examples of Community Development and Cultural Enhancement Approaches*

Several Native-American urban, rural, and reservation communities have begun to implement community development and cultural enhancement programs. These communities have committed considerable time and effort to the development and enhancement of their programs and the people they serve. These communities have assumed ownership of their problems, resources, and growth potential. Each tribal member is viewed as both a participant and a contributor to the common good. Communities are reinforcing the importance of individual worth and cultural identity in the development of these programs. Some examples of programs in which community development and cultural enhancement success are being achieved are described below.

The Oneida Indian Nation in Oneida, Wisconsin, is directing a community effort in behalf of their 3,000 reservation residents (Boyte, 1984). Tribal members have developed economic resources to employ and support their people and community. Bingo games are generating funds to purchase Indian lands that were lost from the reservation some time ago. Cultural reinforcement efforts are promoting

**TABLE 2.1  Process and Outcome Goals**

Recommended for Consideration in Native-American Community Development/Cultural Enhancement Approaches

| *Process Goals* | *Outcome Goals* |
| --- | --- |
| 1. Enhance Community Ownership | A. Identify community problems and resources<br>  1. Invite community participation<br>  2. Review existing research data<br>  3. Conduct needs assessments<br>  4. Determine goals and objectives<br>  5. Select evaluation approaches<br>  6. Report outcomes to the community<br>  7. Revise goals and objectives<br>  8. Repeat evaluation approaches<br>  9. Repeat community reporting measures |
| 2. Enhance Positive Regard—Individually and Collectively | B. Include everyone "in"<br>  1. Hire staff<br>  2. Assign responsibilities<br>  3. Form task committees<br>  4. Recruit, recognize volunteers<br>  5. Implement programs<br>  6. Modify programs in accordance with evaluation data and revised goals and objectives<br>  7. Invite participation from all community members, as appropriate<br>  8. Schedule community activities (formal and informal) |
| 3. Enhance Positive Cultural Identification | C. Emphasize cultural values, beliefs and traditions<br>  1. Form cultural committees<br>  2. Form "Elders" advisory committees<br>  3. Include cultural values & traditions in every component of the program.<br>  4. Program general cultural activities<br>  5. Program tribal-specific cultural activities<br>  6. Emphasize knowledge/wisdom (current and traditional)<br>  7. Enhance leadership skill development |

Oneida language instruction; construction of a traditional "longhouse"; traditional Indian ceremonies and dances; a tribal Indian school; tribal cultural classes; home birthing practices; farming; active involvement of "elders" in community programs; and self-governance after the tradition of the Iroquois Confederacy. This Native-American community emphasizes giving, sharing, and cooperating. Cultural classes provide instruction in traditional tribal medicine; giveaways; activities for community elders; and appreciation for nature and all living creatures. Community ownership, individuality, collectivity, and enhanced cultural identification are all important to this community and its vision.

In other Native-American communities tribal members are implementing collaborative efforts to develop "Heritage Centers" for the benefit of tribal members, other Indian groups and non-Indians. These "Heritage Centers" house (1) pictorial living histories of their tribal heritage; (2) auditoriums for ceremonial and social dances, and pow wows; (3) facilities for hosting traditional games and social gatherings; and (4) ceremonial dwellings such as "longhouses" in which healing and traditional ceremonies are held for the benefit of all tribal members. Some centers also house museums; historical tribal arts; modern arts; giftshops to promote sales of tribal arts; and theaters for local plays, ceremonies, and community events.

One urban community has developed a community approach to enhance the strengths of American-Indian people through a variety of Indian and non-Indian activities developed around a cultural enhancement model that emphasizes "four great powers." The goal of this community is to enhance the meaning of life through traditional values of (1) spirituality—living in harmony with the spiritual teachings of tribal groups; (2) intellectual development—positive use of one's mental capacities through the development of knowledge; (3) emotional well-being—development of self-discipline through respect for nature, family, and clan; and (4) physical well-being—achieving holistic wellness by adhering to principles of good health. Among the activities in which community members can participate are the following: martial arts; cultural arts—including beading, weaving, basketry, and leather work; native language skill enhancement; instruction in traditional herbal medicines; drumming circles; sweat lodge ceremonies; and spiritual and vision quests. Treatment options that can be made available to community members include both modern day medicine/treatment services and spiritual or traditional healers. Respect for "elders" and cultural beliefs are honored through participation in "giveaways" and a variety of tribal ceremonies.

Window Rock, Arizona, High School (Dine Nation—Navajo) has envisioned its student body as a community. Four different types of "Peer Support Groups" are offered to Window Rock High School students. These include: (1) "Staying Straight" groups for those young people in recovery who want to live lives that are chemical-free; (2) "Insight groups" for those young people who are experiencing school, family, or relationship problems as a result of drug and/or alcohol abuse; (3) "Support groups" for youth who are negatively affected by drug/alcohol use of significant others; and (4) "Growth groups" for self-development of young people who are not negatively affected by the drug/alcohol use of significant others. All young people at the high school are welcome to participate in the group of their choice. There is a place for everyone. All of the groups offer a nonusing peer support group philosophy. The groups are organized within the school community, and have the benefit of leadership and support from adults and peers within that community system (*Positive Self-Esteem Can Protect Native American Youth,* n.d.).

Examples of two different Indian communities that have made community commitments to drug-free lifestyles are reflected in the Cheyenne River Sioux Reservation and the Akhiok Alaskan Village on Kodiak Island. The Cheyenne River Sioux Reservation has set a goal to accomplish 100 percent alcohol- and drug-free lifestyles among their 5,000 reservation community members by the year 2000. This is a community effort where a variety of programs are made available to youth and adults to sustain drug-free lifestyles and support accomplishment of this goal. The Akhiok Alaskan Village on Kodiak Island has achieved a 70 percent adult sobriety rate in the past several years. This achievement represents a substantial increase in sobriety from the baseline of 10 percent sobriety before the village promoted this community effort to achieve sobriety (*Pass the Word,* n.d.).

## A Case Study

A case study is presented to illustrate the implementation of the Community Development/Cultural Enhancement Model. This case study details a long-term community development process.

The American-Indian community in Salt Lake County, Utah, has stabilized considerably in the past decade. Many Salt Lake County American-Indian residents are members of one of the eight predominant tribes in the state of Utah. These tribes include the Northern Ute, White Mesa Ute, Dine Nation (Navajo), Paiute, Northwestern Band of Shoshoni, Goshute, Skull Valley Goshute, and San Juan Southern Paiute. The Indian population of Salt Lake County also includes representation from more than sixty additional tribal groups. Many American-Indian people have established permanent residence in Salt Lake County. Some organizations presently serve primarily American-Indian clientele including the Indian Walk-In Center, the Indian Training and Education Center, the American Indian Counseling and Recovery Center, the Indian Health Clinic, and some religious and tribal based organizations. In the recent past, American-Indian community members have come together to address a number of community concerns and to participate in a variety of social, cultural, recreational, and spiritual activities.

In 1988 the Office for Substance Abuse Prevention (O.S.A.P. and now C.S.A.P.—Center for Substance Abuse Prevention) announced funding for community partnership grants. We believed that the Salt Lake County American-Indian community was stable and ready to participate in a collaborative effort of this magnitude. Contacts with the American-Indian community were positive and resulted in cooperative efforts with Salt Lake County Division of Alcohol and Drugs and subsequent funding of a five-year O.S.A.P. (C.S.A.P.) Community Partnership Grant, currently administered by the Salt Lake County Division of Alcohol and Drugs. A Native-American Task Force is responsible for directing the programs available to American Indians through this funding.

This positive experience led to another community effort in response to announcements from the Robert Wood Johnson Foundation of funding for "Healthy

Nations" American-Indian community programs. In anticipation of the R.F.P.'s, the authors invited members of the American-Indian community to participate with us in reviewing the initial announcement. The first meeting was held at the University of Utah's Graduate School of Social Work. Sufficient interest was demonstrated that Native-American community representatives attended one of the seminars sponsored by the Robert Wood Johnson Foundation to learn more about the requirements and whether Salt Lake County would meet the criteria for possible funding. Following the return of these representatives, another meeting was held at the University of Utah and the consensus of those in attendance was that we should proceed with an application.

## Process Goals and Outcome Goals

All the actions taken to this point followed the Community Development and Cultural Enhancement Model we have advocated (Edwards & Edwards, 1988, 1992). The actions are also in keeping with the "Circle of Community Wellness" model (1990) advocated by the American Indian Health Care Association.

## Enhance Community Ownership

Initial interventions were directed toward enhancing community ownership through broad-based community participation.

We believed that in the initial planning process two major concerns would significantly affect community ownership. One was the location of the community meetings. While there was considerable comfort in attending meetings at the University of Utah, parking and traffic were often problematic. These factors would likely limit participation of "Elders" and community representatives who lived some distance from the university, which is located in the northeast section of the Salt Lake Valley. The second decision related to which of our community agencies would be the sponsoring agency. After considerable input from those in attendance, the Indian Training and Education Center (I.T.E.C.) was selected as the sponsoring agency and designated as the site of future community planning meetings. This agency is located in a more convenient location in south Salt Lake and has ample parking.

Several factors contributed to these decisions. We knew that the community meeting location would either encourage or detract from community participation. We also knew, as indicated in the "Circle of Community Wellness" publication that "a gathering of community members to make important decisions is a long-standing tradition among Indian people" (1990, p. 22), and we wanted to support this tradition. We agreed with the authors of the "Circle of Community Wellness" publication that planning community meetings "may involve taking risks; like asking people to come together who have never worked together before or who have fought against each other in the past" (1990, p. 22). We knew this to be true of our community. We didn't know which of these players would fit in these or other categories, but we knew that we wanted to invite broad community participation. We hoped that the project's goals and objectives would bring people together—if not immediately, then sometime during the process.

It has been important for us throughout the community development process to "enhance positive regard" for participants—individually and collectively, and to "include everyone in." We followed community development principles throughout the process and found these to be compatible with our "process" and "outcome goals" and the cultural procedures recommended in the *Promoting Healthy Traditions Workbook* (1990).

We wanted our community meetings to reflect "the tradition of consensus, democracy, and community input" that is a part of American-Indian culture. We agreed, however, with the authors of the *Workbook,* that "for many reasons, many people are not able to work in this tradition" (1990, p. 23). We believed that some community members would develop these collaborative skills as they were positively affected by the vision of this project. Others may choose not to participate at this time. We believed it important to accept the individual decision-making of each prospective participant.

Our community meetings would be attended by Indians and non-Indians. Most participants were familiar with American-Indian cultural traditions—theoretically and emotionally. Our community is made up of representatives from multiple tribal groups, many of whom are long-term residents. Our community has experienced problems both internally and between agencies. How these will be resolved and complicated by future interactions is unknown, but most residents were willing to risk involvement and participation.

We agreed to meet regularly—planning each future meeting with the group as a whole. The meetings were cofacilitated by the authors of this paper and the director of the Indian Training and Education Center. We collaborated in identifying items for the agenda, mailing notices and reminders to nonattendees, and general preparation for the meetings. The authors conducted the meetings with considerable support from the I.T.E.C. director and other group members.

This coleadership relationship was renegotiated several times throughout this process. The authors felt comfortable with the shared planning roles and community committee leadership roles. All three "community leaders" support reinforcing Indian leadership. All community leaders agreed with the position advocated by the *Promoting Healthy Traditions Workbook* (1990) that the chairman of the meetings should be "an experienced facilitator . . . someone who has a neutral role in the community . . . a respected elder." We qualify as experienced facilitators, "Elders," and have a neutral (although supportive) role in the community. It has been, however, important to continue negotiations regarding the process whereby this role is shared within the community planning body.

Our community meetings are accompanied by refreshments—furnished most often by the I.T.E.C.; an agenda that facilitates input from the community members;

updates on work accomplished; appropriate handouts; considerable networking and socialization; extensive good-humored teasing; requests for volunteers for subcommittee assignments; and plans for coming meetings.

## Needs Assessment/Research Data Review

The planning committee reviewed existing data from several resources including the Census Bureau, independent community research studies, social service and community agencies, committee representatives, and two recent Native-American community needs assessments. All these data supported information already known to most of the participants, that is, Indian people in Salt Lake County have health, employment, social service, education, social, and cultural needs. Indian people are often overrepresented in statistics indicating problems with alcohol and drug use, incarceration, juvenile justice and adult correction systems, educational attendance and achievement, and dependence on social service systems.

An interesting finding from both recent "needs assessments" was respondent willingness to participate in programs to identify solutions and develop resources to better meet the needs of Indian people in Salt Lake County. These respondents wanted to be involved in the community through participation in problem solving and positive growth experiences.

After reviewing all these data the "Steering Committee" recommended that a survey be formulated related specifically to the purposes of the "Healthy Nations" funding. The authors designed the survey and asked "Steering Committee" members to complete the instrument in consultation with staff members of their agencies, family members, and other community members. The information was tabulated and summarized for further presentation at the community meetings. At the second community meeting, two subcommittees were formed. One subcommittee was responsible for reviewing all the survey data and recommending goals and objectives for this community project. The second subcommittee was charged with developing "job descriptions" for the project director and the project coordinator. This subcommittee also assumed responsibility for recruiting possible candidates for the project coordinator position and requested vitae from them for inclusion with the grant application.

## Evaluation

All reports were submitted, in detail, at the following committee meeting. The I.T.E.C. staff were responsible for drafting the grant proposal with the authors' participation. The I.T.E.C. staff were also charged with the responsibility for selecting evaluation approaches. Interestingly, research and evaluation were not emphasized in the Robert Wood Johnson "Healthy Nations" R.F.P., but the "Steering Committee" and I.T.E.C. staff believed evaluation to be an important part of the community development process, and assumed responsibility for including this component in the project.

## Reporting Outcomes to the Community

Throughout this process, the community has been informed of the progress to date. This community has included people and agencies represented on the "Steering Committee," coworkers and family members, and people who have been unable to participate or chose not to participate in the "Steering Committee" meetings. Efforts have been made to expand participation at community meetings through written invitations, personal contacts, and shared information. "Steering Committee" members are repeatedly encouraged to invite all interested community residents to participate in the planning meetings. Reports of the work of the "Steering Committee" are given to those who do not attend community meetings.

## Enhancing Positive Regard: Individually and Collectively

Throughout this community development/cultural enhancement process there has been considerable concern that all community members be "included." As community members have learned about this project from others, they have been encouraged to participate. All community members have been invited to submit their ideas for inclusion in the proposal, through the survey and more informal requests. With each contact, we have asked specifically in what ways community residents would be willing to participate and contribute to this program. Letters of support were requested for the grant application that specifically included "in writing" the ways in which community agencies and individual staff and community members were willing to cooperate personally with and provide services to this community project.

Specific goals adopted by the "steering committee" include: (1) to promote prevention of alcohol, drug, and tobacco use through an early identification approach; (2) to provide treatment services to decrease the negative influences of alcohol, drug, and tobacco use on Native-American people and families; and (3) to promote relapse prevention through the provision of culturally enhanced services.

Staff assignments have been made to specific members of the I.T.E.C. staff. Task Committees have been formed to facilitate the application and community development. In addition to the "Goals and Objectives" and "Personnel" subcommittees, the following subcommittees have been formed: (1) Elders Advisory Committee; (2) Cultural Content Committee; and (3) Media Committee. Community members have volunteered to serve as committee members and have addressed a number of other assignments throughout the development of this project.

Invitations to participate were extended to chairmen, and their designees, of the eight major tribal groups represented in Utah. Key professional and knowledgeable people in these tribal groups have also been invited to participate in the project.

A "feast" was held at the authors' home to celebrate the work accomplished and to plan for the Site Visit Team Meetings. "Feasts" are traditionally important to both the "work" and socialization values of American-Indian culture. "Feasts" promote a continued balance in the daily lives of Native-American people. They emphasize cooperation, sharing, industriousness, social interaction, and celebration. The continuing work of subcommittees was discussed at that "Feast." An agenda was established for the Site Visit meetings and additional subcommittee meeting dates were set.

## *Enhancing Positive Cultural Identification*

Throughout this community development process, considerable effort has been extended to affect positively the cultural identification of community participants and the people served by their agencies. All assignments undertaken in this and previous community activities have emphasized incorporation of cultural values, beliefs, and traditions. A "Cultural Content Committee" was formed with volunteers from the "Steering Committee." The Cultural Content Committee is charged with preparing materials that will form the initial cultural thrust of this program. These materials were prepared in advance of the Site Visit meeting. The director of the Utah State Indian Education Department chaired this subcommittee. The cultural content will emphasize, but not be limited to, important cultural information from the eight major Utah tribes.

In addition to this committee, an Elder's Advisory Committee has been formed. This committee will have responsibility for reviewing cultural materials prepared for program use and sanctioning the work, or making recommendations for its modification. Members of this committee will also be invited to participate in all activities sponsored through this community project. They will be informed of the progress of the project through regularly scheduled committee meetings.

All members of the community will be kept informed of community activities through the efforts of the Media Subcommittee. Possible methods to be utilized will include (1) publication of a "project" community newsletter; (2) use of the larger community's media resources; (3) announcements made over the local radio station providing information and programming on a regular basis to the Native-American community; (4) utilization of services of a local American-Indian–owned artistic design studio; and (5) other resources as appropriate.

The cultural content of project programs will relate to general American-Indian values, beliefs, and traditions, but will also present tribal-specific cultural content. For example, the customs observed by Navajo people at the time of death and mourning are quite different from those of the Yurok. Navajos refuse contact with the body of the deceased and traditionally use burial locations some distance from their residences. Yurok people traditionally bury their dead in the center of their villages. Now that Yurok tribal members live on farms and ranches of their own, they often have family burial plots on their own land. These customs will be discussed from both a traditional background and modern-day stance. Sharing of information and the importance of culture and traditions will be emphasized throughout the cultural content of this program. Cultural teachings will enhance the positive identification of Native Americans with their own tribal groups and with American-Indian heritage generally.

A further goal of the "Steering Committee" is to emphasize the attainment and use of knowledge and wisdom—both traditional and current. Traditionally leadership was shared by all tribal members, according to individual and collective strengths and needs. This project seeks to further this tradition for all participants, individually and collectively.

What was accomplished throughout the "enhancing community ownership" process includes emphasis on "enhancing positive regard for self" and "cultural identification." There has been considerable interaction among community participants. As issues and problems are discussed, committee members offer suggestions based on their own tribal values and understanding and acceptance of the values of other tribal groups with which they are aware. Differences of opinion are expressed openly and with respect for the opinions of others. Members believe that the "modeling of these values" can also be incorporated into ongoing community programs for the benefit and learning of all participants.

Throughout this project, a "vision" for the future development of the Salt Lake Native-American community has been clarified and integrated into the minds and hearts of the community participants. The "vision" has been nurtured in community and committee meetings. The community development and cultural enhancement program has brought people together. Personal and professional relationships have been developed and enhanced. Participatory democracy has been experienced through local decision-making. We have learned much about the individual and collective opinions, knowledge, and wisdom of our community members. And we have enjoyed one another's company.

We celebrated the "vision" and goal accomplishment at a dinner party the night before the site visit team meeting in our community. On the following day, the site visit team meeting presented opportunities for Salt Lake and Utah Native-American youth, adults, and elders to describe the needs and strengths of our community and the goals and objectives of our grant proposal. The site visit meeting also graphically demonstrated to all community participants the growth we had individually and collectively accomplished as a result of this "journey." Whether or not this grant is funded, the Salt Lake Native-American community has created a "vision" of what can be accomplished through a community development and cultural enhancement model. We know that we have the motivation and capacity to work together, and we have committed ourselves to continue this effort through interpersonal and professional collaborative "journeys" in behalf of the continued development of the Salt Lake and Utah Native-American communities.

## Community Organization Practice Skills Important to the Community Development/Cultural Enhancement Model

Implementation of this model includes judicious and continuous use of professional community organization skills. None of these should be neglected. Some, however, must take into consideration the cultural values and traditions of American-Indian people.

**1.** *Leadership* positions are not actively sought by many competent, qualified American-Indian people. Leaders are often recruited from the participants on an ongoing basis. Leadership must be shared. Major roles must be fulfilled by those having both the informal and formal sanction of the community. Leadership assignments must be given to those who will follow through and provide a framework that welcomes and involves participation from all community members. Recognition should be given to all participants—one person should not be singled out for recognition more than another—even though that person contributes more significantly to the project. Extensive individual recognition may embarrass traditional Indian people and result in withdrawal from project participation. When people offer suggestions for implementation, they should be invited to provide leadership in developing these suggestions. This is often a way in which American-Indian people offer to "volunteer."

**2.** *Planning* before meetings and subcommittees is imperative. Community meetings must provide opportunities for networking, socialization, feedback from elders, and attention to work. In order to accomplish all these goals, planning and prior task completion are essential.

**3.** *Sharing* the planning, work, and credit is important to maintain participation. Many American-Indian people will not "volunteer" for assignments, especially in front of their peers. Leaders must recognize community members' talents and invite members to assume chairmanship and committee assignments. When committee members do not accept their "share" of the work assignments, it is not unusual for those to be pointed out indirectly in a committee meeting, with some pressure placed on the "reluctant" contributors. Young adults should be welcomed as potential leaders. It is the responsibility of the Native-American adults to train and support youth in the development of their leadership abilities.

**4.** *Communication* is essential. Welcome both nonverbal and verbal communication. Respond to both. "Elders" may take considerable time offering their opinions. Listen. Summarize community meetings. Emphasize assignments, the next meeting, and other matters important to the group's business. Express appreciation for the attendance and participation of everyone. If any one person is singled out, specific mention should be made of all participants.

**5.** *Problem solving* will require attention to *negotiating* and *conflict management.* There is much "history" involved in conflicts among specific tribal groups. Some reservations include more than one tribal group. Some of these tribal "combinations" were pre-reservation "enemies." They have histories of conflict with one another. There are often problems between "enrolled" and "terminated" members of the same tribe. There are family histories that involve cultural conflicts and ill will. Most of these are known to only a few people. But these are barriers to community development. There are differences of opinion regarding the community project itself. Who will lead? Where will the project originate? Who will comprise the "board of directors"? What is our history—individually and collectively—with these people. Two major issues will affect the process of problem solving, negotiation, and conflict management. One of these is the worth and value of the community project. The second is whether the shared leadership includes people with whom there is already a trusting relationship.

**6.** *Goal accomplishment* is greatly facilitated when as many community members as possible are consulted and their input is included in the project. An effective leader must honestly seek consultation from the constituency as well as professional involvement from those who can be supportive of the project. *Consultation* must also be ongoing with the "Elders" of an American-Indian community with both formal and informal role assignments and recognition given to this valued segment of American-Indian people.

**7.** *Decision-making,* like leadership, must be shared. If not, the program may be limited to one agency and one staff—with little involvement or support from the community. If a program operates independently, from a single agency base, it often contributes to the detriment of community building and cultural enhancement.

## Personality Traits Important to the Implementation of the Community Development and Cultural Enhancement Model

The implementation of the community development and cultural enhancement model relies heavily on the maturity and personality traits of all community participants—not just that of the leader(s). American-Indian people are "community oriented." Individually and collectively, their personality strengths must support the community development and cultural enhancement model.

**1.** Community members must be *visionary.* Spiritually, American-Indian people have strong, positive ties to the *visionary* attributes of their personalities. All community members must see the program or components of the program from a committed visionary stance. This means they truly see, feel, and experience the goals, work, and potential accomplishments.

**2.** The community project must be conceptualized as a *journey*. American-Indian people enjoy the journey (process) as much as they appreciate the outcome. Individual growth is valued and subtly recognized throughout the process. Collectivity is nurtured and celebrated. Community members are reluctant to terminate satisfying community "journeys."

**3.** American-Indian community members must continue to build their *inclusionary* traits. Ideally, leaders genuinely "welcome" participation and involvement from others. There is a selflessness in evidence when people recognize the importance of the community project or goals and submit themselves to the "will of the group" in working toward accomplishment of these community goals. One can imagine the conflicts that occur when there are "negative" histories or unresolved relationship issues among Native-American people who are committed to the same community goals. These conflicts may take considerable time to resolve.

**4.** Over time, *honest investment* in goal accomplishment and all aspects of the program's development may appropriately result in subjugation of personal issues to the success of the program.

**5.** All the above may successfully contribute to *understanding, diffusing, and resolving criticism and divisiveness,* which, unfortunately, is altogether too common in programs undertaken within American-Indian communities. There is often legitimate basis for criticism (or unfinished history) which could be addressed. Acknowledging the criticism will do much to diffuse unwarranted criticism. Offering to accommodate or include positive recommendations can propel positive energy toward the program's goals and objectives.

**6.** Motivation and commitment to the American Indian community and project are often framed by the *high energy* investment of community members. All participants should be encouraged to "enjoy" the hard work, the association and togetherness, and the successes and the challenges. *Good humor* and positive interactions will motivate continued involvement and personal growth of community members at all levels of participation. "Feasts" and other socialization activities are appropriate to celebrate accomplishments and redirect community efforts.

## Secondary Community Development

There are often many benefits that communities enjoy in accomplishment of goals and objectives through implementation of "community development and cultural enhancement" models. Primary benefits are the realization of the goals of the specific projects. Secondary benefits are often seen in the community togetherness and enhanced networking of individuals, groups, and agencies. Many secondary benefits have been noted in Salt Lake County since efforts were established to implement this community model. Among these are the following.

**1.** One agency has established an "Elder's Advisory Committee" to identify "Elders" in Salt Lake County and to assess needs and possible programs for this population. Membership consists of a number of committed professional people and community volunteers. One grant has been submitted for possible funding to support these programs. Requests for proposals have been sent to three other funding sources. A needs assessment was developed and conducted among "Elders." Three graduate social work students have volunteered their participation in various aspects of this project.

**2.** Groups for Indian youth have been developed at an elementary school through volunteer efforts of professional social workers and a graduate social work student. Parenting groups are currently in the planning stage.

**3.** The First Annual American Indian Motivational Youth Conference was implemented, as a result of suggestions from American-Indian teens participating in a Youth Leadership program. Representatives from three Western states attended this conference.

**4.** There has been active outreach to all of the major tribal groups represented in Utah.

**5.** Information has been readily shared throughout the community regarding this project and the efforts of community members in the planning stages.

**6.** Youth, adult, and "Elder" participation has been invited and expanded throughout the course of this project. All participants have been encouraged to continue their involvement at higher levels throughout the development of this project.

## Summary

It is important to emphasize both the community development and cultural enhancement aspects of this model. Native-American people have experienced the benefits of "community" in their traditional heritage. They have considerable history, knowledge, and wisdom—much of which can be applied to the community challenges of today. Native-American people are committed to the self-determination and self-governance values that complement community organization principles. They find much satisfaction in identification of "visions" important to the success of their people. They have rekindled the hope of the "journey" (process), which has been so effective in past community accomplishments. Many challenges remain in the broader society and within Native-American communities. This community development approach, with its emphasis on cultural enhancement, has the potential for reenforcing the identification and achievement of the "visions" of Native-American people—individually and collectively.

# References

Boyte, H. C. *Community is possible: Repairing America's roots.* New York: Harper & Row, 1984.

Chavis, D. M., Florin, P., & Felix, M. R. J. "Nurturing grassroots initiatives for community development: The role of enabling systems," in *Community organization and social administration: Advances, trends and emerging principles,* T. Mizrahi & J. Morrison (eds.). New York: The Haworth Press, 1993.

Edwards, E. D. and Edwards, M. E. Alcoholism prevention treatment and Native American youth: A community approach. *Journal of Drug Issues, 18*(1), 1988, 103–114.

Edwards, E. D. and Edwards, M. E. "Native American community development," in Community organizing in a diverse society, F. G. Rivera and J. L. Erlich (eds.). Boston: Allyn and Bacon, 1992.

Khinduka, S. K., "Community development: Potentials and limitations," in *Strategies of community organization: Macro practice,* F. M. Cox et al., (eds.). Itasca, Ill.: F. E. Peacock Pub., 1987.

Martinez-Brawley, E. E., "Power, influence, and leadership in the small community," in *Perspectives on the small community.* U.S.A.: NASW Press, 1990.

McKnight, J. Are social service agencies the enemy of community? *Social Policy.* Winter, 1987.

*Pass the word.* A resource booklet published by the Native American Development Corporation, Washington, DC, n.d.

*Positive self-esteem can protect Native American youth.* A resource booklet published by the Native American Development Corporation, Washington, DC, n.d.

Rothman, J. and Tropman, "Models of community organization and macro practice perspectives: Their mixing and phasing," in *Strategies of community organization: Macro practice,* F. M. Cox et al., (eds.). Itasca, Ill.: F. E. Peacock Pub., 1987.

Scott, S. *Promoting healthy traditions workbook: A guide to the healthy people 2000 campaign.* St. Paul: American Indian Health Care Association, 1990.

# 3

# Chicanos, Community, and Change

## MIGUEL MONTIEL AND FELIPE ORTEGO Y GASCA

As Alice discovered there is nothing "curiouser" than change. Often "change" is viewed as synonymous with "progress": movement toward reason and justice stressing equality as the core of justice.[1] Men and women have power to the extent that they influence the circumstances of the time.

Why do some people resist change while others rush to greet it? William Blake identified resistance to change as "mind-forged manacles." It is true that each of us guards a gate of change most of us are reluctant to open. Nevertheless, each of us makes concessions to change, consciously or unconsciously, with or without consent.

Purposive change—the power of "intervention oriented toward improving or changing community institutions and solving community problems" is the theme of this chapter.[2] We explore the part played by Chicano organizations, particularly since the 1960s, in influencing change.[3]

To understand how change occurs in Chicano communities, consider what is meant by "community." It is simply a group of people sharing similar interests and goals. Warren refers to community as action organized to "afford people daily local access to those broad areas of activity which are necessary in day-to-day living."[4] Often towns and cities are referred to as communities even though the residents may not share common interests and goals. The notions of community—culture, religion, work, education, war, and power—have served "to gratify man's desire for community and for the cherished legitimacy that community alone can give to authority, function, membership, and loyalty."[5]

What has been the process, progress and direction of change in the Chicano community? What part have Chicano organizations played in change? What are the prospects and projections for Chicano communities and organizations? What needs to be done to make things better? These are the questions we will explore. We begin with a brief profile of the Mexican-American community, and the place of the barrio within it, and follow with a discussion of the evolution of organizations and the issues they have attempted to address.

## *The Mexican-American (Chicano) Community*

The population of the United States of Mexican origin is growing rapidly. Hispanics (Mexicans, Puerto Ricans, Cubans, and other Spanish-speaking peoples) now constitute about 9 percent of the total U.S. population or more than 22 million people—an increase of 53 percent over the 1980 count. About 60 percent (13.5 million) are Mexican Americans, and about half of these have arrived over the last two decades. Some experts estimate that perhaps half of the 13.5 million are in the United States illegally. Compared with the general population, Hispanic are more concentrated, with 87 percent living in 10 states as compared with 54 percent in the total population. The highest percentage of Hispanics among the population has remained within the Southwest (Texas, New Mexico, Colorado, Arizona, and California) with the majority (12 million) living in the states of California and Texas.[6]

Compared with the total U.S. population, Mexican Americans are younger (23.8 years vs. 32.9 years); more fertile (3.6 children for women aged 35–44 vs. 2.5 for white women), and more vulnerable (18.8 percent female-headed households vs. 14.3 for the Anglo cohort). Similarly, there are higher rates of delinquency, school dropouts, violent deaths, and alcohol-related diseases even though the life expectancy of Mexican-Americans is similar to that of Anglos. Although Mexican-American males had the highest labor force participation of any group, they had relatively higher rates of unemployment, 9.2 percent vs. 6.1 percent for the total population. Median income was almost $9,000 less than the median of the total population, and women received the lowest wages of any group except Puerto Ricans.[7]

The "bad will" that existed in the early years of Mexican-American interaction continues to some extent. The "English-only" movement attempted to outlaw the use of Spanish in governmental settings (except within the court system) and relations between Mexican immigrants and the U.S. Immigration and Naturalization Service continue to be volatile at times. Immigrants become scapegoats for social problems particularly during times of economic turmoil as evidenced by the strong anti-immigration political rhetoric of Governor Pete Wilson and Senator Diane Feinstein of California.

In many areas of the Southwest, Mexican culture has lingered despite the overwhelming dominance of Anglo society. It is in the barrios, where the culture has been kept alive and vibrant. Louis Wirth described the Jewish ghetto as a transitional enclave that provided temporary continuity to their land of origin.[8] Similarly, barrios, neighborhood enclaves, and the accompanying Mexican-American organizations have served as havens from the vicissitudes of American society.

A barrio, however, is not necessarily a community—that doesn't mean it isn't. The word *barrio* is an imprecise term for a cluster of Chicanos principally because it is fraught with negative perceptions of poverty and impotence. The breakup, or more appropriately the segmentation of barrios, as with ethnic villages, has been created partly because of the movement of the middle class to the suburbs. According to Sennett and Cobb, the integration of white ethnics "meant integration into a world with different symbols of human respect and courtesy, a world in which human capabilities are measured in terms profoundly alien to those that prevailed in . . . their childhood."[9] The same applies to Mexican Americans. Nevertheless, barrios do serve an important function particularly for newly arrived immigrants (legal and illegal). The barrios are the communities with the greatest need for organization and leadership.

## The Evolution of Chicano Organizations in the United States

To understand change and the role that Mexican-American organizations have played in the Chicano community since the 1960s one needs to examine the historical record. The period from 1848 to 1960 can be seen as three stages, each contributing cumulatively to the evolution of Mexican-American organizations and Chicano consciousness.

### Early Mexican-American Period: 1848–1912

This was a period of transition. While no accurate record exists of the number of Mexican citizens in the territory demarcated by the Treaty of Guadalupe-Hidalgo in 1848, estimates range from 75,000 to 350,000.[10] Additional Mexicans became residents of the United States as a result of the Gadsden Purchase in 1853. These were the first Mexicans to face becoming Americans in their own land.

These events marked the end of a historically Mexican community and the beginning of consciousness as Mexican Americans. During this period, Chicanos resisted the one-way process of acculturation and assimilation. Conquest, segregation, a distinct language and culture, and, to some extent, skin color kept Mexican Americans from full participation in the American experience.

There were, of course, many organized groups within the Mexican community before the conquest in 1848. For example, the Penitentes (Brothers of Our Father

Jesus of Nazareth), carryovers from the original Spanish settlers, began organizing in the late 1700s in what is now New Mexico and Colorado. After the conquest, however, Mexican Americans saw the need for organizational strength to ward off Anglo-American onslaughts. The massive land transfers, legal and illegal, from Mexican to Anglo hands, the conversion of Mexican people into a pool of cheap labor, and laws like the California "Greaser Act" of 1855 were some of the tangible effects of discrimination, and resistance organizations were formed in response. In addition to the many mutual aid societies were radical organizations headed by figures like Juaquin Murrieta and Padre Martinez. One such organization, El Guante Negro Mutualista, was a secret organization dedicated to robbing the rich and helping the poor. In 1894, twelve years before the formation of the National Association for the Advancement of Colored People, the first successful organization for Mexican-American rights was formed in Tucson, Arizona, under the banner of Alianza Hispano Americana. Its mission was to defend Mexicans against the bad will in American society. These are the events that set the agenda of the times. The year 1912, when New Mexico and Arizona were admitted into the union, marks the end of this period.

## Later Mexican-American Period: 1912–1940

Between 1912 and 1930, fleeing the turmoil created by the Mexican Revolution of 1910, and attracted by the lure of mining jobs and manufacturing, more than 1.5 million Mexicans crossed into the United States. Ernesto Galarza, a scholar and an early organizer in the farmworkers' cause, called this one of the greatest migrations in world history. Although as many as one-third of them (including bona fide American citizens) were "repatriated" to Mexico during the 1930s, it is from this rapid expansion of the Mexican-American community that the current Chicano population draws its numeric strength.

This period is also marked by Mexican-American efforts to become Americans, shedding, if need be, their "Mexicanness," including their language, to become part of the American mainstream. Leading the effort to promote English and help its members become good American citizens was the League of United Latin American Citizens (LULAC), organized in 1927 in Texas. LULAC, one of the more significant organizational efforts with a membership of approximately 100,000 members, has a long list of civil rights, labor, and educational accomplishments.

## Modern Mexican-American Period: 1940–1960

This was the period when Mexican Americans searched for one America and discovered two—white America and the Other America, as Michael Harrington described it.[11] Some 500,000 Mexican Americans served in the armed forces during World War II and earned a significant number of medals of honor. Yet after the war, Mexican Americans learned painfully that "color" was still the way white America defined good Americans. In the apartheid system of the United States, Mexican Americans could not cross the color line.

In South Texas in 1947, a Mexican-American soldier who died in battle during World War II but whose body had only then been recovered was denied burial in a municipal cemetery. This (and other related events against returning soldiers) precipitated the formation of the American G.I. Forum, a powerful militant organization of Mexican-American veterans.

Two important court cases enjoined by LULAC laid the legal foundation for the involvement of Mexican Americans in the civil rights movement of the 1960s. In 1945, Gonzalo Mendez of Orange County, California, brought suit against the public schools of Westminster to end segregation of Mexican-American students. Judge McCormick ruled for Mendez, and the ruling was affirmed on April 14, 1947, by the Ninth Circuit Court. In 1948 a similar case was affirmed against the Bastrop School District in Texas. Both cases were important precedents in the 1954 Supreme Court ruling, *Brown* v. *Board of Education.*

In 1955, the Alianza Hispano Americana—then more that sixty years old— established a civil rights department headed by Rafael Guzman, an early scholar of the Chicano movement. The Alianza joined with the American Civil Liberties Union (ACLU) and the NAACP to further the civil rights of all minorities.[12] In 1957, for example, *Alianza* magazine informed Mexican Americans that Charlotte C. Rush, Patriotic Education chairman of the Denver Chapter of the Daughters of the American Revolution, didn't "want a Mexican to carry Old Glory" in a parade at the State Industrial School for Boys. She believed that only "American boys" should carry the flag even though the boy originally chosen was an American of Mexican descent.

Only during the civil rights movement of the 1950s and 1960s did Americans began to realize that nineteenth-century theories of acculturation did not tell the full story of minorities in America. An America founded on a homogeneity of values rooted in the English tradition is giving way to an America founded on cultural pluralism.[13]

## *The Sixties and Beyond*

A taxonomy for "Chicanos, Community, and Change" since 1960 does not evolve neatly by decades. The patterns seem to fall from mid-decade to mid-decade. The momentum of the 1950s carries well into the 1960s and the consciousness of the Chicano movement, faint though stirring, begins well before the 1960's. While the beginning of the Chicano movement is not the beginning of the civil rights struggle for Mexican Americans, it begins a time of self-determination and a disruption of the traditional Americanization process. It is out of this resolve that the plethora of Chicano organizations emerged, dedicated to "going it alone" (at least for a while) rather than trying to "satisfy the man." Three organizational epochs since the 1960s are identified: (1) the Chicano Renaissance, (2) economic development and (3) Hispanicity.

## *The Chicano Renaissance*

This period during the 1960s and early 1970s is the beginning of Chicano resistance activities in the arts, academia, and politics. During this period, Chicanos became involved in numerous projects, abortive and successful, in collaboration and in opposition with the "establishment." It was a time of turmoil, confusion, and opportunity. It was a time when Chicanos tried to enter the American system on their own terms.

One of the most effective organizing efforts in the Mexican-American community was led by the Industrial Areas Foundation (IAF), a training network established by Saul Alinsky in 1940. IAF-trained organizers built the Community Services Organization and the Farm Workers' Union in the late 1950s and early 1960s. Cesar Chavez, Edward Roybal, Bert Corona, and many other Mexican-American organizers were influenced by Alinsky's confrontational tactics of the Industrial Areas Foundation, first introduced to the Mexican-American community via the Community Service Organization (CSO), a postwar organization founded on the values of the mutual aid societies of previous years.

In the late 1950s and early 1960s organizers in California and Texas had begun aggressive activities in state and national politics. For example, under the leadership of Bert Corona (and with assistance from the Jewish community), the Mexican American Political Association (MAPA) achieved the incorporation of East Los Angeles and the election of Edward Roybal, an instrumental figure in the formation of several national organizations, to the U.S. House of Representatives. During this time, similar activities were initiated by Henry B. Gonzales, the eccentric and courageous U.S. representative (who became the chairman of the Banking Committee) in San Antonio, Texas.

In spite of strong opposition from growers and the Teamsters Union and a history of failed attempts to organize farm workers, Cesar Chavez established what is today known as the United Farm Workers' Union, an affiliate of the AFL-CIO. Chavez's organizing genius included utilizing powerful religious Mexican symbols like the Virgin de Guadalupe to network diverse groups of farmworkers and appeal to the liberal community, using Gandhian nonviolence and fasting to keep the peace and make it difficult for the growers to retaliate. Chavez maintained a loyal following right up to the time of his death. Shortly before his death in 1993, however, competing unions, lack of enforcement of the Labor Relations Board in California, and litigation setbacks began to affect the power and membership of the Farm Workers' Union.

In the mid-1960s, radical organizations led by charismatic leaders sprang up throughout the Southwest. The most important were Reyes Lopez Tijerina's Alianza

Federal de Pueblos Libres in New Mexico, Rodolfo "Corky" Gonzales's Crusade for Justice in Colorado, and Jose Angel Gutierrez's Raza Unida Party in Texas.

Chavez's nonviolent posture contrasts with the militant tactics of the flamboyant Protestant minister Tijerina, the leader of the Alianza, who fought to have the Spanish land grants restored to the original Mexican settlers in New Mexico, Colorado, and Texas. The Alianza lost its base when violence erupted in a courthouse raid orchestrated by Tijerina's followers in Rio Arriba County in northern New Mexico, which eventually resulted in Tijerina's imprisonment.

Exhibiting a similarly strong nationalistic orientation, Rodolfo "Corky" Gonzales, a former boxer and powerful charismatic leader, inspired the passions of Chicano youth through his Crusade for Justice. The yearly Youth Liberation Conference sponsored by the Crusade of the 1970's had a powerful, long-lasting impact on the more radical elements of the Chicano movement. It is from these conferences that El Plan Espiritual de Aztlan emerged, which outlined a "declaration of self-determination" for Chicanos in the Southwest. "Nationalism," Gonzales claimed "is a tool for organization, not a weapon for hatred."[14]

Under the leadership of the fiery Jose Angel Gutierrez, the Raza Unida Party gained electoral victories in several communities in Texas where Mexican Americans held majorities, thus challenging, at least for a short period, the dominance of the Democratic Party in the Chicano community.[15] Several prominent Chicano leaders have accused the Raza Unida Party of reverse racism. Important during this period also were the organizing activities of the Chicano students under the Movimiento Estudiantil de Aztlán (MECHA) banner, which led to the formation of numerous Chicano studies programs in universities across the country.

The emerging Chicano intelligentsia, some based at fledging Chicano studies departments, began to search for a more accurate depiction of the Chicano community. Until this time, the social sciences had depicted Chicanos as deficient, and policy was aimed at transforming Mexicans into a narrow middle-class success model.[16] Padilla claims that because of diversity and insignificant community participation among Chicanos, however, Chicano studies advocates created an idealized vision of the Chicano community.[17] Focus on community, Padilla argues, reflected a desire on the part of Chicano intellectuals to participate in the struggle for equality at a grassroots level.

During the 1960s and early 1970s, Chicanos proposed bold visions of a bilingual/bicultural society to be maintained by Hispanic institutions; only a handful have survived. The most ambitious was the Hispanic University of America in Denver in 1972. Though headed by New Mexican U.S. Senator Joseph Montoya, the drive to secure funding comparable to that of congressional funding for Black colleges did not materialize. The Chicano movement did not create bilingualism or biculturalism in American society; both were there from the beginning of Anglo-American society on the Atlantic frontier. The Chicano movement (with the significant influence of exiled Cubans), however, did raise discussion of these issues to the level of national policy, culminating in the Bilingual Education Act of 1968.

In the late 1960s, Chicanos began to organize caucuses within various professional organizations. In social work, for example, the Trabajadores de la Raza led by Paul Sanchez helped organize chapters in cities in the Southwest and Midwest. Chicano-oriented schools of social work were established at San Jose State University (where Sanchez became the first dean) and New Mexico Highlands. The Trabajadores also had a part in curriculum changes and redirecting social service delivery systems. Many Chicano agencies began as advocacy agencies, but ended as social service agencies because of their dependence on external funding. Many professional groups organized during this period were institutionalized in the 1980s. Nevertheless, while blatant negative stereotypes of Chicanos have gone by the wayside and institutions give token service to Chicano concerns by establishing ineffective bilingual programs, there is no bilingual/bicultural society.

## The Economic Development Period

The "economic development" era took hold in the mid-1970s and continues to the present. During this time, the focus of reform efforts shifted from global and idealistic aspirations for social justice of the 1960s to gaining economic and political advantage for Chicanos at the national level. Enhanced activity in Washington, D.C., created, at least temporarily, a paucity of leadership at the local level. In the 1970s, a more systematic approach toward solving problems appeared to take place. The tactics of the radicals were rejected. Government and philanthropic foundations like Ford encouraged the establishment of Chicano agencies that would work within the system. There is little question that the rejection of many charismatic leaders led to greater opportunities for the moderate leaders who followed.

Activists (as opposed to agency heads) continued to confront established institutions on many of the same issues raised during the 1960s. Invariably these confrontations lead to concessions, usually not for confronters but for others who waited in the wings. The relationship between confrontation and change is never direct. Institutions never admit that the change results from pressure. As a university administrator stated about a prominent leader, the prize goes to those who are "acceptable to the establishment." The 1970s are filled with examples of this phenomenon. The Raza Unida Party enhanced opportunities for Mexican Americans in the Democratic Party; MECHA opened the universities for newly graduated Ph.D.s; demonstrations and disturbances in the inner cities created opportunities for economic development corporations; the Tierra Amarillo raids in New Mexico enhanced opportunities for Hispanic New Mexican politicians.

The most prominent organizational phenomenon of the 1970s was the formation of community development corporations (CDCs) in poor minority neighborhoods. Their goal was to develop "sources of strength and confidence in those neighborhoods" and to alleviate "the economic and social distress caused by the malfunctioning of the private sector and the shortcomings of the public sector."[18] These corporations were designed to quiet the disturbances in the inner cities. Today, the more than 100 CDCs (some controlled by Chicanos but most by blacks) are supported largely by federal programs and private foundations (especially Ford) although the ultimate goal is to be self-supporting through profit-making ventures.

The Mexican American Legal Defense and Education Fund, (MALDEF) spearheaded by the LULAC network with moneys from the Ford and Marshall Field foundations, came into its own during this period. MALDEF's civil rights activities have touched every area of Mexican-American life from education to women's rights. The Ford Foundation has figured prominently in the organization and funding of other organizations including the Hispanic Policy Development Institute and the Inter-Agency Consortium for Hispanic Research, two national Hispanic organizations. Interestingly enough, these groups are headed by non-Hispanics.

The Industrial Areas Foundation's influence on the Mexican-American community was again felt in the mid-1970s first in Texas, and later in California, and more recently in Albuquerque, New Mexico, and Phoenix, Arizona. There is an strong link between the IAF, at the time led by Fred Ross, and the formation of various Mexican-American organizations (e.g., CSO, MAPA, the Farm Workers' Union and subsequent organizations like the Hispanic Caucus and the National Association of Latino Elected and Appointed Officials, NALEO. The IAF has also served as a catalyst for the formation of various Mexican-American organizations. This pattern is manifested in the formation of other Hispanic organizations. The union organizing efforts of leaders like Barraza and Lacayo spawned ideas for the development of the National Council of La Raza and a string of CDCs such as Chicanos Por La Causa in Phoenix and TELACU in Los Angeles, as well as several offshoots of the Council. Similar threads can be traced to the development of organizations like LULAC, the American G. I. Forum, La Alianza Hispano Americana, and most recently El Concilio de America.

The resources provided by the War on Poverty and the unions helped develop networks that remain to this day. For example, the National Council of La Raza hosted over 125 affiliates and 8,000 participants at their annual meeting in Detroit in 1993. It is not surprising that organizational life in the Mexican-American community is dominated by relatively few individuals connected through a national network; a network, however, that touches a small segment of Chicano and Mexican communities in the United States.

## *The Age of Hispanicity*

In the 1980s many of the concerns of the 1960s were institutionalized. It was the epoch of Hispanicity, a period when many important Chicano leaders of the 1960s became outcasts, when it became possible to form a Hispanic congressional caucus, and when national Hispanic organizations gained prominence. It was also a period when corporations and political leaders at the highest levels saw the convenience of aggregating Spanish-speaking groups, and from one day to another Mexican Americans and other Spanish-speaking groups were referring to themselves as Hispanic.

In the 1980s, "leadership" became important in Hispanic communities. MALDEF, LULAC, and the United Way of America initiated leadership programs to help Hispanics develop the skills needed to serve on boards. In 1988, representatives from various Hispanic leadership programs established the National Network of Hispanic Leadership Programs, aimed at the formation of a national leadership training agenda.

While still important, community-based organizations are giving way to profession-centered organizations. Local and national organizations have sprung up in business, health, education, welfare, and the arts. In the professions there are Hispanic organizations for accountants, for executives, for personnel managers, for psychologists and nurses. The National Hispanic Quincentennial Commission was organized to plan a national program commemorating the 500th anniversary of the Hispanic presence in the Americas. IMAGE (The National Association of Hispanics in Government) established a commission to assess the status of Hispanics in the Department of Defense. Hispanic corporate executives organized the National Hispanic Corporate Council, a Fortune 500 group, to create opportunities for Hispanics within corporations. A similar group of executives, headed by former New Mexico Governor Jerry Apodaca, established the Hispanic Association for Corporate Responsibility. The development of professional groups tied to their mainstream professional organization indicate a shift in strategies for change in the 1990s and beyond. Everywhere Hispanic groups with ties to their mainstream organizations are being formed to tackle specific pieces of the Hispanic agenda.

While general membership organizations like LULAC still "cover the waterfront" in voicing their concerns for Chicanos, more and more of the particular issues of the Hispanic agenda are taken up by organizations with specific rather than general membership. The organizations of the 1980s operate more like pressure groups held together by narrow goals and objectives rather than the broad-based advocacy groups of the past.

Organizations oriented toward promoting individual or professional interests are a recent phenomenon in the Chicano community. They indicate the growing diversity (and fragmentation) of the Chicano community and the emergence of a professional and merchant class. The contrast between the pragmatism of the 1980s and the idealism of the 1960s is a source of great tension between the poor, the working class, and the middle class; between immigrants and Chicanos; and among the various Hispanic groups.

There has been some dissatisfaction with national efforts of organizations like the National Council of La Raza because some critics claim they are removed from the pulse of the local communities, that they are influenced far too much by non-Hispanics and particularly corporate interests, and their advocacy is geared more toward individual interests rather than to that of their affiliates. In many instances national agencies are more involved in running programs rather than advocating local efforts. These concerns have spurred organizing efforts such as those of Miguel Barragan, a pioneer in the development of the Chicano CDCs, who has organized El Concilio de America, an organization in Northern California with over 185 affiliates, some of which belong to both the National Council of La Raza and El Concilio. El Concilio's aim is to establish an Hispanic development fund for Hispanic self-determination, thus avoiding the control agencies like the United Way have exerted on Hispanic organizations. It is not surprising that these maverick efforts have angered those Hispanic groups and individuals who have finally managed to maneuver themselves into the mainstream.

Most Hispanic organizing efforts are staff dominated, and there is little attention paid toward developing leadership within the communities where the organizing takes place. Organizers and agency heads in many Hispanic communities do not live in the communities in which they work and rarely endure the indignities faced by residents of those communities. The dilemma confronting the professional organizer is one of credibility; to have people believe what he or she says about dropouts, segregation, and housing. This is not to derogate the role of community agency organizers but to highlight the inevitable conclusion that while the individual circumstances of many Mexican Americans have changed, the social circumstances of barrios and communities—the targets of community organizers—have not changed dramatically.

Also dissatisfied are many Hispanic women, particularly with their level of participation in organizations of the Mexican-American community. Numerous parallel groups for women like the Chicana Forum, MUJER, and the Mexican American Women's National Association to name just three have emerged in the last few years. Gonzales was one of the first women to raise this issue. Interstate Research Associates (IRA), an important nonprofit research and consulting firm founded on the idea of self-determination, she claimed, was out of touch with the women's movement.

> *Most notable was the lack of female representation in its leadership hierarchy. Mexican American women . . . questioned the lack of women in IRA's decision-making process. More and more they felt that IRA's problem solving excluded the problem of women.* "[19]

Gloria Molina, exploiting the dissatisfaction of women and what Skerry referred to as "elite-network" politics—developed from outside money and with weak community ties—practiced by Los Angeles politicians like Alatorre and Torres, got herself elected to the Los Angeles County Board of Supervisors.[20]

What can be said of the 1980s is that it was a time of institutionalization for Hispanics. This period witnessed the demise of the charismatic leaders of the 1960s; the proliferation of Hispanic professionally oriented organizations; increased visibility of Mexican Americans within the broader community; the seriousness with which they are taken as consumers; dissatisfaction with the status quo among

Hispanic women; the amnesty bill, which at once legalizes illegal immigrants and makes it more difficult for illegal "aliens" to live in the United States; and the "English-only" movement, which attempts to restrict the use of Spanish in the United States. It was the period when ideological and materialistic divisions became apparent.

## Assessments and Reevaluation

In the new science of "chaos," consideration of data focuses on sensitivity to initial conditions. That is, the outcome cannot be predicted from the initial conditions. This is an appropriate consideration in assessing and reevaluating "Chicanos, community, and change" during the last thirty years (1960–90).

The initial conditions that engendered the tumult of the 1960s—poverty, unemployment, housing, failed foreign and domestic policy—are still with us, exacerbated by demographic imperatives that augur the realizations of all past apocalyptic visions, especially those of Malthus.

Have things changed for the better since the 1960s? The individual circumstances of many Mexican Americans have changed dramatically. Many make more money, live in better homes than their parents, are better educated, and generally enjoy a higher standard of living than they did as children. Dramatic changes have occurred at the national level also. National organizations like MALDEF, the National Council, and NALEO have fulfilled one of the most important goals of the 1960s: to get onto the national agenda. In the 1990s we will see national organizations like G.I. Forum and S.E.R. move their headquarters from the Southwest to Washington, D.C., providing further testimony of the prominence of Chicanos in the national scene. There also have been significant gains in national representation in the U.S. Congress, and a proliferation Spanish-speaking radio and television stations, controlled primarily, however, by Cuban and Mexican interests.

In spite of these efforts the situation has not changed appreciably for most Chicanos. The level of Chicano participation in electoral politics continues to be low, and broad-based Hispanic political organizations have not learned how to hold their politicians accountable.[21] And it may be, as Skerry claims that some Mexican-American politicians, because they are beholden to interests outside their communities (like the Los Angeles clique mentioned above), want it that way.[22] The Chicano population is young, poor, growing rapidly, and a significant sector is beset with seemingly insurmountable problems including crime, drugs, teenage pregnancy, and dropouts. Chicano communities have become more segregated; income distribution is lopsided, and indicators of family life are increasingly pathological. Chicanos are living in a society ill equipped to deal with these problems.

Is the relative lack of progress the fault of leadership or of organizations? Both, perhaps. The fault may lie, as Mark Anthony intoned, not in the stars but in ourselves. We expected the miraculous from our ordained leaders and perhaps the impossible from our organizations. We expected a larger response from mainstream America. In 1938 in *Forgotten People* Sanchez wrote about the pledge to his people made by the U.S. government in the Treaty of Guadalupe Hidalgo—a pledge to help his people lift themselves up by their bootstraps. Instead, Sanchez wrote, "it [has taken] away our boots."[23] The Chicano movement, unlike previous Mexican-American movements, made a clarion call for change to come from Mexican Americans themselves, not externally or benevolently from government. This did not mean that government has no role to play. On the contrary, government has a large role to play because it was, after all, government that in 1848 made Chicanos an internal colony.

Chicano organizations did not spring into being sui generis. Though most often formed in opposition to historical oppression, Chicano organizations nevertheless modeled their structures on organizations consistent with their experience in the United States. As Frantz Fanon observed in *Black Faces/White Masks,* having experience with few other models, invariably the liberated turn to models with which they are familiar.[24]

Still, the objectives of Chicano leaders and organizations were sufficiently radical to alarm mainstream America and even some Mexican Americans. That's why the term "Chicano" describes a generation whose sociopolitical directions veered sharply from the historical trajectory of the Mexican-American experience. And it is quite possible that the term "Chicano" will die along with the generations of the 1960s.

Organizations are often ephemeral, chimeras of a hopeful vision. The perduring "artifacts" of change are most often the ideas that give birth to change, ideas written down on clay tablets, or parchment, or codices, or books for future generations to ponder and by which to judge the efficacy of the past.

The most fertile and perhaps the most dynamic period of the Chicano movement was the Chicano Renaissance. Its most enduring contributions are found in education and the cultural arts. The decade of the Chicano Renaissance can be loosely compared to an Iliad of Chicano assaults on mainstream America. By extension, the decade from 1976 to 1985 can be regarded as the odyssey of Chicanos navigating through the rocks and shoals of mainstream American on the "final lap home," as Ricardo Sanchez, the Chicano poet laureate of Aztlan, put it.

Unfortunately, that meaning is being lost as the Chicano community grapples with the notion of Hispanicity introduced in 1986. Are they Chicanos (or Mexican Americans) or Hispanics? More than three-fifths of the Hispanics in the United States are Chicanos. Yet, many are concerned that by subsuming themselves under the Hispanic rubric, they will lose their edge in numbers to Cuban Americans, who make up less than 5 percent of the U.S. Hispanic population but, like Jewish Americans, are influential beyond their numbers in the population. (It should be noted, that unless educated and mobilized, numbers alone are not a good indicator of power.)

Since 1986, Chicanos have been receding to the backdrop of American culture as an ethnic group; they are being culturally if not economically assimilated into the mainstream. High school textbooks still do not reflect the ethnic mosaic that is the American experience, and Chicano high school students do not question this, nor do their parents. The Chicanos of this generation are busy professionalizing their lives, fashioning them on the templates of the dominant culture, and have apparently lost interest in Chicano politics, particularly the politics of protest.

The Mexican-American heteroclites who fashioned and shaped the various canons of the Chicano movement seem forgotten now. Here and there, chispas of those thoughts flow and fan the movement's flame for a flickering moment. The Chicano movement is a distant mirror to a time now denigrated by mainstream thought. Chicano intellectuals fashioned a heuristic tradition for the proper study of Chicano life and culture. Has it all been for naught?

No, we do not think so. The Chicano movement integrates a vision of past and present. The renewed sense of pride in their bicultural heritage has helped Mexican Americans better understand the sociopolitical context of their lives in the United States. More and more, national and local Chicano organizations (in concert with other Hispanic organizations) are affecting the national agenda. This was evident in the Bush appointments of the Texan Lauro Cavazos and the New Mexican Manuel Lujan as the first Mexican Americans to cabinet rank, and the Clinton appointments of Henry Cisneros, a prominent Chicano politician from Texas, to HUD and Federico Pena, the former mayor of Denver, to the Department of Transportation. Skerry raises a critical political consideration for Mexican-Americans: do they follow the immigrant ethnic politics pursued by other ethnic groups or do they follow the racial minority politics of African Americans?[25]

It may be, however, that the demographic imperative will be the demise of the Hispanic agenda. At the moment, there appears to be little planning for that eventuality. When that moment comes, Hispanics will not need an ethnic-specific agenda, because the public agenda will become their agenda. If this does not happen, internecine conflict will surely follow.

## Conclusion

The problems that confront Chicanos are the problems of most Americans— environment, war, education, employment, poverty, the population explosion, and, most recently, unbridled government and corporate corruption. These problems, according to Hans Morgenthau, result from deliberate policies pursued by powerful interests.[26]

Chicano organizations have been influenced by the same forces, perhaps to a greater extent, that influence mainstream culture, and Chicano leaders are vulnerable to the power brokers—interests that set the broad direction of economic and government policy. It is not only the powerful interests that prevent Chicanos from forging a better life, however, it is also the lack of strong families, strong friendships, ethical priests, viable communities and strong vocations. It is the deterioration of these forces that allow "leaders" to lead while separated from the communities they represent. Accountability is absent.

The fragmentation in the Chicano community mirrors that of the larger society. The distorted concept of democracy that sets up a competitive system for the limited societal resources with little concern for the "common interest" makes it most difficult to organize. Chicano organizations often work at cross purposes with one another, and they often miscommunicate one another's motives. Given these circumstances, it is difficult to lay out a strategy for organizing. Noam Chomsky blames a "system of ideological control which aims to make the issues seem remote from the general population and to persuade them of their incapacity to organize their own affairs or to understand the social world in which they live without the tutelage of intermediaries."[27]

However, it is possible to articulate a philosophical and ethical stance on the world that can guide action. It should rightly be an action that confronts the realities of the Chicano experience. And while we have attempted to highlight some of these realities, there are fundamental issues that need to be explored in great depth if the Chicano reality is to be understood in its full significance. The works of Paulo Friere, the Brazilian philosopher, Tomas Atencio, a New Mexican sociologist and activist, and the organizing of the IAF symbolized by the work of Ernesto Cortez are instructive in this regard.[28] At the core of Freire's teaching is the idea that the ontological vocation of man is to be subject. This is a short way of saying that man's reason for being rests on establishing horizontal relationships brought about through a confrontation with the reality of his situation—nature, institutions, and other men. Man can achieve his vocation through a critical consciousness—a depth of understanding in the interpretation of problems that lead toward changing himself, the world, his relationship with others, and his culture. A critical consciousness within the Chicano community is possible, Freire would argue, only through a reflection of man in the context of his cultural environment, that is, the place of Chicanos in American society; the eras both of Mexico and America and the interaction created by the confrontation of two culture; the extent that they are involved in the creation of their own history and culture; and the obstacles that need to be overcome. Education and organizing would need to focus on the development of a critical consciousness, and action would be based on Chicanos viewing themselves as social and political beings capable of accessing and acting on the world.

Atencio's reflections expand on an understanding of Chicano consciousness.[29] He believes that the core of the problem facing Chicanos is the disharmony between Anglo and Chicano values. One set instrumental (e.g., goal-oriented), legitimate and systematic; the other moral, nonlegitimized and unsystematic, but linked to myth. He refers to myth as the primal forces of society that serve to give meaning to cosmic and social phenomenon. It is the separation of modern culture from its myth that has led to distorted ideologies that support negative irrational political motives. Cultural action must be based on the Chicano experience uncovered through personal history, oral history, folklore and art—*el oro del barrio.*

It is through dialogue that people become aware of their myth and of the external forces that lessen or aid "fulfillment and freedom." Atencio uses the idea of the "resolana"—sunlight reflecting light off the walls where men gather to talk—as the metaphor for enlightenment.[30] The spiral of thought and action that evolves from individuals to groups leads to consensual validation objectifying a body of knowledge from everyday experiences. It is "this body of knowledge that is used as education and ultimately objectified as a basis for action," an action where people respond (and not react) to their world. Atencio has been implementing these ideas in one of the barrios of Albuquerque in the "Resolana Learning Center."

The tedious organizing process of the IAF as described by Skerry consists of transferring "informal, primary groups between friends and neighbors into the instrumental ties binding members of a formal organization."[31] The process requires an understanding of the disjunctures between democratic and Judeo-Christian values and the reality facing not only Mexican Americans or Hispanics but all segments of American society, black or white, rich or poor. Thus Cortez argues that people's concerns transcend ethnicity, and has criticized Mexican-American civil rights activists of the late 1960s and early 1970s because of their "ethnic exclusivity."[32]

In San Antonio, Houston, and El Paso people were concerned with flooding and deterioration, education, and utility bills. Cortez's method of organizing is based on organizing people and not communities. Power relies on broad-based organizing that requires money and many organized people, not single individuals. What is needed is a strategy and vision that Cortez claims "comes out of our institutions and . . . Judeo Christian tradition and democratic values."[33] IAF's goal is to establish self-governing institutions and a political culture that can hold institutions accountable. It is not surprising that IAF organizing depends on linkages with religious organizations, particularly the Catholic church.

Realistically, given the existing power arrangements and the available means to counter them, it is difficult to envision anything from American institutions other than token changes. There are no quick fixes or Chicano messiahs. In the final analysis, it is Chicanos who must set the example of just and democratic behavior. Only then can the example be set for the next generation.

## *Endnotes*

1. M. Ginsberg, *The idea of progress: A reevaluation* (London: Methvens, 1953), p. 68.

2. F. M. Cox, J. L. Erlich, J. Rothman, and J. E. Tropman (eds.), *Strategies of community organizing: A book of readings* (Itasca, Ill.: F. E. Peacock Publishers, 1979), p. 3.

3. The information on organizations comes from S. A. Gonzales, *Hispanic American voluntary organizations* (Westport, Conn.: Greenwood Press, 1985) and from M. S. Meier, *Mexican American biographies: A historical dictionary, 1836–1987* (New York: Greenwood Press, 1972). The authors, who have witnessed many of the organizational developments over the years, also draw on their own experiences. Hispanic dictionaries include only a

fraction of Hispanic organizations because many organizations spring into being between the time a directory is submitted for publication and the time it appears in print.

4. R. L. Warren, *The community in American* (2nd ed.) (Chicago: Rand McNally & Co., 1972), p. 1.

5. F. M. Cox, J. L. Erlich, J. Rothman, and J. E. Tropman (Eds.) *Tactics of community practice* (Itasca, Ill.: F. E. Peacock Publishers, 1977), pp. 1–11; B. E. Mercer, *The American community* (New York: Random House, 1956), p. 27; R. Nisbet, *The social philosophers, community and conflict in western thought* (New York: Thomas Y. Cromwell Co., 1973), p. 446.

6. U.S. Bureau of the Census, *Race and Hispanic origin: 1990 census profile* (Washington D.C.: GPO, June 1991).

7. F. D. Bean, E. H. Stephen, and W. Optiz, "The Mexican origin population in the United States: A demographic overview," In R. O. de la Garza, F. D. Bean, C. M. Bonjean, R. Romo, and R. Alvarez (Eds.), *The Mexican American experience: An interdisciplinary anthology* (Austin: University of Texas, 1985), pp. 57–75; P. Skerry, *Mexican Americans: The ambivalent minority* (New York: The Free Press, 1993); U.S. Bureau of the Census (June 1991).

8. L. Wirth, *The ghetto* (Chicago: University of Chicago Press, 1928).

9. R. Sennett and J. Cobb, *The Hidden injuries of class* (New York: Vintage Books, 1972), pp. 17–18.

10. C. McWilliams, *The Mexicans in America: A student's guide to localized history* (New York: Teachers College Press, 1968); F. D. Ortego y Gasca, *Backgrounds of Mexican American literature* (Austin, Tex.: Caravel Press, 1981).

11. M. Harrington *New York Times,* January 29, 1978, p. E-17.

12. Gonzales, *Hispanic American voluntary organizations,* pp. 8–17.

13. R. W. Lubomyr, *Encyclopedic directory of ethnic organizations in the United States* (Littletoy, Colo.: Libraries Unlimited Inc., 1975).

14. C. Marin, "Rodolfo 'Corky' Gonzales: The Mexican-American movement spokesman, 1966–1972," *Journal of the West, 14*(4) (1975), pp. 107–120.

15. M. S. Meier and F. Rivera, *The Chicanos: A history of Mexican Americans* (New York: Hill and Wang, 1972).

16. M. Montiel, *Hispanic families: Critical issues for policy and programs in human services* (Washington D.C.: National Coalition of Hispanic Mental Health and Human Service Organizations, 1978).

17. R. V. Padilla, "Chicano studies revisited," Occasional Paper #6 (El Paso: University of Texas, Chicano Studies Program, 1987), pp. 9–10.

18. Search, *A Report from the Urban Institute, 5* (Winter, 1975), pp. 5–6.

19. Gonzales, *Hispanic American voluntary organizations,* pp. 106–7.

20. Skerry, *Mexican Americans.*

21. R. O. de la Garza, F. D. Bean, C. M. Bonjean, R. Romo, and R. Alvarez (Eds.), *The Mexican American experience: An interdisciplinary anthology* (Austin: University of Texas).

22. Skerry, *Mexican Americans,* 1985.

23. G. I. Sanchez, *Forgotten people: A story of New Mexicans* (Albuquerque: C. Horn, 1967).

24. Frantz Fanon, *Black skins, white masks,* trans. Charles Lam Markmann (New York: Grove Press, 1967).

25. Skerry, *Mexican Americans.*

26. H. Morgenthau, The end of the republic? *New York Review of Books,* September 24, 1970, pp. 39–40.

27. N. Chomsky, *Language and responsibility* (New York: Pantheon Books, 1977), pp. 4–5.

28. P. Freire, *Pedagogy of the oppressed* (New York: Herder and Herder, 1970); T. Atencio, "Phenomenology and social research: A theoretical discussion of a proposed method" (paper presented in partial fulfillment of the requirement for Sociology 580, University of New Mexico, 1978); idem, "Resolana: A Chicano pathway to knowledge," *Ernesto Galarza Commemorative Lecture,* Stanford Center for Chicano Research. Stanford University, 1988.

29. Atencio, "Phenomenology and social research."

30. Atencio, "Resolana."

31. Skerry, *Mexican Americans,* p. 210.

32. E. Cortez, Jr., "Changing the locus of political decision making," *Christianity and Crisis, 47*(1) (February 1987), pp. 18–22.

33. Ibid.

4

# Organizing for Violence Prevention: An African-American Community Perspective

*WYNETTA DEVORE*

> *Violence is as much a public health issue for me and my successors in this county as smallpox, tuberculosis, and syphilis were for my predecessors in the last two centuries.*
> —FORMER SURGEON GENERAL C. EVERETT KOOP, M.D., AUGUST 1986

> *Jessica Bradford knows five people who have been killed. It could happen to her, she says, so she has told her family that if she should get shot before her sixth-grade prom, she wants to be buried in her prom dress. . . . "I think my prom dress is going to be the prettiest dress of all." . . . When I die, I want to be dressy for my family." (Brown 1994)*

## *The Family and Community Context for Violence*

"GETTING READY TO DIE YOUNG Children in Violent D.C. Neighborhoods Plan Their Own Funerals" (Brown 1993). This front-page headline caught the attention of a national audience including the president. Jessica was among a group of about thirty-five African-American youth and adults interviewed by Brown, a reporter for the *Washington Post*. These self-reports reveal life of urban violence such that in the past five years, 224 children younger than eighteen have been killed in Washington, D.C., the nation's capital. These youngsters have been either targets of shootings or merely bystanders, on the street at the wrong moment.

Brown (1993) provides an update of instances of violence in urban African-American communities. Earlier reports provide similar evidence of the impact of violence on this community. "Black men living in Harlem are less likely to reach the age of 65 than men in Bangladesh"; "Reported aggravated assaults have increased by 40 percent or more in many large urban areas" (Battle 1991).

In 1988 Gibbs provided evidence of what she considered to be a new morbidity, which she defines as "life-threatening diseases or disabilities which are primarily caused by social rather than biological factors," which evolve from social, cultural, and economic forces that foster high-risk activities along with destructive behaviors and deviant lifestyles. Her report suggests that in 1977 more young black men (5,734) died from homicide than were killed from 1963 to 1972 in the Vietnam War (5,640).

Examples of these activities include drive-by shootings, gang wars for "turf" rights, homeless young drug addicts exchanging dirty needles, college athletes who die of cocaine overdoses, and suicide. Each act is one of violence to individuals and the community at large.

While the media pay considerable attention to the activities of young African-American males, they focus little attention on the incidence of violence within the family, including spouses, children, siblings, and the elderly. Banks's (1987) discussion of family violence in the course of family life mentions that at the earliest stages the family may be dazed by conditions that set the stage for dysfunction and violence, including pregnancies, planned and unplanned, death of infants, crowded living conditions, and substance abuse.

Increases in family size, without sufficient income, present greater potential for family violence that may include sibling rivalry expressed by hitting new-born infants and younger siblings, regressive behavior, or attention-getting behavior. Such are the roots of later sibling-to-sibling violence.

Parents respond to the stressful events related to employment and unemployment, personal losses, or encounters with various social institutions with behavior that is abusive to their children and other family members.

Corporal punishment is often seen as an appropriate tool for disciplining children. Parents wonder why children do not obey no matter how much they shout and threaten; they question the use of spanking as effective discipline (Comer and Poussaint 1992). At the same time the community appears to support harsh punishment for disobedience and other childhood offenses. Comer and Poussaint (1992), commenting on the tasks related to raising black children, recognize that parents need to understand that they are neither masters nor servants of their children. Banks (1987) reinforces this, acknowledging that a factor in child abuse may be inadequate knowledge of normal child development and an understanding of the roles of parent and child. At the same time environmental pressures dictate the choice of techniques or practices as well as the skills and behavior that are to be acquired.

Considerable attention continues to be invested in adolescent males in trouble, particularly those in single-parent homes. But this does not take account of all youth in this age group. Many live with their single mothers in harmony. They make appropriate adaptations to the normative struggles of adolescence.

However, negative institutional responses place many other African-American youths at considerable risk. While the literature highlights the experience of males, young women in this cohort also suffer as a result of institutional insensitivity.

Three elements in the disintegration of urban social structures have been identified as structural shifts in the economy placing the entire community at risk, and young people at particular risk (Taylor 1991). First, service industries have replaced manufacturing. Remaining industrial plants have moved from the core of the city to suburban industrial parks and out of the country. A second factor is the deterioration of the inner-city economy, a major force behind negative social changes in the community, such as a large population of single mothers and their children and a disproportionate number of youth concentrated in these communities.

Finally, Taylor identifies the exodus of working-class and middle-class families. These families provided a "social buffer" against the advance of various forms of social dislocation. Researchers claim that these families afforded "much of the fine texture of organization and patterned activities that allowed previous generations of urban Blacks to sustain family, community and collectivity even in the face of continued economic hardship and unflinching racial subordination."

Social and spatial concentration of poverty in urban centers and identified social ills such as family disruption, school failure, drugs, violent crime, and housing deterioration have quantitatively and qualitatively altered the psychosocial and material foundations of life for residents of all ages. These ills and others intensify economic marginality and social isolation.

For many youths, male and female, the changes and the need to adapt may be extremely intimidating, thereby producing a "subculture of disengagement" from the social mainstream. This process of disengagement is not unique to African-American youth; it may be observed among poor white and Hispanic youth whose affiliation with family, educational, and economic institutions is faulty. One researcher continues that the influence of the subculture is "most pernicious" among African-American children and youth. It is evident in the rise of youth gangs and violent behavior; it is the "the new morbidity" introduced by Gibbs (1988).

The sparseness of positive male role models is a problem for male adolescents. Again, female adolescents receive scant attention. Each adolescent, male or female, may benefit from a relationship with models from whom they may acquire knowledge, guidance, values, and skills that are the foundation for positive self-definition and a sense of direction.

In another work Taylor (1989) studied middle-class and low-income black male adolescents and discovered that a sense of self-determination, confidence in the future, and willingness to explore alternative possibilities for self-actualization and achievement could be related directly to role model identification, or the lack of such identification. Low-income, inner-city males lacking the gratification from such relationships showed a lack of confidence and trust in their social environment. Because they lack a role model their perceptions, experience of restricted alternatives, or opportunities for assuming responsible adult roles were limited. This population of adolescent males could find no relationship between role model identification and their immediate or long-range goals.

Experiences at home, in school, with peer groups and the larger community generate a discontinuity and conflict in relationships. Because of the nature and quality of the interactions in these particular contexts, poor African-American males are more likely to experience difficulties than female members of their cohort. Difficulties surface in reconciling the contradictory values, expectations, and demands of the environment and in negotiating the difficult transition to adulthood. Too often they drift toward delinquency, crime, drugs, and other antisocial behavior (Gibbs 1988).

Many single young mothers find it difficult to assume adult responsibilities and roles without having had the opportunity to complete the traditional tasks of adolescence. Indeed, they too are at risk, unable to accomplish instrumental and expressive tasks. The lack of success provides the base for child abuse and antisocial behavior similar to that of their male friends.

At each transition point in individual and family life, urban African Americans, young and old, are likely to have experiences that may be identified as violent.

Homicide and violence have been identified as contemporary health problems for the African-American community (Prothrow-Stith and Spivak 1992). This chapter began with an overview of violence in the community. Prothrow-Stith and Spivak begin by identifying violence as a health problem that takes a toll on African-American men who are more likely to be poor and young. Homicide is the leading cause of death for African-American men between the ages of fifteen and forty-five. These urban men are overrepresented among the indicators of violence, emergency room and arrest rates, and school suspensions, as well as the homicide rates mentioned.

Poverty and race continue to be dominant factors in the examination of incidents of violence. Urban African Americans are overrepresented among the poor and among the victims of fatal and nonfatal violence. Although the media are partial to reports of stranger, gang, and racial violence, these are not the most common incidents of violence. Correlates of violence include the use of alcohol, cocaine, other drugs and handgun availability (Prothrow-Stith and Spivak 1992).

Our national response to violence has been management through the legal, juvenile justice, and criminal justice systems, which are largely reactive, pursuing a morality of blame, retribution, and punishment (Earls 1991). The evidence of success of such punitive responses is elusive, as citizens and legislators call for more institutions of "correction," places to hold the offenders.

Earls (1991) and others (Cron 1986, Cohen and Lang 1991, Trafford 1992) call for the realization that these penalizing responses have not served us well. They present violence as a community as well as a public health problem. Trafford (1992) is more forceful, identifying violence as a public health emergency. In 1986 public health professionals were alarmed, reporting that "violence is a public health problem because it exacts in injuries and death, especially among young people. Too many victims are victimized again and again" (Cron 1986).

With the identification of violence as a public health emergency there has been a "medicalization" of violence, removing actions such as murder and assault from the realm of crime to the territory of disease. Former Surgeon General Antonia Novello set forth the public health perspective, declaring, "The prevention of violence . . . is as much a responsibility as is the treatment of its victims" (Trafford 1991).

Alex Gitterman (1987) has set forth the public health social work perspective in relation to prevention as a mode of intervention, stating that the primary objective of intervention is to forestall and anticipate some undesirable event or condition that might otherwise take place and spread. The National Association of Social Workers' definition is more expansive, defining public health as a science and art of preventing diseases, prolonging life, and promoting health and efficiency through organized community efforts (Leukefeld 1987). This public health social work perspective serves as the foundation of this chapter.

## Social Work Foundations for the Prevention of Violence

Calls for community focus on the prevention of violence comes from many directions, but the messages are similar.

> We need to take a comprehensive, community based approach to the needs of both direct, and indirect victims of assault and homicide. . . . We need to improve communications and collaboration among victims service agencies, religious institutions, the criminal justice system, and all relevant provides of health. (Cron 1986)

> We should have conversations on how we can revitalize the community organization tradition of our profession. Community organizing is essen-

*tial for both instrumental accomplishments . . . [and] important for the experience of challenging the imbalance in power relations. (Gitterman 1987)*

Indeed, community organization techniques have been a bulwark in the empowerment of the African-American community. A glance at the history of the civil rights movement in the United States reveals that the Montgomery bus boycott of 1955 and 1956 was a successful community action initiative. Not only were patterns of segregation in public transportation changed but nonviolence was affirmed as a viable tool for social change (Devore 1992).

Rivera and Erlich (1992) have suggested that perhaps the three classic models of community practice—locality development, social action, and social change—are not as "color-blind" as we have assumed them to be. It is their contention that several additional factors must be addressed when working with communities of color: (1) the racial, ethnic, and cultural uniqueness of people of color; (2) the significance of these unique qualities in relation to variables such as kinship patterns, social systems, power and leadership networks, religion, the role of language, and the economic and political configuration within each community; and (3) the process of empowerment and the development of critical consciousness.

Devore (1992) suggests that work in African-American communities would be enhanced if social workers were guided by the layers of understanding for ethnic-sensitive practice including a respect for the values that guide the profession, basic knowledge about the community, knowledge, and skills in public welfare polices and services, an awareness of one's own ethnic heritage, the impact of the "ethnic reality," race, and social class upon daily life in the African-American individual, family, and community, and the need to adapt and modify familiar skills and techniques to the community (Devore and Schlesinger 1991).

Rivera and Erlich (1992) have presented a framework for community practice using language that is similar to public health language related preventive strategies. The terms are primary, secondary, and tertiary. Public health primary prevention efforts are those that focus on preventing the condition from occurring; secondary efforts involve early detection and treatment; and tertiary prevention has been defined as rehabilitation (Schlesinger 1985).

Community organizers, like other social workers involved in the helping process, must continually make decisions related to appropriate strategies and tactics for intervention. Rivera and Erlich (1992) contend that these decisions are made within the context of each situation. The context will determine the degree and nature of contacts on the three levels. These levels of contact and intensity will be examined here within the context of the African-American community.

The primary level of involvement is the most intimate, requiring racial, ethnic, cultural, and linguistic identity with the community. This level requires intimacy and influence to engender trust. Entry into the community, the contact phase of the helping process, is enhanced by ethnic solidarity. The African-American social worker would be the most appropriate for the development of strategies to address violence in the community as a public health problem. Much like public health strategy intervention, this initial level concentrates on efforts to prevent violence from occurring.

The second level of intervention in the community requires contact beyond personal identification with the community and its problems. In this position the worker takes on the role of liaison or community advocate with the larger community fighting for the rights and needs of the community. The broker role, requiring a knowledge of community resources and the ability to create needed resources, may be added to the roles identified at this level.

The roles of conferee, broker, or mediator may be assumed during the change process. As conferees social workers join with others, members of the African-American community or appropriate persons from the larger community. Conferences set the stage for work to be accomplished in the future, while the mediator helps to resolve conflicts that may arise at any point in the helping process. Those involved in the conflict may be members of the community or a combination of African-American community members and representatives of institutions and agencies in the larger community (Wood and Middleman 1989).

The third level of contact, the tertiary, is with the outsider who works for the common good of the community. Tertiary activity need not be assigned to a person with the racial or cultural similarity that is suggested for the primary and secondary levels of contact. Their commitment to the community qualifies them for tertiary roles.

Although it appears that the community levels of contact and intensity do not immediately compare with the public health levels of intervention we must recognize that public health strategies for intervention are the foundation for public health social work (Leukefeld 1987).

## Violence: The Presenting Problem

Violence has been identified as a public health emergency in African-American communities. Evidence has been cited earlier, beginning with Jessica Bradford's plans for her funeral. At a meeting of the Minority Health Professions Foundation, former Surgeon General Novello (1991) confirmed the high instance of violence against children, noting that violence kills more children than does pertussis and harms more of them than does the measles.

Noting homicide rates among young men, she voiced concern that the homicide rate is three times higher among African-American women than among white women. These women are often the victims of intimate violence, they may rebel or participate in violence as the price for association with a man. The judgment of other women may be impaired by substance abuse, leaving them to live in violent situations.

The evidence of individual and family association with violence in its many forms is compelling. Community and family life are at risk. No one escapes; children, youth, adults, men, or women. The public health perspective views the need as being prevention.

## Modes of Intervention

### The Boston Experience

Prominent among the public health strategies for violence prevention are the "Violence Prevention Curriculum" established in the Boston public schools and the "Violence Prevention Project" of the Boston Department of Public Health and Hospitals (Prothrow-Stith and Spivak 1992; Wilson-Brewer 1991). A significant portion of these programs falls within the public health and community development areas of primary prevention. In combination the two perspectives call for community education to be carried out by persons who have close ethnic ties to the community. Dr. Prothrow-Stith meets this expectation.

The community based program has three components: community-based outreach and education, clinical treatment, and a media campaign. The stated goals include:

1. Preventing interpersonal violence among adolescents.
2. Generating service supports for youth already involved with violence.
3. Creating a new community ethos supportive of violence prevention (Wilson-Brewer 1991)

Other community efforts include attention to school-based violence. Prothrow-Stith's experience in hospital emergency rooms provided more than enough evidence of violence among adolescent African-American males. These acts made homicide the leading cause of death of these urban poor, unemployed young men.

Again addressing the primary level of contact suggested by Rivera and Erlich (1992) Prothrow-Stith, an African-American professional, worked with students at Dorchester High School, a predominantly African-American high school (Wilson-Brewer 1991). The result of the effort was a course on anger and violence, the "Violence Prevention Curriculum for Adolescents."

Based on the premise that anger is a normal, essential, potentially constructive emotion and that creative alternatives to fighting are available; the curriculum is designed to:

1. Provide facts that alert to their high risk of being the victim *or* the perpetrator of an act of violence

2. Create a need in students to find alternatives to fighting by discussing the potential gains and losses
3. Offer positive ways to deal with anger and arguments, the leading precipitants of homicide
4. Allow students to analyze the precursors of a fight and to practice alternative conflict resolution using role play and videotaping
5. Create a classroom ethos that is nonviolent and values violence prevention behavior (Wilson-Brewer 1991).

In addition to the curriculum, community support is required in order for children to combat the social pressures in the community that have a negative impact on their daily lives. The community-based "Violence Prevention Project" provides the needed primary and secondary prevention initiatives.

## The Kansas City, Missouri, Experience

In Kansas City, Missouri, the response to the murders of young African-American males came from the community itself. A grassroots organization, The Ad Hoc Group Against Crime, led the community as it addressed the loss of its young men to homicide (Mitchell and Daniels 1987).

This ad hoc group was established in 1977 after the murders of nine African-American women. The murders remained unsolved, and the dissatisfied community responded by organizing. Members of the group include volunteers from various occupations and professions including social work. The response will be examined in relation to frameworks suggested by Netting, Kettner, and McMurtry (1993) and the paradigm of Rivera and Erlich (1992).

The Kansas City Health Department, understanding that work is best accomplished at the primary level of the community, approached the leader of the ad hoc group seeking assistance in dealing with the increase in homicides within the African-American community. They understood that working at the more intimate primary level would give greater assurance of success. The leader, a member of the community, was familiar with community customs, traditions, social networks, and values (Rivera and Erlich 1992).

During the data collection phase of the work, the demographics of homicide in Kansas City were presented by the chief of the Homicide Division. The result of the presentation and ensuing discussion led the ad hoc group to create a task force to study and document the instances of "black-on-black" homicide and present the ad hoc group with recommendations.

Local media, including African-American radio and newspapers, announced the creation of a task force and invited applications and nominations for membership in it. This process used the resources in the community, institutions that understood the culture of the community. The media served as secondary contacts, forces that have contact outside the community with the ability to provide resources and technical expertise. The press indeed has the ability to inform the local community as well as the community at large.

Among the seventeen persons selected to serve on the task force were consultants, outsiders to the community, who were able to provide expertise needed for a competent study of the problem of violence in the community. When finally constituted, the task force membership included persons from the primary, secondary, and tertiary levels of the community (Rivera and Erlich 1992).

The data collection phase of the task force's work included research. A random sample of 102 homicides were selected from available data covering the years 1980 to 1986. The analysis included demographic, descriptive, and the social context of the homicide.

A second data collection task was review of services presently available to families of homicide victims in order to prevent the duplication of services and to identify any gaps in services needed. A third data collection tool, the community survey, was used. Data was collected relating to the personal characteristics that may differentiate homicide victims from nonvictims. The final step in the data collection process was "brainstorming" of the recommendations committee. The exercise produced 100 recommendations; twelve were given priority status for implementation in the community.

Again, the media were used to inform the local community and the community at large. This tactic is supported by Netting, Kettner, and McMurtry (1993) for its ability to influence public opinion and pressure decision-makers, who are tertiary contacts, into favorable responses. In this instance it is the community resolve to decrease violence among its citizens.

After the work of the task force was completed, the Ad Hoc Group Against Crime assumed responsibility for implementation of the recommendations. The most active and visible committee was "Headlights for Life."

In Kansas City, as in many other communities, homicide and other acts of violence are ordinary and expected occurrences. Yet many are unaware of the frequency of violence and their personal risk for homicide. To heighten awareness the committee, using radio and newspapers, asked the community to drive with their headlights on all day after instances of one or more homicides. The headlights were to indicate that these acts of violence were not acceptable to this African-American community.

At 6:00 P.M. on the day of headlights a vigil is held. This "Community Circle" serves as a community forum in which there are expressions of concern over the loss of potential contributors to the community and the whole of humanity. It provides an opportunity for education as the gathered community is provided with profiles of those who commit violence and guidelines for decreasing personal risk.

Mitchell and Daniels (1987) caution that although the community organizing process has many positive aspects in relation to the public health problem of violence, it has drawbacks as well. Among the positive aspects are community ownership of the project, commitment on the part of leadership, knowledge of the community, and creativity of intervention approaches. Noted among the deficits of the process are the familiar ones of unrealistic expectations, lack of staff, continuity, foresight and planning, and the differing agendas of group members. Despite these deficits, the Kansas City effort addressed the problem of violence in the community in a systematic way, using tactics and process appropriate for a community organization response to a public health problem of violence.

## The Syracuse, New York, Experience

The Southwest Community Center in Syracuse, New York, proudly declares in a banner beneath its name that it this is a "DRUG-FREE ZONE." The message to the community is that in this place we care about the health of the community. Despite this declaration the community suffers from the troubles of other urban African-American communities; there is poverty, despair, and continual incidents of violence in homes, in school, and on the streets.

A meeting room in the center displays another banner identifying it as the "LETHAL WEAPONS ROOM." Activity in this room is designed to nurture and cultivate the minds of young people with positive messages and information about the contributions of African Americans to the world (I.Y.M. 1990).

In this process of reframing, young adults have begun to attack the violence in their lives and community using their minds as weapons combating the intruder. The change was initiated by an organizer who fits the Rivera-Erlich (1992) profile of the community organizer. He is an activist who can identify with the community culturally, racially, and linguistically, having an intimate knowledge of the public and private language of the community.

In what may be identified as part of the problem definition phase, the organizer identified a group of young people who would "hang around the center." Although they used the play areas of the center they were not involved in any particular program activities. Calling the young people together, the organizer offered an opportunity for involvement. He had specific goals in mind: the development of skills for survival in the community, structured activities requiring discipline, and the development of a sense of empowerment.

Although the organizer's initial task was drug counseling, a new program, "Intelligent Young Minds," grew out of his investment in young adults. At a time when significant amounts of attention are given to African-American males, "Intelligent Young Minds" includes young men and women, a significant statement about the center's commitment to all children in the community.

Using "brainstorming" techniques the organizer and other staff members sought to answer the unusual questions: where to begin, how will we be different, how can we capture and keep the attention of youth? The result of this technique was a recognition that young people like to make money. Thus, processes began to establish a small business.

Looking again to the Rivera-Erlich (1992) paradigm for organizing and the public health prevention model, one may identify intervention at the primary and tertiary levels as this enterprise began. Primary-level intensity and influence is exerted by persons familiar with the community having the same racial identity. Other staff members took on secondary roles as liaisons with other center programs and the community. Tertiary-level work in this project has been accomplished by so-called outsiders who may or may not be African Americans.

The small business product was silk-screened T-shirts. Tertiary contacts included a silk screen artist, a professional sales person, and a bank executive who helped the youths to open a business account. During 1992 the group earned $9,000 from sales of T-shirts and other fund-raising activities. Plans are under way for the development of a computerized business that will produce stationery and business cards, again with the support of "outsiders."

The organizer's skills in empowerment, program planning and development, assessing community psychology, and understanding organizational behavior, along with a keen sense of self-awareness (Rivera and Erlich 1992) have provided support to this innovative community program.

In 1992 "Intelligent Young Minds" received one of seven state awards recognizing innovative and creative programing for youth along with the Onondaga Council on Alcoholism and Addictions award as the substance Abuse Prevention Program of the Year (Eimas 1994).

Two particular activities of I.Y.M. provide contacts with community professionals and children who frequent the center. Each helps I.Y.M. members to gain a sense of empowerment and an opportunity to develop communication skills. Tertiary-level professionals, bankers, doctors, pharmacies, and painters, have provided opportunities for learning and employment during the summer months. In the second activity I.Y.M. members serve as peer counselors to younger children whom they claim as family members. In this mentoring role they begin to take responsibility for change needed in the community.

They discover children who have dreams of basketball as the gateway to college and success as the new Michael Jordan. Through mentoring they attempt to "give them a different perspective on things like going to school for school, getting an education instead of just playing sports . . . see both sides of the picture, letting them know that not all of their brothers and sisters are doing the wrong thing" (Eimas 1994). Peer counselors are bound by a pledge of responsibility:

*As a peer counselor I realize that I have a major responsibility to myself and my community. By maximizing my daily efforts to be the best person that I can be, I realize how both my family and my community would benefit.*

*To help me, keep a daily focus on maximizing my potential as Peer Counselor I take this pledge of responsibility.*

1. *I will remain drug free.*
2. *Put forth an honest effort to get the most out of my education, and seek help when necessary.*
3. *To be a positive role model in my community.*
4. *To participate in the structured education and activities of my peer counseling group.*
5. *Once established in life, I will return to my (any) community to share the gifts life has afforded me. (I.Y.M. 1990)*

The I.Y.M. logo contains outreached hands, symbolizing an attitude of reaching for responsibility and independence. The hands are surrounded by an array of stars, symbolizing goals and blessings, with an understanding that there are no limits to what may be accomplished for themselves and the community (Moss 1992). The pledge and symbols give the group a sense of cohesiveness.

Unlike the Boston and Kansas City programs, which have very clear goals related to violence prevention, the Syracuse program has redefined lethality. In this mode the young men and women accomplish significant social change in their community. The leader fits the profile of a community organizer and has the skills needed to accomplish the goals set forth; although violence prevention is not included among the stated goals, there is a recognition of the impact of violence in the community. Much like the Boston Prevention Curriculum (Prothrow-Stith and Spivak 1992) the target population is adolescents and young adults.

The I.Y.M. group has clearly developed skills in behavior modification as members challenge one another in discussion and debate. Although some issues may provoke anger, they understand that anger is normal and have learned to work together in ways that are exciting and creative.

As mentors to community children, they endeavor to change behavior as it relates to setting personal goals. These activities fall within the public health model of education and behavior modification, in the hope that persons involved will not have contact with the criminal justice system.

The group continues to have a significant impact on the development of its members. Graduates attend local colleges and return to the center to work with their colleagues and with the younger children, fulfilling their pledge to be a positive role model and return to the community to share the gifts that they have received.

## *Public Health and Social Work*

This chapter began with a public health perspective, providing evidence from public health and social work professionals that violence is indeed a public health problem that must be addressed by individuals, institutions, and communities. Gitterman (1987), cited earlier, develops the potential implications for public health and social work as he presents three aspects of primary prevention that may be seen in the Boston, Kansas City, and Syracuse programs as they respond to the disease of violence in their communities.

The first aspect is *specific protection;* an explicit procedure for disease prevention in which a population at risk is identified and something is done to strengthen its resistance. The second aspect, *health promotion,* places emphasis upon improving the quality of life and raising the general health level of the population. *Environmental change,* the third aspect, calls for the social worker to do something about the social condition that is the host and fosters the identified problem.

Recalling former Surgeon General Koop's (1986) declaration that "Violence is as much a public health issue for me . . . as smallpox, tuberculosis, and syphilis were for my predecessors," we should review the history of public health social work. Social workers were involved with families in 1918 when tuberculosis and venereal disease were spreading among the general population. They were present in 1938 when the Venereal Disease Act was passed, and in 1962 when the Vaccination Assistance Act enabled states and communities to conduct immunization programs against poliomyelitis, tetanus, diphtheria, and whooping cough (Leukefeld 1987). Social work is present now, able to use classic techniques of preventive intervention along with public health prevention strategies to combat the present epidemic of violence in our communities.

## References

Banks, J. (1987). A developmental perspective on black family violence. In R. L. Hampton (ed.), *Violence in the black family: Correlates and consequences.* Lexington, MA: Lexington Books, D.C. Heath & Company.

Battle, S. (1991). Health and social considerations of young African American males. In K. Jaros & G. C. St. Denis (eds.), *Use of public health social work leadership tools and the strategies: Addressing health issues of black male adolescents. Proceedings of the Annual Public Health Social Work Maternal and Child Health Institute* (pp. 1–14). Pittsburgh: University of Pittsburgh Press.

Brown, D. L. (1993, November 1). Getting ready to die: Children in violent DC neighborhood plan their own funerals. *The Washington Post,* pp. 1, A8.

Cohen, S., and Lang, C. (1991). Application of the principles of community-based programs. *Public Health Reports,* 106(3): 269–270.

Comer, J. P., and Poussaint, A. F. (1992). *Raising black children: Questions and answers for parents and teachers.* New York: A Plume Book Published by the Penguin Group.

Cron, T. (1986). The Surgeon General's workshop on violence and public health: Review of the recommendations. *Public Health Reports,* 101(1): 8–14.

Devore, W. (1992). The African American community in the 1990's: The search for a practice model. In F. G. Rivera and J. L. Erlich, *Community organizing in a diverse society.* Boston: Allyn and Bacon.

Devore, W., and Schlesinger, E. G. (1991). *Ethnic-sensitive social work practice* (3rd ed.). New York: Merril, an imprint of Macmillan Publishing Company.

Earls, F. (1991) Understanding and controlling violence. *Journal of Health Care for the Poor and Underserved,* 2(1): 156–166.

Eimas, L. (1994, February 3). We're the now. *Syracuse Herald-Journal,* pp. H6–7, 11.

Gibbs, J. T. (1988). The new morbidity: Homicide, suicide, accidents, and life-threatening behaviors. In J. T. Gibbs (ed.), *Young, black and male in America: An endangered species* (pp. 258–293). Dover, MA: Auburn House Publishing Company.

Gitterman, A. (1987). Social work looks forward. In G. C. St. Denisa (ed.), Proceedings *Implementing a Forward Plan: A Public Health Social Work Challenge* (pp. 3–13). Pittsburgh: University of Pittsburgh Graduate School of Public Health.

Koop, C. E. (1986). Surgeon General's workshop on violence and public health. (DHHS Publication No. HRS-D-MC 86-1, pp. 35–43). Washington, DC: U.S. Government Printing Office.

Intelligent Young Minds (1990). *I.Y.M. Yearbook.* Syracuse, New York, p. 7.

Leukefeld, C. G. (1987). Public health services. In *Encyclopedia of Social Work* (18th edition) Vol. 2, 409–417. Silver Spring, MD: National Association of Social Workers.

Mitchell, M., and Daniels, S. (1987, October). Black community mobilization to decrease homicides in Kansas City, Missouri. Paper presented at the annual meeting of the American Public Health Association.

Moss, J. (1992). Introduction. *I.Y.M. Yearbook.* Syracuse, New York.

Netting, F. E., Kettner, P. M., and McMurtry, S. L. (1993). *Social work macro practice.* New York: Longman.

Novello, A. C. (1991) Violence is a greater killer of children than disease. *Public Health Reports,* 106(3): 231–233.

Prothrow-Stith, D., and Spivak, H. (1992). Homicide and violence: Contemporary problems for America's black community. In R. L. Braithwaite and S. E. Taylor (eds.), *Health issues in the black community.* San Francisco: Jossey-Bass Publishers.

Rivera, F. G., and Erlich, J. L. (1992). *Community organizing in a diverse society.* Boston: Allyn and Bacon.

Schlesinger, E. G. (1985). *Health care and social work practice.* St. Louis: Times Mirror/Mosby.

Taylor, R. L. (1991). Poverty and adolescent black males: The subculture of disengagement. In P. E. Edleman and Joyce Ladner (eds.), *Adolescence and poverty: Challenge for the 1990s.* Washington, DC: Center for National Policy Press.

Trafford, A. (1992, Fall). Violence as a public health crisis. *Public Welfare.*

Wilson-Brewer, R. (1991). Violence prevention and African American males: Promising strategies. In K. J. Jaros and G. C. St. Denis (eds.), *Use of public health social work leadership tools and strategies: Addressing black male adolescents and children. Proceedings of the Annual Public Health Social Work Maternal Child Health Institute.* Pittsburgh.

Wood, G. G., and Middleman, R. R. (1989). *The structural approach to direct practice in social work.* New York: Columbia University Press.

# 5

Community Social
Work with Puerto
Ricans in the
United States

*JULIO MORALES, PH.D.* *

## *Ideology, Values, and Social Change*

In the late 1950s and early 1960s, the Puerto Rican Association for Community Affairs (PRACA) sponsored youth conferences for Puerto-Rican high school and college students. The theme of the conferences was "Aspire and Attain," and the organizers, many of them social workers, contributed their time to reach young Puerto Ricans and involve them in community work. PRACA's efforts served as a backdrop to the creation (in 1962) of ASPIRA, the first Puerto Rican–controlled private social service agency in the United States. Both groups stressed the importance of a college education, a positive sense of identity, knowledge of Puerto-Rican history and culture, and a commitment to contributing to the Puerto-Rican community.

*Dr. Morales's C.O. skills have facilitated his founding Puerto Rican Studies Projects and numerous social service agencies or programs in New York, Massachusetts, and Connecticut.

By the late 1960s and early 1970s, as Puerto-Rican studies programs began to take root in New York and New Jersey colleges, a more progressive ideology developed.[1] This ideology urged a rejection of traditional learning and teaching. It encouraged more collective methods of working, defined new sources of knowledge, discarded ideologies that condoned colonialism, and designed theoretical constructs that look at the power of macro forces on poor and powerless people.[2]

Community social workers need to confront their and others' tendencies to blame victims and look for new ways to empower poor and oppressed people while validating their contributions and struggles. As part of their community organization processes, workers should plan group discussions of oppression that are meaningful to the everyday reality of people's lives. For example, a group of elderly Puerto Ricans could be encouraged to talk about their lives in Puerto Rico and why they migrated to the United States. Many will say that they had to try elsewhere because of the inadequate employment opportunities in Puerto Rico. The organizer could facilitate further discussion by asking provocative questions to stimulate people to open up about their experiences—"You mean you did not come here to get on welfare? That's what a lot of people think"; and "Why were employment opportunities so limited?" Such discussions with older Puerto Ricans yield interesting anecdotes that underscore their hard work and high aspirations for themselves and their families. This type of exchange is emotionally charged and can act as a springboard for confronting other stereotypes and helping Puerto Ricans to become more assertive about their rights.

Some Puerto Ricans may not view themselves as oppressed, while others may blame themselves for their personal problems. Organizers need to address both beliefs and connect private troubles to public problems and foster positive identities within the larger Puerto-Rican community.

An ideology that empowers clients must also question societal priorities and forces that have led to large discrepancies in income and wealth distribution among Americans. In the 1980s, poor people in America experienced a 9.8 percent decrease in income while the affluent enjoyed a 15.6 percent increase, according to a congressional study.[3] Similar studies document that 35 percent of America's wealth is owned by half of one percent (.5 percent) of the population, while 44 percent of Americans share just 2 percent of the wealth.[4] In the United States 40.6 percent of Puerto Ricans live below the federal poverty level.[5]

Community social workers need to project genuine caring for people and strive continuously to enhance, integrate and interpret knowledge, skills, and values when working with Puerto Ricans and other oppressed groups. To some extent, this skill parts from the social work ethos of impartiality, neutrality, and objectivity. It means placing the problems of an individual or community within the context of larger social, economic, and political problems and generously sharing such knowledge with the client and action systems.

## History of the Americas and Puerto Rico

Many historical accounts of Puerto Rico, Latin American nations, and the United States start with Columbus's "discovery" of a "new world" in 1492. These accounts reinforce a decidedly European perspective on history and exemplify institutionalized ethnocentrism and racism by dismissing the fact that Native Americans preceded Columbus by thousands of years.

The Europeans who settled in North America brought back from Africa millions of black African natives, whom they sold as slaves in the Americas and the Caribbean. In the United States and other countries, white men justified the killing of the people they called Indians and the enslavement of Africans by viewing these populations as subhuman heathens. Later, white Americans would view the descendants of Africans and Indians as racially inferior, a misperception that exists to this day.

Puerto Ricans are a racially mixed people of Taino Indian, European, and African heritage. The United States began to occupy Puerto Rico in 1898 after winning the Spanish-American War. The U.S. government and military establishment had long viewed the island as an attractive territory because of its strategic location and economic value.[6]

The Foraker Act of 1900 established an American-controlled government in Puerto Rico. The U.S. president appointed the governor of the island and the upper chamber of the legislature. Economic control followed, and a diversified agricultural society was turned into an economy based on a sole crop—sugarcane—dominated by absentee businesses. The low-paying and seasonal nature of work in the sugarcane fields, shipping monopolies, and a tax system that favored U.S. businesses led to poverty so severe that by 1940, Puerto Rico became known as the "Poor House of the Caribbean."[7]

> An effort to industrialize Puerto Rico's economy, called Operation Bootstrap, was seen as a remedy. American capital quickly moved in to enhance a factory system that guaranteed owners seven years of tax exemptions, a cheap labor force and political stability not associated with other Third World countries . . . Operation Bootstrap did not provide enough of the labor-intensive work it had promised. Instead, it has favored pharmaceutical, computer and other capital-intensive industries. Factory owners often leave Puerto Rico when their tax exemptions expire and find cheaper labor in other Third World countries.[8]

In Puerto Rico, unskilled workers often compete with one another and undocumented workers from neighboring Caribbean nations. In the United States, they compete for scarce jobs as the manufacturing and farm work they were recruited to do after the 1940s has dried up. Ironically, even though Puerto-Rican migrants now tend to have more formal education than past immigrants, the jobs available today require more specialized education, training, and skills than those in the past. In 1910, 90 percent of Americans did not finish high school, but they could still find jobs. That is no longer true. Skilled jobs such as clerical work and bank tellers, which provided upward mobility in the past, are almost obsolete as personal computers and electronic banking have replaced workers.

## Culture and Practice Issues

The Indian, European, and African mixture, the geography and topography of the island, and a history of oppression and colonization by both Spain and the United States have combined to create a culture that is different from American, Spanish, and other Latino cultures.

For 400 years, until the United States moved in after the Spanish-American War, Spain imposed its language, religious beliefs, values, and culture on Puerto Ricans. These systems were altered, however, by influences of the African and Indian cultures. Dominated by one powerful nation and then another, Puerto Ricans have long lived as a colonized and oppressed society.

From this history of colonialism, Puerto Ricans have developed powerful survival mechanisms that are reflected in their culture. These include a spirit of resiliency, a strong sense of peoplehood, and a readiness for action when organizers tap the leadership and resourcefulness of the Puerto Ricans. To avoid stereotypical thinking, we should stress that Puerto-Rican communities and individuals vary. Certain socioeconomic factors such as urbanization, social class, levels of formal education, and length of residence in the United States affect the varying relation to traditional cultural patterns between Puerto Ricans living in Puerto Rico and in the United States.

## Respect, Honor, Dignity, Hospitality

Traditionally, Puerto Rican feelings of pride and self-esteem are rooted in community and culturally related to the concepts of respect and honor. Respect is shown by being polite, attentive, discreet, and sensitive to the needs and feelings of others. Respect is shown to neighbors and acquaintances, even vulnerable ones such as clients, by addressing them as Don or Doña (Sir or Madam) followed by their first name (i.e., Doña Juana, Don José); by using the formal *you* (Usted); by not joking or "jiving" without all people involved feeling comfortable; by calling adult strangers Mr., Miss, or Mrs.; by avoiding eye contact when culturally appropriate; by specific dating rituals; and by showing that one cares about other people's opinions, contributions, and feelings. For example, many Puerto Ricans demonstrate honor for parents, grandparents, aunts and uncles, and godparents by asking for their blessing (*bendición*) when entering or leaving from their presence. A strong sense of family honor is demonstrated through achievement and work, service to the community and a willingness to take care of and become responsible for other members of one's family and community. A sense of obligation for the family is culturally expected and hospitality is captured in the phrase "mi casa es su casa" (my house is your house).

## Extended Family, Espiritismo

The mixed heritage of Puerto Ricans has led to a blending of Indian and African religious customs with Catholicism. American Protestantism has also strongly influenced spirituality and religion in Puerto-Rican communities. The majority of Puerto Ricans identify themselves as Catholic, but many, especially the poor, practice Pentecostalism—an evangelical form of Protestantism.

African and Indian religious influences are evident in many Puerto-Rican communities, where many people frequent *botanicas*—shops that sell candles, statues, incense, body oils, herbs, and other paraphernalia used to ward off evil and heal the body, mind, and soul. These practices are part of *espiritismo,* and *espiritistas* need to be recognized in social work practice because of their influence in the lives of many Puerto Ricans.[9]

The extended family system, until recently, has been overshadowed by the nuclear family, even in Puerto-Rican communities in the United States *compadres, comadres, padrinos, madrinas,* and close friends are also seen as part of the family. Most Puerto-Rican families will include *hijos de crianza.*[10] The traditional extended family or the new combination of extended and nuclear family is for the most part patriarchal and often hampered by traditional male/female roles that are also tied to concepts of dignity, honor, and respect.[11]

## Personalismo—Confianza

*Confianza* means trust and culturally established acceptable boundaries for interpersonal behavior. *Confianza* evolves and allows for *relajo* (joking around) and for bonding. *Confianza* must be earned; assuming prematurely that one has it is often culturally unacceptable. Establishing trust, an essential component of social work practice with Puerto Ricans and others, requires approaches that may be new to social workers who have never worked with this population.

*Personalismo* is a culturally supported expectation of "personalizing" individual contact in important relationships. For example, Puerto-Rican children complain that their teachers, guidance counselors, and social workers do not seem to care about them as individuals. In frustration, these children often say such things as, "They are just doing their job. They don't really care." No matter how much a social service system says it is concerned about people, Puerto Ricans may need to feel the caring personally. Community workers need to understand this pattern because getting Puerto Ricans to become involved in local organizing efforts may depend on their feeling connected, in a personal way, to the organizer. Face-to-face contact is important in all community organization work, but it can be crucial in organizing Puerto Ricans.

Organizers are more likely to "win over" the people by demonstrating they care. An effective way of demonstrating this is by socializing in the Puerto-Rican community and spending time with the action group involved in the organizing efforts. This may mean drinking coffee together; sharing pictures of each other's families; attending parties and church services; shopping at local stores; and eating lunch in neighborhood restaurants.

## Self-Oppression

As a result of centuries of oppression and colonization under Spain and the United States, many Puerto Ricans have internalized stereotypes of themselves as passive and dependent beings similar to those described by Paulo Freire in his discussion of the oppressed and by Frantz Fanon in his writing of the colonized mentality.[12] Many Puerto Ricans blame themselves for their fate because they do not realize that their sense of alienation and helplessness and lack of control are attributable to poverty, racism, and discrimination. These systemic forces have taken over many aspects of Puerto Ricans' lives for 500 years.

Community organizers and other social workers need to consider the implications of certain behaviors and beliefs that are best understood within the context of religious, linguistic, social, political, and economic colonization and oppression. Certain patterns emerge when one attempts to organize Puerto Ricans:

- Dependence on or unwarranted respect for authority can make organizing people against school systems, law enforcement bodies, the medical establishment, and other societal institutions difficult.
- The expectation that leaders and "experts" will solve their problems.
- A fatalistic approach to life and reliance on saints, God, the Virgin Mary, and spirits.
- A belief that *pala* (influence, connections, or political pull) is necessary for self-advancement and that confrontation is to be avoided. Doing things *a la buena* (without conflict) and if necessary using *la pelea monga* (passive fighting) may mean telling people what they want to hear but not necessarily meaning it.[13] This may include their giving the impression that they intend to come to a meeting when that is not the case. Some people might confuse culturally sanctioned behavior with what appears to be acceptance of injustice.

## Machismo, Marianismo, and Other Isms

Puerto-Rican society, like all others, oppresses certain members within its own group. For example, most adult males have more privileges than most women. Homophobia and heterosexism may be more overt in some Puerto-Rican communities than in most non–Puerto-Rican communities in the United States. The cultural concept of machismo sanctions male privilege and superiority. It strongly emphasizes adult male financial responsibility and protection of the wife and other women and children in the family. Husbands and fathers, particularly poor men, often feel a sense of shame and dishonor if they cannot provide adequately for their families, even if they are un- or underemployed. This feeling may explain some pathological behavior in Puerto-Rican and other Latino males. Desertion, abuse, or neglect may stem from a perceived demasculation due, for example, to women's obtaining welfare benefits. Sometimes, however, males will pretend to "disappear" so that their families can become eligible for government support. Organizing these men to channel their anger and frustrations constructively is a challenge that very few organizers have undertaken.

*Marianismo* is a cultural institution that, like the whore-madonna complex in other cultures, divides women into two mutually exclusive categories: the saintly, devoted wife, mother, sister, virgin (until marriage) female and the sinful, cold-hearted, promiscuous "other." Although these values are less dominant than in the past, like the more global malady of male sexism, *marianismo* and *machismo* persist. Strong traditional gender roles often lead to overt heterosexism and homophobia in Puerto Rico and Puerto-Rican communities in the United States. Although sexual taboos have relaxed in recent years and an increasing number of young unmarried women are becoming sexually active, strict gender roles and close supervision of female children may still lead to marriage at young ages and early common-law and consensual living arrangements.

## Strengths

An a society, Puerto Ricans value hospitality, cooperation, and sharing, as well as a collective humanism that appeals to a sense of justice and fairness. Because of the racial mix that comprise this population, racism may be less of an issue than in other client groups.[14] These culturally sanctioned patterns and principles enhance community organizing.

The tradition of close-knit extended families serves as a source of community strength and stability. This cultural strong point can be used effectively by involving family members in community organization activities, such as adolescents in tutoring programs and adults in tenant organizing. Organizing projects involving housing, jobs, education, and other macro issues that benefit entire families, especially their children, have a better chance of attracting Puerto-Rican participation.

## Problems and Programs—Strategies and Tactics

Puerto Ricans in the United States face many problems, most of which are rooted in poverty and discrimination. If, for example, most Puerto Ricans were middle class, housing problems would diminish as could other poverty-related problems such as low levels of education and poor health. Middle-class Puerto Ricans tend to hold jobs that pay enough to cover basic needs and provide fringe benefits such as health insurance, paid vacations, and medical leave. Poverty is associated with political powerlessness that, in turn, minimizes the ability to compete for resources. The traditional American values of competition and individualism, along with America's history of ethnic and racial rivalries, clash with Puerto Ricans' values of cooperation and collectivism.

> *More importantly, competition in the United States is less than perfect . . . politicians and bureaucrats often side with those having greater access to power, not those having greater needs . . . A society needing less unskilled work, stressing profit and middle-class comfort, and generally accepting cuts in social programs and services will have little empathy for Puerto Ricans and other oppressed populations. The high price of housing and necessities; national trends of unskilled jobs moving out of large cities where Puerto Ricans are concentrated; gentrification and continued automation add to Puerto Rican poverty.*[15]

Homelessness; a lack of decent and affordable housing; a high school dropout rate; AIDS; chronic unemployment or underemployment; substance abuse; discrimination; teen pregnancy; attacks on bilingual and affirmative action programs; the English First movement; limited access to society's resources and institutions; and a deficit of culturally and linguistically sensitive health and social services—an endless list of problems confronts Puerto Ricans in the United States. While this list seems overwhelming, all lend themselves to community-organization intervention. Mobilizing in the 1990s and beyond needs to capitalize on the efforts of past struggles; coalition building, not competition with other oppressed groups, is necessary for success. The political process must be targeted for attack because that is where decisions affecting Puerto Ricans and other poor people are made. Organizers need to address and challenge prejudices such as sexism and heterosexism that characterize certain oppressed communities. These attitudes, however, must be confronted with sensitivity to cultural norms and values and only after a relationship of trust and *confianza* have been established.

## Specific Strategies

Ideally, social workers in the Puerto-Rican community are bilingual, bicultural, and progressive advocates with strong community roots. They make community empowerment a community goal, have a repertoire of community-organization skills, and a theoretical understanding of macro forces and dynamics. Such organizers need to familiarize themselves with the different value systems and factor them into their organizing strategies. These specific problems and possible solutions include not only the worker's own values but those of the community, action group, sponsoring agency, target group, and client group.

The way a problem is defined determines the way it will be responded to and inevitably is grounded in a framework of basic values. For example, teen pregnancy can be viewed from many perspectives. Some regard it as a crisis in morality, a health-care issue, or a reflection of the hopelessness of underprivileged young people. Based on problem definition, possible solutions include pastoral counseling, family planning education, expansion of prenatal health services, and advocacy for progressive abortion policies. Conflicts that arise from the emotional, value-laden definitions of a particular problem are difficult to address and may lead organizers to either work on less controversial issues or to tackle tough ones and accept the consequences. Sometimes, depending on the issues, working on a research project or establishing or supporting a coalition where Puerto Ricans are one of several entities may be an effective and appropriate strategy for addressing problems that Puerto Ricans confront.

It is equally important for organizers to assess and try to increase resources available to Puerto Ricans while realizing the resistance they likely will face from constituencies at the neighborhood, local, regional, or national levels. At times, organizers will face opposition from Puerto Ricans who may feel threatened by a potential loss of their own leadership as new leadership emerges.

Organizers with the characteristics and skills described are not plentiful. The challenge for schools of social work, therefore, is to actively recruit, retain, and graduate Puerto Ricans and teach culturally sensitive community organization skills that will enable Puerto-Rican and non–Puerto-Rican social workers to work effectively with Puerto Ricans.

## *Organizing Strategies*

Poverty, powerlessness, racism, and numerous social ills such as homelessness, substance abuse, and criminal activity that grow out from these forces have led to the "full-plate syndrome" facing many Puerto Ricans and other ethnic and racial minority communities. Efforts to counteract this syndrome, such as community-based social service programs for Puerto-Rican families and culturally validating school curriculums are either inadequate or nonexistent. To effect meaningful change for Puerto-Rican communities, organizers need to focus on certain pressing issues such as intercommunity rivalries and power imbalances stemming from greater levels of need, lack of political representation, tokenism, or invisibility of Puerto Ricans on agency boards and their administrative units. For example, addressing educational issues for Puerto-Rican children in public schools may be more difficult when Puerto Ricans are not proportionately represented on school boards or as school principals.

The saliency of issues in a specific community obviously influence this work. Crisis, for instance, may lead to decisions around short-term organizing efforts that can, in turn, serve as springboards for other work. Clearly, an agency employing community social workers can respond to a local tragedy by encouraging residents to collectively express their feelings about the event and harness the emotional energy to call attention to injustices and challenge policy. For example, when a young Puerto-Rican girl in Hartford was killed by a hit-and-run driver who held an influential job, the Puerto-Rican community was outraged at the lenient treatment of the driver. The anger led to forums on racism and classism and to organized marches and vigils. As a result of that process, new leaders emerged and the criminal justice system was assailed with criticism. While immediate changes did not result, the experience of responding in a unified and organized way—one voice for the entire community—was empowering.

The tragedy of Hurricane Hugo led many community organizers to help raise money for grassroots agencies wishing to contribute to help hurricane victims. Such efforts make agencies and organizers more humane and caring in the eyes of a community of people whose friends and relatives may have suffered from the violence of the storm.

The shock and pain of gang-related deaths in Puerto-Rican communities has prompted organizing activities around safety programs and increased Puerto-Rican involvement in combatting violence.

It is appropriate and important for organizers to "seize the moment" and build on the momentum created by the unifying forces of a community tragedy or success. Obviously, organizers cannot rely on trials, hurricanes, or other calamities to facilitate organizing. Organizers in the Puerto-Rican community must gather much information about the community they are involved with. Demographic information on age, gender, employment, poverty, housing, and other matters is necessary. Knowledge of the community, history, neighborhood associations, human services, cultural groups, religious institutions, perceived leadership, and how the community is viewed by Puerto Ricans and non–Puerto Ricans should be gathered and understood.

One cannot overstate the importance of selecting appropriate locations and meeting times, assuring transportation and child care, and utilizing effective communication skills in the organizing process. At times, speaking in Spanish only is effective. Other times, English may be more appropriate when addressing second-generation Puerto Ricans. Even then, however, using Spanish phrases helps create an ethnic atmosphere. Often, both languages may need to be spoken. Translations must be accurate. Communication means being clear and not assuming that people understand what is being expressed. This goes beyond the language(s) being spoken. The language must be appropriate to the group one is working with. This may mean addressing people as Don or Doña, avoiding or explaining professional language and technical terms, and utilizing idiomatic expressions.

Organizers must be willing to knock on many doors and go to where the client and action systems live, socialize, or gather. This may mean visiting many neighborhoods and human service groups and asking to speak at PTAs, church services, clubs, or organizations. Working with and through community leaders and identifying and helping to promote emerging leadership is crucial. Involving people in agenda setting, translations, designing leaflets, making phone calls, or writing letters empowers them. Giving people credit for their efforts and their work encourages participation.

Much organizing demands working long hours and planning or being at evening meetings. Planning fun activities and celebrating small victories is part of the community organization process. Sometimes, providing snacks during a meeting is appropriate; at other times it takes away time and energy from the meetings. However, ethnic food and music make fun activities and celebrations more meaningful.

The following cases are examples of organizing efforts that this author has been part of and that highlight these and other skills and strategies that proved appropriate in direct community social work with Puerto Ricans in the United States or in community social work from which Puerto Ricans and others have benefited.[16]

## Organizing Church Constituents— A Pentecostal Example

"I knew that I needed to get people to trust and like me. Singing, and playing my guitar at the services helped a lot," said Ada Suarez, an energetic and highly committed second-year community organization student at the University of Connecticut School of Social Work (UCSSW) who wanted to harness the potential strength of the members of a large Puerto-Rican Pentecostal Church in Hartford, Connecticut. Ada had been raised as a Pentecostal in Puerto Rico and believed organizers could cultivate the spiritual mandate of Pentecostals to do "God's work" and use it as the basis for organizing strategies around church and community improvements.

Churches are not typical social service agencies. They usually have no social workers on staff. Therefore, as a member of the Puerto-Rican Studies faculty at UCSSW, I agreed to supervise Ada.[17] Culturally, college professors are respected as experts, and Ada's pastor welcomed access to this valuable resource along with Ada's help.

In addition to singing at church services and helping the pastor with clerical tasks, Ada visited the homes of people she identified as potential community leaders, met with church elders, and served as a mentor to some of the church's youth. She distributed questionnaires to the membership at various meetings and church gatherings asking them to provide information about their needs and concerns. Ada shared the survey responses with the congregation during a church service and recommended solutions. "Some brothers and sisters want to write better in Spanish, some want to learn English and others want help in finding work or better jobs . . . Some committees want help in functioning better at meetings and others want to know more about how to help people . . . The youth want to discuss school issues and some church elders wish to learn how to be better leaders in and out of the church."

Ada brought teachers from the public school system into the church to teach literacy and English as a second language. With assistance from the Puerto-Rican studies faculty: Latino students at UCSSW, and community leaders, Ada organized workshops in leadership skills development, vocational training, résumé writing, job interviewing skills, and public assistance eligibility. Ada made sure church members were involved in planning and, wherever possible, in conducting the workshops.

Ada also introduced controversial projects such as AIDS workshops. She encouraged young people to talk about their feelings of isolation in school and community as a result of the church's strict moral codes, which forbade such typical adolescent behaviors as listening to rock music and going to the movies. In addition, she encouraged the women of the congregation to become more assertive and independent and to seek equal representation with men on the Board of Elders. Some church members were not comfortable with the graphic language used by AIDS workshop speakers and the attitude changes Ada proposed for the adolescents and women. In response, she explained diplomatically that since members worked with drug addicts and prisoners, some had expressed interest in knowing more about the AIDS epidemic. Ada then led a discussion of why certain language might he appropriate for certain subjects and asked members to suggest less offensive words.

As a result of Ada's work, women did join the Board of Elders and the youth group continues to meet. Ada consciously used culturally relevant strategies: maximized participation of groups of people that had not been previously involved, and respectfully tackled controversial issues. She imparted community organization skills to church members by helping them articulate their needs, involving them in agenda setting and sharing leadership. She also moderated struggles emanating from changes, helped church members design and disseminate flyers, and led discussions on forming committees and selecting community organization strategies. To spark discussion and increase member involvement in these sessions, Ada employed colorful visual aids such as videotapes and slides. Such images can leave a lasting impression and emphasize points more effectively than words.

## English First/Only

Few issues have mobilized Puerto Ricans as much as fighting Against the English First/Only bill that was introduced in Connecticut in 1987 and again in 1989. A massive organizing effort in February 1989 duplicated and amplified strategies used two years earlier to defeat this legislation. Opponents of the bill acknowledge that its intent initially sounded appealing, for learning English is essential for acclimating to American society. But English is already the dominant language, and the bill took on ethnocentric and racist overtones; it could have curtailed civil rights and eliminated or tightly restricted necessary bilingual services such as emergency health and police responses. Organizers spoke against the bill at schools, colleges, and Latino agencies. They mobilized Spanish-speaking media, wrote letters and editorial responses to local and state media, organized debates, and created a coalition of Latino leaders who had access to the community and to resources. The emphasis was on a multiplicity of community organization strategies that included calling attention to the adverse effects of what appeared to be sound legislation. Motivating people to attend and testify at hearings on the bill and bombarding neutral members of the legislative committee with calls, letters, and telegrams proved effective. Rallies were organized before and during the hearings to call further attention to the Puerto-Rican community's outrage. Never in Connecticut had so many Puerto Ricans walked, carpooled, or chartered buses to be present at any state hearing. The bill was defeated in committee, but may be brought back in the future. Mobilization needs to continue against the English First/Only movement in Connecticut, and elsewhere.

## *Research, Consultation, and Evaluation as C.O. Tools for Action*

In 1992 this author was hired by the Bridgeport school system as a consultation/researcher to study why Puerto-Rican youngsters drop out of school. As an organizer, I knew that if the research was to lead to changes, a strong and diverse community team to which I would be accountable had to be organized. Fortunately, the Ford Foundation, which sponsored the study, insisted on broad community participation. A collaborative team, with heavy Puerto-Rican representation, was formed. My reporting directly to them and seeking their involvement in all aspects of the research project empowered them. They were encouraged to help develop all research instruments and were trained to interview Puerto-Rican youths who had dropped out, young Puerto Ricans who were at risk of dropping out, and those who were achieving. Parents, teachers, administrators, social workers, and other staff were also interviewed in order to obtain the broadest level of participation and supports, as well as raise awareness. All questionnaires addressed community and school factors attributed to students and their families. Numerous community forums were organized to disseminate findings and gain more input on problems and solutions. The collaborative "owns" the study, continues meeting, advocates for programs flowing from the study's recommendations, and monitors them. Programs addressing school policies, teacher training, and a Puerto-Rican studies curriculum have been initiated as a direct result of the study.

## School Integration

On April 26, 1988, legal action was taken by the Puerto Rican Legal Defense League, the Connecticut Civil Liberties Union, and other legal entities on behalf of Hartford's school children against the State of Connecticut. About 48 percent of Hartford public school children are identified as poor by the U.S. Census. Ninety-one percent of these children are black or Latino. The Hartford school system is overwhelmed by the demand to educate a student population drawn almost exclusively from the poorest families in the Greater Hartford region, while neighboring towns and suburbs are primarily white and upper or middle class. The court case is known as *Sheff* v. *O'Neill*. (Sheff is an African-American student and O'Neill was governor of Connecticut in 1989.) Latino students, overwhelmingly Puerto Rican, comprise more than 50 percent of Hartford's public school enrollment, and yet no information was available about what Puerto-Rican parents knew about this important case, which could change public education in Hartford and elsewhere.

A research class I taught in the spring of 1993 became involved in interviewing Puerto-Rican parents in an effort to determine Puerto-Rican awareness of the case, attitudes toward integration, and knowledge about potential integration strategies.

Students and I interviewed 187 people in Hartford's El Mercado, a Puerto-Rican shopping center, and during parent-teacher organization meetings in two of Hartford's schools. Generally Puerto Ricans with children in the public schools knew almost nothing about *Sheff* v. *O'Neill* and could not define concepts such as mandatory vs. voluntary busing, magnet schools, regionalization, or vouchers. After each interview, interviewees were given definitions of concepts used during the interview. The findings have been publicized, and schools have been encouraged to hold meetings (in Spanish and in English) on the topic. Because integration is often viewed in black and white terms, we asked Puerto Ricans how they identified in terms of color. They were given the choices of white, black, or *trigueño* (tan). Seventy percent identified as *trigueño*.

Research can be a powerful strategy for alerting community about important issues, for learning about the Puerto-Rican community, and for advocacy. Carefully translated instruments must be used, and interviewers must ask interviewees which language they prefer to use during the interview. Conversing with people after the interviews is an excellent tool for raising consciousness related to issues addressed by the research.

## Addressing AIDS

Puerto Ricans in Connecticut and elsewhere are almost four times more likely than whites to be AIDS patients.[18] The need to organize around AIDS prevention, education, and services in Puerto-Rican communities cannot be overstated. Sometimes this can best be done by concentrating solely in Puerto-Rican neighborhoods. Other times, depending on the goals or issues, working jointly with other communities can be more effective and lead to future collaborations.

Traditional and nontraditional methods of bringing attention to this pandemic should be utilized. Between 1986 and 1990 Puerto-Rican students in a research class used research as a tool for raising consciousness around AIDS. Puerto-Rican store-owners or employees of Puerto-Rican grocery stores, beauty parlors, or other businesses in Puerto-Rican neighborhoods were interviewed to assess their knowledge of AIDS. They were given information on AIDS and asked to share it with their customers. Hundreds of Puerto-Rican church goers were interviewed after Sunday services. The information obtained as a result of this research effort was brought to the attention of policymakers, AIDS activists, and AIDS organizations. Much of the findings have also been disseminated at conferences and published in *Multi-Cultural Services for AIDS Treatment and Prevention,* edited by the Puerto-Rican Studies faculty involved in this research.[19]

Working with a community organization class in 1990, this author helped organize the Greater Hartford Coalition for Needle Exchange. This was a very controversial undertaking, with attracted organized and fierce opposition. AIDS often forces people to confront their values and moralistic judgments. Coalition members reviewed and summarized the sparse literature on needle exchange, wrote position papers, lobbied Hartford city council members, testified at community meetings, and met with elected state representatives. This coalition is often credited for expediting legal needle exchange programs in Hartford and elsewhere in Connecticut.

Latinos(as)-Contra-Sida (Latinos Against AIDS), a Hartford community-based organization, has pioneered innovative methods to mobilize AIDS awareness in communities. Among these is a yearly AIDS radiothon utilizing local radio stations and national and statewide Puerto-Rican entertainers, who perform during an entire day in late spring. A street in the heart of the Puerto-Rican community is closed off. Stages are erected and local leaders are mobilized to spread the message of AIDS prevention. Merchants contribute money, food, prizes, and other resources. Stores are encouraged to distribute AIDS information, and volunteers are organized to canvass buildings, streets, and other places where people gather. Puerto Ricans are asked to contribute their pocket change to support LCS. Approximately $8,000 is raised. Radio stations ask people to go to Park Street and enjoy the music and dance and become involved in the fight against AIDS.

A broader collaborative strategy utilized over the past six years has been organizing AIDS vigils. Recently, high school choirs and church youth choruses have been asked to perform during the vigil to ensure the participation of youth. Collaboration in AIDS work has been facilitated by having the vigils sponsored by four key community-based organizations offering AIDS services in Hartford. The agencies are: LCS, AIDS Project Hartford, AIDS Ministries Program, and the Urban League of Greater Hartford. Those organizations invite other private and public groups to cosponsor the vigil. Cosponsors are expected to duplicate and distribute flyers, commit themselves to sending more than five people to the vigil, and not hold other AIDS activities on the eve of the vigil.

The vigil is a helpful tool for minimizing conflict and rivalry among the primary sponsors. Other strategies for enhancing cooperation and collaboration include having joint socials for staff and board members and expecting board membership in the organizations to share representatives. In this manner, secrecy is minimized and successful strategies are shared and duplicated.

## *Summary of Strategies and Conclusions*

The community organization strategies discussed above stress coalition building, consciousness raising, educating clients on their own oppression and the oppression of others, political awareness, and empowerment. The importance of cultural sensitivity, knowledge of specific communities, strong research skills, and alternative explanations of history and political power have been highlighted. Advocacy tools include "educating" potential funders and boards of directors and agency personnel of human service agencies that work with or should be working with Puerto Ricans; having experts and grassroots organizers testify at public hearings; holding public demonstrations; and training and developing community leaders. All have been included in the preceding case studies. Personal involvement and involving friends, relatives, neighbors, and clients in the political arena must be part of community organization.

Organizing is political. At times, personnel in Puerto-Rican and non–Puerto-Rican agencies will choose not to initiate or participate in organizing efforts if the activities are perceived as potentially risky to their programs, their own agencies, or agency funding. Ada Suarez was successful in much of her work, but churches can be a tool for either supporting victim-blaming ideology, dependency, sexism, and heterosexism or for helping to liberate Puerto Ricans. Many institutions may never mobilize to directly confront employers, politicians, landlords, schools, or other powerful systems that may discriminate or oppress Puerto Ricans. It may be easier for some agencies or churches to support affirmative action, increased access to employment, education, business opportunity, bilingual and multicultural education, more equitable welfare benefits, and strict health and sanitary housing codes. Given the needs of most Puerto-Rican communities, organizers need to accept such support. Most important, they need to continuously question a system that seems to need poor people at the bottom of the social and economic ladder and to address short- and long-range goals for human liberation for all oppressed populations.

Future C.O. work with Puerto Ricans must also include organizing to support national health insurance, guaranteed child care, employment at "living" wages, decent housing, quality education, and women's and lesbian/gay civil rights. More than 50 percent of Puerto Ricans are women and 10 percent are gay or lesbian.

Validating diversity within the Puerto-Rican community strengthens us as a people. Organizing the unemployed, the "disappearing male" referred to earlier, the homeless, and the uninsured are challenges community organizers must pursue. Day care, affordable health care, and housing must be made available to everyone.

Schools of social work have a special responsibility to hire Puerto-Rican faculty and administrators and to actively recruit Puerto-Rican students. Puerto-Rican course content in social work school curriculums must be visible. Social work students must also bring back community organization as a prominent social work method; it was not given adequate attention in the late 1970s and the 1980s. The 1990s must make up for it. Organizers in the 1990s and beyond must project confidence and demonstrate that they appreciate and are comfortable with cultural diversity. Furthermore, just as caseworkers often must address macro forces as they respond to individual client needs, organizers must consciously address the importance of organizing style and the culture, class, and values of the clients they work with. This implies learning how to address victim-blaming ideology at all levels. Liberating the minds of oppressed people is as challenging and as important as attacking the problems they confront.

## Endnotes

1. See Julio Morales, "Puerto Rican Studies and Social Service Careers," and Josephine Nieves et al., "Puerto Rican Studies: Roots and Challenges," in *Toward a Renaissance of Puerto Rican Studies,* ed. Maria Sanchez and Antonio M. Stevens-Arroya (Highland Lakes, NJ: Columbia University Press, 1987); also see Julio Morales, "Puerto Rican Studies: An Example of Social Movements as a Force Towards Social and Economic Justice," in *Towards Social and Economic Justice,* ed. David Gil and Eva Gil (Cambridge, Mass.: Schenkman Publishing Co., 1985).

2. Ibid.

3. Martin Tochlin "Study Shows Growing Gap Between Rich and Poor," *New York Times,* March 2, 1989, p. A-24; also see Robert Pear, "Study Shows Health Gap Widens Between the Affluent and the Poor," *New York Times,* July 8, 1993, p. A-1; and "Evidence Indicates the Rich Got Richer During the '80s," *San Juan Star,* March 5, 1992, p. 1.

4. See Bob Kaplan, "Who's Worth More—Americans Richest 400 Families or Its 40 Million Poorest," *New England Prout Journal,* December 1986.

5. United States Government, *U.S. Census 1990* (Washington, DC: General Accounting Office, 1990).

6. Manual Maldonado-Denis, *Puerto Rico: A Socio-Historic Interpretation* (New York: Random House, 1972).

7. John Gunther, *Inside Latin America* (New York: Harper & Brothers, 1941).

8. This is extracted from Julio Morales's "The Elusive American Dream," written for the *Hartford Courant,* pp. C-1–C-4; *Commentary,* August 10, 1986; also see Julio Morales, *Puerto Rican Poverty and Migration* (New York: Praeger, 1986).

9. *Espiritistas* are either male or female, and some Puerto Ricans may "consult" them when seeking a cure for health (or mental health) problems or advice on other problems. See

Melvin Delgado, "Puerto Rican Spiritualism and the Social Work Profession," in *Social Casework* (October 1977)

10. *Compares* and *comadres* are close friends among the adults, established as a result of the baptism of a child. Padrino means godfather, and madrina godmother (of the baptized child). *Padrino* and *madrina de boda* are best man and maid of honor at a wedding. *Hijos de crianza* means "children by raising" and is usually translated as stepchildren.

11. See Emelicia Mizio, "Puerto Rican Culture," in *Training for Service Delivery to Minority Clients,* ed. Emelicio Mizio and Anita J. Delaney (New York: Family Service Association of America, 1981).

12. Frantz Fanon, *Black Skin, White Mask* (New York: Grove Press, 1967); also, idem, *The Wretched of the Earth* (New York: Grove Press, 1968).

13. See Mizio, op. cit., and Karl Wagenheim, *Puerto Rico: A Profile,* 2nd ed. (San Francisco: Holt, Rinehart and Winston, 1975).

14. Puerto Ricans on the island and the United States are not totally free of racism. For example, in his autobiography, *Down These Mean Streets,* Piri Thomas describes the pain he experienced because he was the darkest child in the family. Jon Longres's article "Racism and Its Effects on Puerto Rican Continentals," *Social Casework* 55, no. 2, (1974) discusses a preference among many Puerto Ricans for lighter skin. Nevertheless, it is next to impossible to be racist in the North American sense when there is so much variation in skin color (and hair texture) within Puerto Rican families. Puerto Ricans will often call someone *negro* or *negra* (black) as a sign of affection and love. Referring to someone as *negro(a)* has nothing to do with color, and to be *jincho* (too white) is perceived as unattractive.

15. Competition for resources—jobs, housing, scholarships—can lead to conflict between oppressed groups, and organizers must be conscious of such possibilities. See "Black Puerto Rican Conflict: The Inevitable Systemic Outcome," chapter 2, in Morales, *Puerto Rican Poverty and Migration,* op. cit.

16. For further organizing and advocacy strategies see Julio Morales, "The Clinician as Advocate: A Puerto Rican Perspective," in Mizio and Delaney, op. cit.

17. The Puerto Rican Studies Project at the University of Connecticut School of Social Work was founded by this author to address the need for culturally sensitive social work practitioners in the Puerto-Rican community, to recruit, retain, and graduate Puerto-Rican and other Latino graduate social work students, and to train social work providers throughout Connecticut and southwestern Massachusetts. Before the project was initiated in 1980, the University of Connecticut School of Social Work had graduated 25 Latino students (1946–79). From 1980 to 1990 it graduated 140.

18. Julio Morales and Marci Bok, eds., *Multicultural Human Services for AIDS Treatment and Prevention* (New York: Hayworth Press, 1992).

19. Ibid.

# 6

# A Feminist Perspective on Organizing with Women of Color

*LORRAINE M. GUTIERREZ AND EDITH A. LEWIS*

Although the presence of women of color in the United States is growing, (Armott & Matthaei, 1991) our distinctive perspectives, problems, and potentials have rarely been addressed within the field of community organizing. As educators, activists, and practitioners of community practice and multicultural social work, we believe that this limited perspective can have negative effects both on women of color and on those who wish to work within their communities. In this chapter we present one approach to organizing with women of color, which suggests a way in which race and gender issues can be worked on simultaneously. The issues and practice principles we present here are relevant for both women of color and European-American woman organizing in communities of color.

## Women of Color: Who Are We?

The term *women of color* has been adopted by many African-American, Latina, Asian, and Native-American women in the United States as a way of unifying what we have seen as commonalties between us, especially in contrast to the experiences of European-American women in our society. However, the acceptance of this umbrella term does not indicate that we do not recognize the differences between and within racial and ethnic groups in our society. Understanding the specific historical experiences and cultural expressions of different groups of women of color is as important as understanding ways in which we are similar. All women of color have been affected by the domination of the larger society, but this has taken different forms with different groups: the experience of reservation life creates a different social context from that of slavery or forced deportation. Women of color have drawn strength from their ethnic minority communities, but this can be expressed quite differently within each group. Therefore, although this chapter is written about women of color in general, differences exist between these groups that must be recognized and used when working within specific communities. Understanding differences and similarities is particularly important in the development of multiethnic coalitions or when the organizer is from a different background than the majority of the women involved.

Although the specific ethnic and racial groups encompassed by this umbrella term differ in many respects, together we share similarities in terms of our strengths, low status, and power. Women of color experience the "double jeopardy" of racism and sexism in our society. We are hampered by average earnings lower than that of white women, by overrepresentation in low status occupations, and by a low average level of education (Armott & Matthaei, 1991). Correspondingly, women of color are underrepresented in positions of power within our government, corporations, and nonprofit institutions (Gordon-Bradshaw, 1987; Zambrana, 1987).

These statistics suggest ways in which our powerlessness as a group has direct and concrete effects on our daily experiences. Lack of access to many social resources is both a cause and effect of the powerlessness of this group. The poverty rate of women of color is two to three times that of white women: 36.5 percent of all black women and 31.2 percent of all Latinas live below the poverty line, in contrast to 12.7 percent of all white women (1990 Census, 1992). Therefore, women of color are more likely than are white women to suffer from conditions of poor or no housing, insufficient food and clothing, inadequate access to health and mental health services, and to be located within low-income and physically-deteriorating communities (Gordon-Bradshaw, 1987).

Women of color also share similarities in terms of strengths and coping strategies. Within our own communities we have developed values and behaviors that have allowed us to survive in the face of oppression. Economic necessity has led women of color to participate in the labor market at higher rates than white women. Although this role has not always been voluntary, it has helped us to develop ties and a sense of self outside the family and has reduced our economic dependency on men. Women of color are also likely to have strong family ties and ties with other women in our community upon which we can go for concrete and emotional support. These informal ties can be a form of strength. Another commonality is a strong connection to spirituality, through formal or informal religion, which has helped us to survive (Gilkes, 1986; White, 1981). This history of coping and surviving within a hostile world has led many women of color to perceive themselves as strong and capable of dealing with adversity.

Existing models of community practice need to recognize these ways in which women of color differ from white women and from men of color. Organizers have most often recognized the impact of powerlessness on women of color from the perspective of institutional racism while overlooking the role of gender inequity in influencing the life chances of women of color. Similarly, the strengths of women of color are also often ignored in community work. When women of color are viewed solely as members of their racial or ethnic group and gender is not taken into account, community organizers may alienate women of color and reinforce ways in which sexism, both in the larger society and within ethnic minority communities, is a form of oppression (Aragon de Valdez, 1980; Armott & Matthaei, 1991; Weil, 1986; Zavella, 1986).

A feminist perspective, which assumes that issues of power and powerlessness are integral to the experience of women of color, can address this oversight. It proposes concrete and specific ways in which community organizers can work with women of color by increasing their power on different levels and by drawing upon their strengths. The goal of this approach is to eliminate the social conditions that are oppressive to women of color by increasing their influence in our society. However, the historical tension between white feminists and communities of color has led some to reject this method without looking closely at ways in which differences can be dealt with and used constructively to the benefit of women of color. In this chapter we attempt to bridge this gap by outlining the assumptions of the feminist perspective and the practice principles it involves, describing ways in which feminist organizing has excluded women of color, and present a reformulation of feminist organizing for use with women of color. Although we anticipate that our ideas may be controversial, we believe that feminist methods provide one useful framework for ensuring that attention be given to both sexism and racism when organizing with women of color.

## Defining Feminist Organizing

Feminist organizing developed from efforts by feminists to improve the lives of women. Community work has always played an important role within the feminist movement in this country. Nineteenth-century feminists were leaders in the abolitionist movement, the suffrage movement, in community settlements, and in the progressive movement. Community organizing has been equally important in more recent feminist movements, especially those coming from a radical rather than liberal perspective (Nes & Iadicola, 1989; Weil, 1986). It has focused primarily on work for improving women's health, for ending violence against women, and for increasing economic opportunities for all women (Morell, 1987; Schechter, 1982; Withorn, 1984).

The overarching goal of feminist organizing is the elimination of permanent power hierarchies between all people that can prevent them from realizing their human potential. The goal of feminist organizing is the elimination of sexism, racism, and other forms of oppression through the process of empowerment, which "seeks individual liberation through collective activity, embracing both personal and social change" (Morell, 1987).

Recent research on feminist organizing has begun to identify ways in which it differs from other models of community practice. Most often this research has used participant observation methods to identify the values and practice principles upon which feminist organizing is based. The following factors have been found to be common to most feminist organizing:

**1.** *A gender lens is used to analyze the causes and solution of community problems.* Sexism is assumed to be an important force in the experiences of all women and at the root of many problems. All women are thought to be a part of a "community" of women, as well as members of their own specific community (Bricker-Jenkins and Hooyman, 1986; Gould, 1987; Hyde, 1986; Kopasci and Faulkner, 1988; Morell, 1987; Zavella, 1986).

**2.** *Attention is paid to the process of practice, in an effort to create organizations based on feminist principles* (Hyde, 1990). As described by the Women Organizers Project (Joseph et al., 1989): "Feminist organizing is based on values and actions carried out in a democratic, humanistic framework . . . [it] must affect the conditions of women while empowering them." Efforts are made to make feminist movement organizations "safe spaces" where women can escape the larger and more oppressive external social environment. This has most often involved developing feminist organizations based on the principles of collectivity and gender equality in which women can support and develop the confidence and skills necessary to increase their political power (Bricker-Jenkins and Hooyman, 1986; Hyde, 1990).

**3.** *Empowerment through consciousness raising* is characteristic of feminist organizing efforts. Empowerment is a process of increasing personal, interpersonal, or political power so individuals can take action to improve their lives (Bricker-Jenkins and Hooyman, 1986; Gould, 1987; Gutierrez, 1990; Kieffer, 1984; Longres and McLeod, 1980; Morell, 1987; Pernell, 1985; Pinderhughes, 1983; Schechter, Szymanski, and Cahill, 1985; Simmons and Parsons, 1983). Empowerment theory assumes that society consists of separate groups possessing different levels of power and control over resources (Gould, 1987). Recognizing the way in which power relationships affect daily reality and understanding how individuals can contribute to social change is the process through which empowerment takes place (Friere, 1970; Gutierrez, 1990; Longres & McLeod, 1980).

Consciousness raising contributes to empowerment by helping individuals to make this connection between personal problems and political issues. By examining the nature of their lives, women can begin to understand the commonality of their experience and its connection to community and social issues. Consciousness raising can be carried out in one of two formats: group discussion or praxis, the integration of action and reflection. An important outcome of consciousness raising is an understanding of ways in which women, individually and in groups can begin to change the social order (Bricker-Jenkins & Hooyman, 1986; Friere, 1970; Gutierrez, 1990; Rosenthal, 1984).

**4.** *A major assumption is that the personal is political, therefore organizing often takes a "grass-roots," bottom-up approach.* Organizing efforts must often grow out of issues that are impinging on women's daily lives. The development alternative services for women is integral to this method. As described by Withorn (1984) "for the past 15 years, to be a feminist has meant to engage in service work as much as it has meant to do the things which are normally defined as political." Alternative services such as support networks, health clinics, shelters and hotlines are critical elements of feminist organizing (Hyde, 1990; Withorn, 1984).

**5.** *Efforts are made to bridge differences between women based on such factors as race, class, physical ability, and sexual orientation with the guiding principle that diversity is strength.* According to this model "feminist practitioners will not only strive to eliminate racism, classism, heterosexism, anti-semitism, ableism, and other systems of oppression and exploitation, but will affirm the need for diversity by actively reaching out to achieve it" (Bricker-Jenkins & Hooyman, 1986). As described in the following section, this principle has often been difficult to put into practice.

**6.** *Organizing is holistic.* It involves both the rational and nonrational elements of human experiences. Emotions, spirituality, and artistic expression are all used as tactics for unifying women and expressing issues. Involvement in social change is considered organic, not an adjunct, to women's lives. The use of puppets and street theater in the women's disarmament movement is one example of this tactic (Linton & Witham, 1981).

This brief discussion of feminist organizing indicates some of the ways in which it can be used when working with women of color. Feminist theory provides a means for understanding ways in which racism, sexism, and classism have an interactive impact on the lives of women of color (Armott & Matthaei, 1991). It also suggests a method for directly addressing how we are affected by conditions of powerlessness. By placing a value on multiethnic and racial coalitions, it assumes that women of color should play an important role in the movement. However, as discussed in the following section, this coalition has historically been the exception, rather than the rule.

## Problems and Issues for Feminist Organizing with Women of Color

The feminist movement of the United States has excluded women of color in three ways: by not acknowledging its racist tenets and foundations; by ignoring the issues that primarily affect women of color; and through difficulties with integrating other "voices" into the formulation of feminist theory and practice. Lack of attention to these three conditions relegates the feminist movement in the United States to providing a platform for European-American women on issues that have been addressed by women of color in other arenas.

The inability to address racism in the feminist movement has been documented by numerous scholars (Dill, 1987; Giddings, 1984; Hooks, 1981; Solomon, 1982; Spelman, 1989). While the movement has advocated paying critical attention to the domination of women in their historical and political contexts, only recently has it done so when examining its own formation. Hooks (1981) notes two instances of this historical racism. Elizabeth Cady Stanton, a leader of the suffrage movement of the turn of the century, identified the rights of white women to vote as being distinct from those of other men or women of color in this way:

> *If Saxon men have legislated thus for their own mothers, wives and daughters, what can we hope for at the hands of Chinese, Indians and Africans? ... I protest against the enfranchisement of another man of any race or clime until the daughters of Jefferson, Hancock are crowned with their rights.*

In the early 1900s, during a meeting of the General Federation of Women's Clubs, the president, Mrs. Lowe, stated her own reluctance to integrate black women into the clubs on the following basis: "Mrs. Ruffin belongs among her own people. Among them she would be a leader and could do much good, but among us, she can create nothing but trouble." Yet during this era, black male scholars and activists such as Frederick Douglass and Henry Garnett were welcome in white women's social circles as speakers.

Recent feminist scholarship demonstrates how racism in the contemporary women's movement has interfered with the involvement of women of color. Although many white leaders of the women's liberation movement gained an awareness of gender inequity through their involvement in the civil rights movement, they were unsuccessful in working collaboratively with women of color (Evans, 1980). Because feminist movements have often presented gender as the sole form of oppression, women of color have perceived their experiences with racism or ethocentrism as being ignored (Reid, 1984; Gould, 1987b). Only recently have efforts been made to incorporate issues of racism and other forms of oppression into the women's movement (Gould, 1987b; Weil, 1986).

A second impediment to the involvement of women of color has been the nature of the issues selected for mobilization. Because the majority of the leaders of the movement emerged from the European-American middle class, their life experiences have influenced the direction of the movement (Kopasci and Faulkner, 1988). Women of color, who have traditionally had high rates of labor force participation, often could not identify with the emphasis placed by feminists on the right of women to enter the workplace. Many of these women attributed their low wages to racism, rather than sexism, therefore the issue of comparable worth based on gender had little meaning.

A recent example of the exclusion of women of color and their problems from the women's movement of the United States is given by Williams (1988). In describing incidents of sterilization of women of color, she noted:

> *I was reminded of a case I worked on when I was working for the Western Center on Law and Poverty about eight years ago. Ten black Hispanic women had been sterilized by the University of Southern California-Los Angeles County General Medical Center, allegedly without proper consent, and in most instances without even their knowledge. Most of them found out what had been done to them upon inquiry, after a much-publicized news story in which an intern charged that the chief of obstetrics at the hospital pursued a policy of recommending Caesarian delivery and simultaneous sterilization for any pregnant woman with three or more children and who was on welfare. In the course of researching the appeal in that case, I remember learning that one-quarter of all Navajo women of childbearing age—literally all those of childbearing age ever admitted to a hospital—have been sterilized.*

Feminist organizing regarding reproductive rights has more often focused on issues of access to abortion than on the sterilization of women of color. A more inclusive formulation of the issues involved in reproductive rights would involve both access to contraception and abortion *and* the ability to exercise one's reproductive capacity.

The third impediment to the participation of women of color is the willingness to acknowledge other "lenses" or "voices" through which the experiences of women can be analyzed. The emergence of several theories about the status of women in the United States have been criticized for their lack of application to those other than white women (Spelman, 1989; Giddings, 1984; Hooks, 1981; Solomon, 1980). Contemporary theories of the women's movement are only now acknowledging the existence of an ethnic labor market structure, as in the case of Chinatown women (Armott & Matthaei, 1991; Loo and Ong, 1987). They further fail to acknowledge fully the oppression of men of color, or differences in family or gender roles in some ethnic communities (McAdoo, 1981; Solomon, 1980; Segura, 1987).

## *Community Organizing by Women of Color*

Lack of participation in feminist movements does not mean that women of color have not been active in their own communities: organizing by women of color in the United States has a rich and diverse history. An example of this involvement is the organization of Black Women's Clubs in the United States a century ago. Through women's clubs African-American women, such as Ida B. Wells Barnett, took leadership roles in the organization of their communities. At the end of the nineteenth century, these clubs organized nursing homes, daycare centers, and orphanages because the need for assistance with the care of children and the aging were of critical concern to African-American women in families during this period. Women's clubs were also involved in social action against lynching and sexual assault. The National Urban League, in which women had an important founding role, was another example of a community of color organizing nationally to address the problems and concerns of people of color in the United States.

These organizations, supported and developed by women of color, aimed at benefiting all society, not just their own target ethnic group. Macht and Quam (1986) note:

> the contributions of these groups did not stop with the Black community. They also played a vital role in World War I. The Committee on Women's Defense Work of the Council for National Defense consisted mainly of Black women. It helped care for families of absent soldiers, gave comfort kits to the soldiers, helped conserve and enlarge the food supply, and formed canning clubs. The Committee also brought attention to the high infant mortality rate in this country. It discovered a need for better community health services. To correct these problems, the Council set up programs to weigh and measure infants and provide them with milk. In addition, the Committee sought to improve recreational facilities available to youth and pushed for nurse's training for Black women. Medical personnel for Black people had always been woefully inadequate; the committee compiled and circulated a list of hospitals where Black women could be trained. (p. 96)

Women of color in these and other organizations did not view their work as affecting only their constituencies. Their work allowed for the incorporation of additional perspectives to assist all families.

Organizing by women of color has been based upon existing networks of family, friends, or informal and formal *ethnic community* institutions. Gilkes (1981, 1983) notes in her research on African-American women community organizers that these women were deeply embedded in black communities and became active because of their commitment to their communities. Barrera (1987) describes the extra activities willingly taken on by Latina professionals and paraprofessionals.

These individuals, he notes, have developed organizations and political interest groups and have served as interpreters of the wider society to those Latinos with limited access to it.

Other examples of community organization in long-standing ethnic communities are the mutual aid societies. The Hui, among the Chinese, the Ko among the Japanese, and the Tribal Councils among the Native Americans have all served as vehicles for assisting individual ethnic group members, families, and entire communities through the establishment of business loans, funerals, and community programs. Organizing with women of color from a feminist perspective must acknowledge, work within, and build upon these rich traditions.

## Examples from the Field

Feminist organizing methods place a high value on experience-based knowledge. Effective feminist organizing with women of color builds upon this base by drawing upon two sources: techniques based in feminist efforts and those from the tradition of women of color organizing within their own communities. The following examples indicate ways in which these traditions have been integrated:

### The Network Utilization Project (NUP)

The NUP project was developed by one of the authors in her work with women in a small Midwestern city. The purpose of the project was to use the strengths of African-American families as an intervention for empowerment. We did this in a variety of ways. First, the project was designed to be community-based. All participants lived in the same geographic proximity and had frequent interaction. Secondly, the project focused on the small group as a primary form of interaction. In this way, women had an opportunity to meet with one another on a weekly basis in a small group, which did not require that they either physically or psychologically remove themselves from their community of origin.

A third principle underlying the NUP project was that women of color in communities of color were a part of both those communities, as well as, extended family networks. It was necessary for these networks to be acknowledged in any change effort undertaken by the women, either individually or in groups. Each decision for change was met with an analysis of its possible consequences for the participants, their families, and the host community.

Lastly, it was assumed that experiences with individual problem resolution could be expanded to community problem resolution. It was in this effort that the program was most effective (Lewis, in press). NUP participants, through group meetings, organized a Tenant's Council in one of the city's low-income communities, were instrumental in closing down a city-funded agency that had not provided service to the community although it was being paid to do so, and participated in the organization of a citywide organization for low-income women's rights in the city. The Network Utilization Project activities moved participants from developing a sense of personal empowerment to bringing about change in their communities as well.

## *Project Oasis*

Safe homes networks were created early in the battered women's movement to provide short-term emergency shelter to victims of abuse and their children. The core of such a program is volunteers who agree to shelter battered women and their families within their homes for a limited period of time (Schechter, 1982). Safe homes programs have most often been used in white middle-class areas and rural areas and have rarely been developed within low-income, minority, or urban settings.

Project Oasis was an attempt to bring this form of feminist organizing into multiracial and multiethnic urban communities. The goal of Project Oasis was to end violence against women in these communities through the provision of advocacy, counseling, and shelter services; and through community education, legal advocacy, and the development of self-help networks. The program was initiated by one of the authors while working with a larger organization that offered counseling and community organization programs for all victims of crime in a large Northeastern city.

Developing a safe homes network for women of color involved modifying the structure it had taken in other localities. The organizer was able to draw upon the natural support networks of women of color within each community. She found that it was not unusual for women of color to shelter sisters in need, but that this sheltering was often done with expectations of reciprocity. Few low-income families could afford to provide financial support for a woman and her children. Therefore, this program gained funding that allowed them to reimburse volunteers for room and board so women who had the desire to help others were given the financial means to do so.

The program was ethnically and racially integrated in terms of staff on all levels, and efforts were made to administer it collaboratively. The director and 50 percent of the staff were women of color. Personal attributes and a commitment to using a feminist perspective in working with women of color were considered more important qualities for staff and volunteers than academic training. Staff and volunteers were involved in all aspects of administration, particularly in program planning and outreach. The goal was to develop a structure in which the women on the staff could grow and learn from one another.

Working within this multiethnic environment was a challenge for all those involved in the program: many of the white staff and volunteers had never worked in an environment in which women of color had the leadership roles, and many of the women of color had never been in a position in which they were allowed to take a major role in the development of programs. In an effort to deal with these issues, and others that emerged in this kind of program, much attention was paid to staff development and training. Based on principles of feminist management (Hyde, 1990) every month full-day staff retreats were scheduled in which team building and organizational activities were carried out. Responsibility for these meetings rotated among the different staff and units. These efforts were successful to the degree to which they opened up lines of communication and provided a structure for shared responsibility and collaboration among staff and volunteers. However, they did not prevent or eliminate the emergence of conflicts or issues present in any multiethnic organizing effort.

The multiethnic and urban nature of this program also affected the location and development of safe homes. Many safe homes networks established within white middle-class settings have focused their efforts for volunteer recruitment within the feminist community. Project Oasis was most successful when focusing outreach to organizations within minority communities: churches, Asian merchant associations, schools, health clinics, Head Start centers, and multiservice community centers. These organizations saw Project Oasis as an asset to the community and provided us with support and assistance. As a method of feminist organizing, Project Oasis was most successful in educating the community regarding violence against women and providing shelter. It also was effective in empowering individual women to became involved in helping others, volunteering, and testifying at public hearings. In these ways, women of color became more directly involved in ending violence against women.

## Future Directions for Feminist Organizing with Women of Color

### Practice Principles

The purpose of this chapter is to explore ways in which knowledge concerning feminist organizing methods and an understanding of the issues relevant to women of color can be integrated into a new and more inclusive organizing strategy. What do these examples and the preceding discussion tell us about feminist organizing with women of color? We believe that the following practice principles can provide directions for future work:

**1.** *Organizers must have intricate knowledge of and willingness to participate in the woman's ethnic community.* This first involves knowledge of its institutions and how they work for or against women. Churches, community centers, schools, and social clubs can be avenues for accessing women of color and affecting change within the community. Organizing requires an analysis of social institutions, including the one represented by the organizer, and how they might ultimately benefit or hurt the women being organized. Gaining this knowledge could involve learning more about specific communities of color through reading, and participation in community events (Kopasci and Faulkner, 1988). Working with women of color requires an understanding of the cultural context.

In an effort to become involved in the community, one of the group facilitators of the NUP project participated in activities sponsored by the local community center. She worked weekly with the children of the community in enrichment programming for several months before proceeding to organize the women. During this time, she became aware of community members' patterns of interaction, their relationships with agencies in the city, and other potential issues in the community. Community members, and group participants had the opportunity to meet and talk with the community worker and to watch her interact with their children. Many initial participants later mentioned that their decision to participate in the project was directly related to their approval of the facilitator's work with their children and presence in the community.

**2.** *Effective feminist organizing with women of color requires that women of color be in leadership roles.* Too often attempts to use these techniques with women of color have taken the unidirectional "outreach approach": communities of color are targets of feminist efforts, rather than active participants. When this approach is used, women of color often resist these efforts or can undermine them (Schechter, 1982; Kopasci & Faulkner, 1988). In both case examples described here, women of color acted as organizers of the activity within the community and used "community expertise" to guide their work. Although we were outsiders, our experience as women of color assisted our entrée into community. As women of color we were capable of assessing strategies of feminist organizing and making them more compatible with the minority community in which she worked. This is similar to Rivera and Erlich's description of secondary-level contact within the community (Rivera & Erlich, 1992).

Feminist organizations that would like to carry out more organizing with women of color should incorporate women of color as active participants and leaders *before* taking on this kind of work. This kind of collaboration may require redefining the kind of work they do and their attitudes toward institutions such as the church and family. The history of attempts at collaboration suggest that effective work involving European-American feminists and women of color requires identifying how racism and goal setting may exclude women of color from feminist efforts. Therefore successful collaboration requires that European-American women change their interactions with women of color. This kind of organizational work embraces the tenet of feminist organizing that "diversity is strength."

**3.** *The organizer must be willing to serve as a facilitator and to allow the problem to be studied through the "lens" or "vision" of women of color.* This requires allowing this vision to alter the way the organizer herself views her work and sharing that new information with others who hope to organize and work within communities of color. An organizer who is from a different racial, ethnic, or class background than the women must recognize how her life experience has influenced her perceptions. Her definitions and perceptions should not dominate the organizing effort. It is important that her work involve secondary or tertiary contact with the community: taking the role of facilitator or consultant while developing and working with local leadership.

In the Network Utilization Project described earlier, the initial intention of the project was to separate individual from community concerns. We initially believed that the group members would work on individual problem resolution for eight weeks and then, having established a pattern of interaction within the group, be able to work cooperatively on analysis and resolution of a community concern. It became clear during the first two meetings that the project could not separate individual from community concerns. As one participant put it: "My individual problems *are* the community's problems." The flexibility to alter the design based on the realities of the community allowed the group to continue to work toward resolution of its identified goals, not those of the facilitator/researcher.

**4.** *Utilize the process of praxis to understand the historical, political, and social context of the organizing effort.* This means that the organizing process will inform not only the organized community but the "community" of the organizer as well. Praxis involves an analysis of the process and outcome of organizing efforts. When this technique is used the outcome of a tactic is often less important than what the community and organizer learn about the nature of the problem being addressed. In this way community issues are often redefined.

Community organizers must engage in ongoing praxis in their work in order to recognize their own biases and assumptions in working with communities. How, for example, do their own social, historical, and political experiences influence their understanding of the communities they are working in, and their assumptions about which strategies are effective in these communities? How does the organizer change his or her own behavior and communicate that transformation to members of the wider society as a result of community work? How are effective strategies developed within the community of color transmitted for use to the wider society?

The involvement of women of color in the battered women's movement provides another example of this principle. When many feminist shelters observed that they were unsuccessful in reaching women of color, many defined the problem as that of inadequate outreach. When outreach was unsuccessful, women of color in some localities provided feedback to many shelter programs that their approach was alienating and foreign to communities of color. Those programs that have been most successful with women of color have been those that addressed their own racism, classism, and ethnocentrism in the development of alternative programs (Schechter, 1982).

**5.** *An effective strategy for organizing women of color is the small group.* The literature on empowerment and feminist organizing suggest that small group interaction can play a critical role (Gutierrez, 1990; Pernell, 1985). The small group provides the ideal environment for exploring the social and political aspects of "personal" problems and for developing strategies for work toward social change (Schechter et al., 1985). Therefore, feminist organizing often begins with interactions between women in small groups (Hyde, 1985).

On a national level, women of color have used this strategy to improve conditions in ghettos and barrios, based on a "house meeting" strategy (Sunday Chicago Tribune Magazine, 1988). For example, Clementine Barfield's work with SOSAD (Save Our Sons and Daughters) in Detroit began with a small group of mothers who had experienced the loss of a child through a violent death in the inner city. The formation of many similar small groups has built coalitions that have become an influential force in lobbying for gun control and related issues.

**6.** *Women of color who are involved in feminist organizing must anticipate the possible backlash from within their own community of origin, the wider society, and the feminist movement.* These sources of conflict will affect the outcomes of the organizing effort. The extent to which the worker/organizer anticipates conflict related to group interaction, the possibility of internalized oppression, wider society strategies to destroy the community change effort, and similar issues will often determine whether the efforts are successful.

Women of color have often worked effectively as organizers, but often at great expense to their physical and emotional health (Gilkes, 1983). Organizing around issues shared with European-American women may place the organizer in additional jeopardy within the ethnic community, because of the notion that organizing groups of women can be divisive (Aragon de Valdez, 1980). Strategies such as mapping out the benefits and drawbacks of sharing a community change effort are necessary when these linkages are desired. Efforts often require dealing directly with incidents of homophobia or sexism within communities of color.

When the negative consequences outweigh the benefits, alternatives to the proposed organizing effort must be identified. In some cases, this may mean that organizers who are not community members must continue their work outside the ethnic community and share strategies with organizers who are inside the ethnic community (Kopasci and Faulkner, 1988).

Women of color inside the community can also look to other women of color across the country involved in organizing effort for support. Pat Collair's efforts at organizing rural poor southern women rely not only on work with these women, but also with other women involved in similar grass-roots change efforts. This continued communication is one way of dealing with the problem of the emotional drain related to issues of racism and sexism in community organization.

**7.** *Feminist organizers must recognize ways in which women of color have worked effectively within then own communities.* Women of color have traditionally been involved in activities to benefit their community. Feminist organizers should work with these indigenous leaders and learn from them the most effective ways to work in particular communities. Working with existing leaders may involve feminist organizers in different types of activities than those in which they may usually engage. For example, existing community leaders may be active in church-related activities or in working with municipal agencies (Bookman & Morgan, 1986) to provide necessary survival services. Organizers can learn from these women ways in which they have found to survive and leverage political power.

It is more important than ever to recognize and facilitate effective organizing efforts among women in communities of color. Poverty levels in the United States, which have always disproportionately affected families of color, are at pre-1965 levels for women and children. Homelessness, originally theorized to be a problem of unemployed men, is now a serious problem for poor women and their families as well. Many of the reasons for organizing efforts of the 1800s for people of color, have been resolved (inability to vote, restricted access to banks and insurance companies, etc.). The mutual aid societies and African-American women's clubs, however, may be still be used as entry-level points to women of color. Just as the early African-American Women's Clubs of the 1880s began with a concentration on antilynching strategies and later expanded to problems facing the general society, so can the mutual aid societies form a basis for organizing on both the micro and macro levels for women of color.

## *Conclusion*

A feminist perspective on organizing with women of color is one way to address how sexism and racism have a profound effect on our lives. Knowledge based on feminist organizing suggests specific ways in which organizers can move individual women from feelings of powerlessness and apathy to active change. However, this model of feminist organizing must be modified when working in communities of color. Feminist organizers must recognize how their life experience might differ from that of community members and therefore be willing to accept the problem definitions and strategies developed by women of color. Another technique requires recognizing how historical conflicts between feminist and antiracist movements may affect interactions between white women and women of color and point to ways of opening up a dialogue that will work toward creative resolution of these conflicts.

Traditional feminist organizing has usually moved in one direction only: from the organizers representing the white middle-class community to the community of color. For example little of the literature on feminist organizing or community organizing describes the activist roles of women of color within our communities. As students, we learned of our contributions to social change only through reading the popular African-American press (e.g., *Ebony, Essence, Black Digest*), local ethnic press, or through oral tradition within our communities.

As suggested by Rivera and Erlich in this volume, the most appropriate role for European-American organizers with woman of color is that of consultant rather than direct grassroots organizer. In this chapter we reinforce this perspective by suggesting that in order for this work to be effective, the flow of information about the best ways to engage in organizing activities with women of color is to adopt a multidirectional approach: from the individual women of color, through their families, informal institutions, and back to the feminists representing the wider society. In this way, feminist community organization techniques can contribute to the empowerment of individual women and to their involvement in solving the problems of all women of color.

## *References*

Aragon de Valdez, T. (1980). Organizing as a political tool for the Chicana. *Frontiers*, 5: 7–13.

Armott, T., & Matthaei, J. (1991). *Race, Gender, & Work: A Multicultural History of Women in the United States.* Boston: South End Press.

Barrera, M. (1987). Chicano class structure. In R. Takaki (ed.), *From Different Shores: Perspectives on Race and Ethnicity In America* (pp. 130–138). New York: Oxford University Press.

Bookman, A., & Morgan, S. (1986). *Women and the Politics of Empowerment.* Philadelphia: Temple University Press.

Bricker-Jenkins & Hooyman, N. (1986). *Not for Women Only: Social Work Practice for a Feminist Future.* Silver Spring, Md.: NASW.

Dill, B. T. (1987). Race, class and gender: Prospects for an all-inclusive sisterhood. In R. Takaki (ed.), *From Different Shores: Perspectives on Race and Ethnicity in America* (pp. 204–214). New York: Oxford University Press.

Evans, S. (1980). *Personal Politics.* New York: Vintage Books.

Friere, P. (1970). Cultural action for freedom. *Harvard Educational Review,* 40: 205–225, 452–477.

Giddings, P. (1984). *Where and When I Enter: The Impact of Black Women On Race and Sex in America.* New York: William Morrow and Company.

Gilkes, C. (1986). Building in many places: Multiple commitments and ideologies in black women's community work. In A. Bookman and S. Morgan (eds.), *Woman and the politics of empowerment.* Philadelphia: Temple University Press.

———. (1983). Going up for the oppressed: The career mobility of black women community workers. *Journal of Social Issues,* 39(3): 115–139.

———. (1981). Holding back the ocean with a broom: Black women and community work. In L. F. Rodgers-Rose (ed.), *The black woman* (pp. 217–233). Beverly Hills: Sage.

Gordon-Bradshaw, R. (1987). A social essay on special issues facing poor women of color. *Women and Health,* 12: 243–259.

Gould, K. (1987a). Life model vs. role conflict model: A feminist perspective. *Social Work,* 32: 346–351.

———. (1987b). Feminist principals and minority concerns: Contributions, problems, and solutions. *Affila: Journal of Women and Social Work, 3:* 6–19.

Gutierrez, L. (1990). Working with women of color: An empowerment perspective. *Social Work, 35:* 149–154.

Hooks, B. (1981). *Ain't I A Woman: Black Women and Feminism.* Boston: South End Press.

Hyde, C. (1990). A feminist model for macro practice: Promises and problems. *Administration in Social Work, 13:* 145–181.

———. (1986). Experiences of women activists: Implications for community organizing theory and practice. *Journal of Sociology and Social Welfare, 13:* 545–562.

Joseph, B., Mizrahi, T., Peterson, J., & Sugarman, F. (March 1989). Women's perspectives on community organizing: A feminist synthesis of theory and practice. Paper presented at the annual program meeting of the Council on Social Work Education, Chicago.

Kieffer, C. (1984). Citizen empowerment: A developmental perspective. In J. Rappaport, C. Swift, & R. Hess (eds.), *Studies in Empowerment: Toward Understanding and Action* (pp. 9–36). New York: Hawthorn Press.

Kopasci, R., & Faulkner, A. (1988). The powers that might be: The unity of white and black feminists. *Afflia, 3:* 33–50.

Lewis, E. (in press). Ethnicity, race and gender: Training and supervision issues in the treatment of women. In B. De Chant, J. Cunningham, J. Lazerson, & R. Perls (eds.), *Women, Gender and Group Psychotherapy.* New York: American Group Psychotherapy Association Monograph.

Linton, R., & Witham, M. (1981). With mourning, rage, empowerment and defiance: The 1981 Women's Pentagon Action. *Socialist Review, 63:* 11–36.

Longres, J., & McLeod, E. (1980). Consciousness raising and social work practice. *Social Casework, 61:* 267–627.

Loo, C., & Ong, P. (1987). Slaying demons with a sewing needle: Feminist issues for Chinatown's women. In R. Takaki (ed.), *From Different Shores: Perspectives on Race and Ethnicity in America* (pp. 186–191). New York: Oxford University Press.

McAdoo, J. (1981), Black father and child interactions. In L. Gary (ed.), *Black Men* (pp. 115–130). Beverly Hills: Sage.

Macht, M., & Quam, J. (1986). *Social Work: An Introduction.* Columbus, Ohio: Merrill.

Morell, C. (1987). Cause is function: Toward a feminist model of integration for social work. *Social Science Review, 61:* 144–155.

Nes, J., & Iadicola, P. (1989). Toward a definition of feminist social work: A comparison of liberal, radical, and socialist models. *Social Work, 34:* 12–22.

1990 Census of the Population. (1992). *Volume 1: Characteristics of the Population.* Washington: U.S. Department of Commerce.

Pernell, R. (1985). Empowerment and social group work. In M. Parenes (ed.), *Innovations in Social Group Work: Feedback from Practice to Theory* (pp. 107–117). New York: Hawthorn Press.

Pinderhughes, E. (1983). Empowerment for our clients and for ourselves. *Social Casework, 64:* 331–38.

Reid, P. (1984). Feminism vs. minority group identity: Not for black women only. *Sex Roles, 10:* 247–255.

Rosenthal, N. (1984). Consciousness raising: From revolution to re-evaluation. *Psychology of Women Quarterly, 8:* 309–326.

Schechter, S. (1982). *Women and Male Violence: The Visions and Struggles of the Battered Women's Movement.* Boston: South End Press.

Schechter, S., Szymanski, S., & Cahill, M. (1985). *Violence against Women: a Curriculum for Empowerment.* (Facilitator's Manual). New York: Women's Education Institute.

Segura, D. (1987). Labor market stratification: The Chicana experience. In R. Takaki (ed.), *From Different Shores: Perspectives on Race and Ethnicity in America* (pp. 175–185). New York: Oxford University Press.

Simmons, C., & Parsons, R. (1983). Empowerment for role alternatives in adolescence. *Adolescence,* 18(69): 193–200.

Solomon, B. (1982). Empowering women: A matter of values. In A. Weick & S. Vandiver (eds.), *Women, Power and Change* (pp. 206–214). Silver Spring, Md.: NASW.

———. (1980). Alternative social services and the black woman. In N. Gottlieb (ed.), *Alternative Services for Women* (pp. 333–345). New York: Columbia University Press.

———. (1976). *Black Empowerment.* New York: Columbia University Press.

Spelman, E. (1989). *Inessential Woman: Problems of Exclusion in Feminist Thought.* Boston: Beacon Press.

*Sunday Chicago Tribune Magazine* (1988, Oct. 16). Fighting back: Frances Sandoval and her mother's crusade take aim at gangs (pp. 10–24).

Weil, M. (1986). Women, community and organizing. In N. Van DenBergh & L. Cooper (eds.), *Feminist Visions for Social Work* (pp. 187–210). Silver Spring, Md.: NASW.

White, B. (1981) Black women: The resilient victims. In A. Weick & S. Vandiver (eds.), *Women, Power and Change* (pp. 69–77). Washington D.C.: NASW.

Williams, P. J. (1988). On being the object of property. *Signs: Journal of Women and Culture,* 14(1).

Withorn, A. (1984). *Serving the People: Social Services and Social Change.* New York: Columbia University Press.

Zambrana, R. (1987). A research agenda on issues affecting poor and minority women: A model for understanding their health needs. *Women and Health,* 12: 137–60.

Zavella, P. (1986). The politics of race and gender: Organizing Chicana cannery workers in Northern California. In A. Bookman and S. Morgan (eds.), *Women and the Politics of Empowerment.* Philadelphia: Temple University Press.

# 7

Organizing in the Chinese-American Community: Issues, Strategies, and Alternatives

*PETER CHING-YUNG LEE*

Asian and Pacific-Islander Americans are a diverse and rapidly growing minority population in the United States. This phenomenon is due primarily to the large influx of immigrants from China since the late 1960s; from Korea, the Philippines, and India since the early 1970s; and more recently from Southeast Asia. In many ways, the major Asian or Pacific-Islander groups are different from one another as well as from other races. As a people of color who represent a multitude of distinctive languages and cultures, Asian and Pacific-Islander Americans also face political and economic oppression, which results in problems and issues associated with discrimination. Community organization practice is one professional field in which efforts can be made toward resolving these problems. While the human services literature related to people of color has received much recent attention, the scarcity of literature on community organization practices of minorities, and on organizing strategies and tactics of Chinese Americans in particular, created the need for this chapter.

The framework and content of this chapter are based on three areas of knowledge: (a) sociocultural and political-economic dynamics of minority populations; (b) theoretical frameworks; and (c) knowledge and strategies relevant for professional action. Accordingly, the chapter is divided into three major sections. The first part examines the status of Chinese Americans in terms of historical background, sociodemographic changes, cultural values, problems and issues, and human service needs. The second part provides an introduction to community organizing of Chinese Americans by identifying key elements of a basic framework. The purpose here is to analyze further the state of community organizing among Chinese Americans by focusing on Santa Clara County in Northern California to illustrate the wide range of areas that can be subsumed under the community organization practice. This chapter also diverges from current community organization literature in one important respect—its emphasis on practice. Its focus is mostly an analysis of transcultural practice technology. Therefore, the chapter concludes with a discussion of community intervention strategies from social development and cross-cultural perspectives and the prospects for the future.

## Chinese Americans: A Profile

Ethnicity in itself is a complex variable that involves knowledge, expectations, attitudes, social norms, and experiences. At the same time, it is not a stable variable since its significance changes as persons become socially adapted to the dominant culture. For persons or groups in varying stages of adaptation, ethnicity could have subsequent varying effects upon their changing problems and needs. One particularly relevant target population in this context is Chinese Americans, whose cultures, traditions, assimilation patterns, and coping mechanisms may have profound implications for the professional practice of community organization. Over the last two centuries, Chinese Americans have immigrated to the United States from different parts of the world in their search for better lives. Although policymakers, researchers, professionals, and the public often stereotype that Chinese as all alike, the reality is that the Chinese population is a heterogeneous one with diverse cultural, political, economic, and social circumstances. Discussing community organizing requires an outline first of general trends and characteristics of Chinese Americans as an ethnic group in the United States.

## Current Sociodemographic Characteristics

Reliable statistical data on Chinese Americans in the United States are either rare or nonexistent. Yet this group is one of the fastest growing ethnic minorities in the country today. Since the 1980 Census, the Chinese-American population, up 85 percent since 1970, has emerged as the largest group among Asian and Pacific-Islander populations in the country.[1] According to the 1990 Census, Chinese Americans, who have an average annual growth rate of around 7 percent, numbered 1,645,472, accounting for 0.7 percent of the total U.S. population.[2] If current trends continue, the Chinese-American population will number over 3 million by the year 2000, over 1 percent of the total projected U.S. population.

The 1990 Census also provided basic sociodemographic information on Chinese Americans. Chinese Americans are primarily urban-oriented and concentrated in metropolitan areas. A majority of Chinese Americans lived in three states: California (about 40 percent), Hawaii (10 percent), and New York (20 percent), with the other 30 percent or so scattered over the remaining forty-seven states. The concentration of Chinese Americans in the West is not surprising because large Asian and Pacific-Islander populations already reside there.[3]

Given prior and ongoing accelerated Chinese immigration to the United States, it is not surprising that more than two-thirds (70 percent) of the current Chinese-American population is foreign-born. As for those who were born outside the United States—the so called first generation Chinese Americans—nearly two-thirds of them came from Taiwan or mainland China (65 percent), while 12 percent came from Hong Kong, 16 percent from Southeast Asia, and remaining 7 percent from other parts of the world.[4]

The average age of Chinese Americans is nearly the same as the national average (median age of 29.6 years for Chinese compared with thirty years for the nation).[5] The Chinese family composition of 3.7 persons, on the average, is slightly higher than the national average of 3.3 persons, partly because a higher percentage of Chinese elderly and children live with family members.[6] Chinese women have a lower fertility rate than do U.S. females in general, as well as a lower divorce rate.[7] In addition, out-of-wedlock childbearing, as measured by the ratio of births to unmarried women per 1,000 total live births, occurs least often among Chinese women.[8]

Chinese are among the highest-ranked Asian-American groups in terms of socioeconomic status. For example, the 1980 Census documents that most Chinese Americans were middle class, with an average family income of $22,600, higher than the national median income of $19,900. A similar trend was also observed in the 1990 Census. However, this difference is somewhat misleading because it is partly a function of their having more working family members. And a disproportionate number of Chinese Americans reside in areas with a high cost of living (California and Hawaii, for instance), which may force many individuals to work at more than one job. In addition, the poverty rate among Chinese was only slightly lower than the national average (14.5 percent) in 1993, because of persistent nationwide unemployment, low wages, and a slow recovery from the last recession.

The Chinese-American emphasis on education is well known and is clearly reflected in the Census data. In educational attainment, Chinese Americans are one of the best-educated groups in the United States. For example, nearly three-quarters of Chinese Americans who are twenty-five years of age and older have graduated from high school. Respectively, more than two-fifths (44 percent) and nearly one-third (30 percent) of Chinese men and women in the United States have completed college education, thus far exceeding the national rates of 20 percent and 13 percent for men and women.[9]

## *Changing Values and Behaviors: What Are We?*

What does it mean to be Chinese in America? This question would no doubt invite a wide variety of responses. When a profile of a given ethnic group is presented, it may stray across the invisible boundary that separates profiles from stereotypes. With this caution in mind, the following general description explores some cultural values and behavioral norms that may be helpful in understanding Chinese Americans and their community.

   **1.** When trying to understand Chinese-American values and behaviors one must begin with the concept of self in Chinese-American terms. While Western concepts of self place the individual at the center, with all other relationships arranged around the self, the Chinese people perceive the self as part of a set of interpersonal relationships of which the family system is the core. Contemporary Chinese families in America are predominantly nuclear ones consisting of a married couple and their children; their role composition is simpler when compared to the traditionally extended ones. For the great majority of Chinese Americans, the provision of a sense of security, intimacy, unity, acceptance, and mutual support by the family is still considered indispensable to modern life.[10]

   **2.** With their social organization revolving around family and kinship, Chinese have traditionally held on to the concept of *ren,* or benevolence, which encompasses filial piety and fraternal love. In etymology as well as in interpretation, *ren* is always concerned with human relationships. Basically, *ren* is translated variously as goodness, benevolence, humanity, and human-heartedness. *Ren,* therefore, is rooted in human sentiment as well as in a fundamental orientation of life. It is associated with loyalty (*zhong*)—loyalty to one's own heart and conscience, and reciprocity (*shu*)—respect of and consideration for others.

   **3.** Within the traditional Chinese community system, the well-known five relationships include that of ruler-subject, father-son, husband-wife, elder-younger brothers, and friend-friend.[11] Three of these are family relationships, while the other two are usually conceived in terms of the family models. For this reason, Chinese society regards itself as a large family. Thus, familial relations provide a model for Chinese social behavior. The responsibilities ensuing from these relationships are mutual and reciprocal. They have been the reason for the strong sense of solidarity not only in the Chinese family, but also in social and community organizations. Thus, the group, rather than the individual, is the major unit of society. In addition, the parent-child relationship (that is, father-son relationship in the traditional sense) often take priority over the husband-wife spousal relationship. The parent-child relationship tends to be characterized by mutual obligation within a vertical power hierarchy. Benevolent parents are those who do what is best and appropriate for their children, even at the expense of personal needs. While the extent of Chinese parental sacrifice and fulfillment of duties vary, Chinese culture perpetuates powerful pressure on parents, as well as children, to think of the family first.[12] For example, divorce is generally considered a social embarrassment and only as a last alternative, an attitude that may be changing among the younger generation of Chinese Americans.

**4.** The concept of obligation in Chinese culture is also crucial in the context of community. In American society, the tendency toward reciprocity, for example, is weighed heavily toward contractual obligation. Within Chinese culture, obligation is important and is generally incurred through ascribed roles or status, even through kindness or helpfulness received from other people. Therefore, obligation often becomes the basis for reciprocal relationships between peers and within families, as well as community social networks. While social relationships are based primarily on the preservation of harmony and suppression of conflict, obligation to different individuals, families, or groups may conflict and can become a source of great anxiety. In Chinese culture, where interdependence is emphasized, the perceived or actual withdrawal of support may shake an individual's basic trust and confidence and raise one's anxiety over being alone. Thus, the fear of losing face or support can be a strong motivating force in favor of conformity, and family or group-oriented behavior is strongly approved.

**5.** Of further importance is the great emphasis on mutual dependence rather than individual independence and antagonism. That is to say, role fulfillment is of cardinal virtue in Chinese culture. This means that everyone should learn to play his or her proper role in various interpersonal relations in society. Establishing right interpersonal relationships in all aspects of life is the way to achieve an orderly and peaceful society.

**6.** Many of those first-generation Chinese Americans feel that they must be the last generation in America to feel a strong connection with traditional values and customs.[13] They are in many ways a link between the past and future and feel a sense of responsibility for passing on the traditional ways of thinking, although they often find this a difficult task. Their own children, as products of a different environment, tend to be much more individualistic in their decision-making. Still, most first-generation Chinese Americans consider it their obligation to be good role models for the younger generations.[14]

**7.** Although most new immigrant Chinese accept responsibility for the welfare of their aging parents, they do not expect their children to take care of them. In fact, today's Chinese immigrants are perhaps the first generation to assume that they will be on their own after retirement, and many are beginning to make financial preparations for their old age. By the same token, many also expect their children to fend for themselves when they grow up, a marked change in attitude from their parents' generation. While many first-generation Chinese Americans do not want to exert as much influence over their children's lives as their own parents did, they still have high expectations for them. And whatever they may expect of their children, Chinese Americans still consider their families a valuable source of moral support.

**8.** Their children's education is another paramount consideration for Chinese-American parents. Central to Confucian thinking is belief in the perfectability and educability of human being. This is why the emphasis on education became one of the most prominent features of Chinese culture. This is particularly true for many first-generation Chinese immigrant parents who worry when their children do not excel academically and often invest generously in education-related programs and activities.

## Chinese Community: Then and Now

We now turn to an overview of the historical dynamics of Chinese immigration to the United States. Even though the United States has traditionally identified itself mostly with Europe, an important component of the political or social change perspective has been an increased awareness and understanding of cultural diversity. Therefore, within the cross-cultural framework proposed here, it is crucial to understand particular behaviors of Chinese Americans in the context of contemporary American society. Many Chinese Americans are still victims of discrimination and social prejudice. By tracing some historical facts, we will examine examples of some of the most important racist legislation that significantly hindered the political, social, and economic development of the Chinese-American community.

## Historical Background

### 1. The Pioneer Chinese
Since the Chinese began to arrive in the United States as early as the mid-seventeenth century, the nature and size of the Chinese population have varied widely.[15] Before the 1800s, the number of Chinese immigrants remained relatively small, and many of them served as "imported Chinese workers" in Hawaii. However, the unstable political and miserable social conditions in China, along with the discovery of gold in California during the late 1840s motivated Chinese immigration in increasing numbers. By 1860, the Census reported 34,933 resident Chinese, a figure that rose to 63,199 in 1870, 105,465 in 1880, and peaked at 107,488 in 1890.[16] But a more significant fact is that these early Chinese immigrants were mostly male (94.9 percent according to the 1860 Census) and were frequently praised for their cleanliness, thrift, industry, and orderly behavior.

Most of these newest minority were poorly educated, strong, young, single males from rural areas in China, who were attracted by labor contractors, steamship companies, and plantation owners. But from the time of their arrival, these immigrants suffered from economic exploitation, political oppression, social and legal injustice, and subhuman treatment. For example, the California Foreign Miner's Tax Law of 1853 allowed for the collection of taxes almost exclusively from Chinese miners between 1853 and 1870. During the first four years of its enforcement Chinese miners paid 50 percent of the total revenues obtained from working in gold mines. During the next thirteen years, the rate was increased to 98 percent.[17] The Exclusion of Chinese Witness Act of 1854 (reaffirmed in 1871) prohibited Chinese persons from serving as witnesses in actions or proceedings in which a white person was a party. In addition, no Chinese were permitted to testify or present evidence in favor of or against any white person. Clearly, this legislation put Chinese in a judicially unprotected situation.[18]

## 2. Continued Oppression

Before the turn of the century, there were about twenty-seven men for every woman among the Chinese in America. This is primarily the direct result of the so-called Restriction of Chinese Female Immigrants Act of 1870, which prevented the entry of Chinese females into the United States. What this meant for white perceptions of Chinese newcomers is probably familiar enough. Forced into Chinatown ghettos, these men joined together in clan associations and secret societies to obtain familiarity, security, and solidarity. Meanwhile, the alarming imbalance in the sex ratio also meant that the Chinese communities in America at the time were almost incapable of producing a second generation of American-born Chinese. It was not until 1950 that the American-born made up more than half the total Chinese population in America, and even this growth only came about through the much larger number of immigrants who entered since the 1940s, thanks to gradual but important relaxations of the immigration laws.

In the economic depression of the mid-1870s, the Chinese became scapegoats for white laborers who lost their jobs. Legal and legislative action was taken in an attempt to diminish Chinese competition in the labor force. In fact, the Naturalization Act of 1870 excluded Chinese from obtaining U.S. citizenship and forbade the entry of laborers' wives. Subsequently, the Chinese Exclusion Act of 1882 was passed to stop the immigration of Chinese laborers and to continue the denial of citizenship to the Chinese. A series of laws followed the Act of 1882, culminating in the 1924 Asian Exclusion Act designed to shut out all Asian immigrants, a clear-cut case of institutional racism.

The Geary Act of 1892 (upheld by the Supreme Court in 1893) extended all existing laws restricting Chinese immigration and was later extended further to restrict all Asian immigrants. In 1913, California became the first state to pass the Alien Land Law, also called the Webb-Henry Act of 1913. This Act prohibited landownership and limited to three years the leasing rights of aliens ineligible for citizenship. It was not until 1943 that the so-called Magnuson Act finally repealed the Chinese Exclusion Act of 1882. Finally, the McCarren-Walter Immigration Act of 1952 changed exclusion to restriction for all Asian immigrants and gave them the citizenship that had long been denied. For more than a century and through repressive legislation, the result of injustice was a steady decline in the Chinese population and a concomitant repression of their basic human rights and fair participation in the dominant white society.

### 3. A Turning Point

Time has brought more social equality and opportunities. Consequently, the old stereotypes have waned, and the image of Chinese Americans as a group has improved considerably in recent decades. This change gained increased momentum in the mid-1960s as a result of the most radical immigration law, passed in 1965 (Public Law 89–236), finally giving fair and equal immigration opportunities to Chinese. The abolition of the quota system through this 1965 legislation established an annual ceiling of 20,000 immigrants for each Asian country. As a result, an influx of immigrants arrived from all walks of life and different parts of Asia.

The law's emphasis on family reunification attracts thousands of new Chinese immigrants who are either parents or children of U.S. citizens. Unlike Chinatown residents, the majority of these more recent immigrants from Taiwan, mainland China, or Hong Kong came to the United States as students pursuing advanced degrees. And the policies of admission based on occupational preference also absorbs a large proportion of professional immigrants. Many of these students who became qualified professionals actually formed a second wave of Chinese immigration to the United States, beginning in the 1950s. This 1965 law was based on a shift in the American public's image of Asian Americans from yellow peril to model minority.

### 4. Starting from Zero

Since the end of the Vietnam War in 1975, another distinct ethnic Chinese group from Southeast Asia began to arrive in the United States in large numbers as refugees under the so-called Indochina Migration Refugee Assistance Act of 1975. The majority of these ethnic Chinese are refugee populations resembling other refugee groups (e.g., Vietnamese and Cubans) who were forced to leave their homelands and settled in the United States. Further, their resettlement experiences are similar in many ways to those of other Asian immigrant groups in this country. This population has faced adjustment problems such as cultural change, acculturation stress, and intergenerational conflict, including negative public attitudes in the United States.[19]

## Changing Problems and Needs: From Chinatown to the Suburbs

The marked increase in the Asian and Pacific-Islander American population, especially since 1965, has created a fluid, rapidly changing mixture of peoples. The

Asian and Pacific-Islander American populations are now becoming more hetero-geneous as new immigrants alter the composition and cultural unity of the total Asian and Pacific-Islander American population. By the same token, the Chinese communities in America are perhaps much less homogeneous than they appear to the casual observer. As the largest Asian group, the overall picture for the Chinese-American community, then, is that the Chinese-American population has continued to increase substantially since 1965 because of immigration and that this influx of Chinese immigrants has concentrated itself in a relatively small number of urban areas.

The earliest immigrants came as coolie labor to work on farms, in mines, and on the railroads. They came with no expectation of staying, but they ended up settling down in North America. Originally, the Chinese community was expressed in the term "Chinatown," which continue to have both a geographic and social reality. Early immigrants stayed and raised their families in Chinatowns, where the old ways held sway. Chinatown first grew out of a desire to maintain closeness, preserve cultural values and traditions, and help its residents become self-sufficient. However, misunderstood and mistrusted by the mainstream, the Chinese who lived there did so as a society within a society. Ironically, the anti-Chinese movement forced the entrenchment of Chinatown, which in turn strengthened the controls of traditional associations, resulting in the establishment, rather than the destruction, of the Chinese community.

Although many Chinese immigrants have succeeded in making their dreams realities, they, like earlier immigrants, live in two worlds. Their workplace is often predominantly white, but they live in a "Chinese community," where Chinese goods, Chinese newspapers, and Chinese television programs are readily available, including a special Chinese edition of the yellow pages. This is what could be called a divided existence: they work in one culture, but live in another. As a result, many new immigrants are not forced to venture outside the Chinese community. Conse-quently, the conflict between personal identity and social identity may affect first-generation Chinese Americans and their children. It can be a trying emotional struggle.

Furthermore, successes of Chinese immigrants have also led to an interesting new phenomenon—the rise of a new stereotype of Chinese Americans as over-achievers in science or business. Now greater numbers of young Chinese Americans are entering nontraditional fields outside science and business. They are gaining recognition in music (cellist Yo-yo Ma and violinist Cho-liang Lin), literature (the novelist Amy Tan rose to fame with *The Joy Luck Club*), broadcasting and journal-ism (CBS-TV anchor Connie Chung), and in public service (California State Secre-tary March Fong Eu; Julia Chang Bloch, the first Chinese American to serve as a U.S. ambassador; and Elaine Chao, the head of the United Way of America, to name a few). Like earlier immigrants to America, Chinese Americans are now striking a balance between maintaining their cultural heritage and assimilation, and everyone is the richer for it.

The American-born generation faces unique problems of its own as well. They naturally assimilate much more readily into the mainstream of American life than their parents. The Chinese language is almost extinct among children of Chinese immigrants. Having been brought up in America's predominantly English-speaking environment, they have little motivation to learn the language of their parents. Loss of linguistic heritage is not the only problem faced by the Chinese in America. In the eyes of their parents, younger Chinese Americans are losing touch with their cultural roots and traditional values. It is generally agreed that the strong family ties and filial piety so cherished in traditional Chinese culture have lost their authority with younger Chinese Americans.[20]

The model minority myth, coupled with the rising economic prowess of Pacific-Rim Asian countries and the corresponding downturn of the American economy, has given rise to an increase in anti-Asian sentiment and violence. The case of Vincent Chin sadly demonstrated the impact of such campaigns. Chin, a twenty-seven-year-old Chinese-American engineer, was bludgeoned to death by two white unemployed auto workers in Detroit. The two men, who were merely fined and put on probation by the judge, mistook him for Japanese, whom they blamed for their unemployment. In recent years, violence against Asian refugees and immigrants who compete for scarce resources in low-income communities has also dramatically increased.

Among other new issues facing the Chinese-American community is the emerging phenomenon of so-called little overseas students from Taiwan and Hong Kong.[21] Many of these families brought their children here for the sake of better education and the security of property and investment in America. The burden of care for these youngsters, ranging in age from six to fifteen in most cases, often rested upon the shoulders of the mothers, friends, and relatives, while the fathers returned to their jobs in Taiwan or Hong Kong most of the time. Most of these families left their homelands with high hopes, only to face the grim reality of adjustment in American society. As young and inexperienced immigrants, many of these students faced legal problems when their visas expired, in additional to language difficulty and learning barriers. Some juvenile delinquency and gang activities have emerged among the new Chinese youth in junior and senior high schools around the urban communities.

Therefore, the human service needs of the current Chinese Americans stem from an aggregate of new and old problems. On the one hand, there are the problems of incomplete structural assimilation common to a visible minority group like Chinese Americans, who have coexisted uneasily for several generations with a white majority that has never totally accepted it. On the other hand, the fact that current Chinese-Americans are overwhelmingly foreign-born may lead to problems arising from a lack of cultural assimilation. For example, the new immigrant Chinese may not know how to utilize social services; the second-generation Chinese American may still be asked when he or she immigrated to United States.

Because of the large proportion of recent immigrants among most Asian-American groups, it is important that we have a clear notion of the community experiences of these people. For example, what is the nature of the ethnic community and its social support system? Does such a community support system exist, and if it does, has it managed to remain viable in view of the great influx of immigration since 1965? Can the organizing experience of Asian-American communities (such as the Chinese), which do have well-established community organizations, be generalized to the more recently arrived groups? How important are the family and the ethnic community in providing help? Do Chinese Americans fail to utilize social services provided by the majority community? Has community organization been successful in working with Chinese Americans? What effect has the new immigration had upon the older Asian-American communities? It is also important to know what specific community organizing strategies and tactics have been applied to the Chinese-American community. This may affect the overall service needs of these communities. From this overview of what we need to know about Chinese-American community, it should be clear that determining how strategies and tactics are practiced is one of the most critical factors in community organizing.

## Chinese-American Community Organizing Experience

### Theoretical Framework

An analysis of literature in the field of community organization indicates that some of the most common theories include system theory, conflict theory, theories of political economy, theories of group politics and influences, theories of social change, theories of personality and attitude formation, and theories of management and administration. The importance of a sociocultural perspective in community organizing strategies has now begun to be explored. It cannot be assumed that the strategies and tactics that are effective with the majority community will be applicable to the same degree with ethnic communities. Synthesizing some of this recent body of knowledge indicates several working principles relevant to the Chinese community. From an application perspective, the current changing patterns of the Chinese-American community may be understood in terms of these theoretical perspectives.

#### 1. Empowerment as a Relevant Paradigm
The first fundamental assumption upon which the theoretical framework is based is: there is a limited number of basic human problems for which all peoples at all times and in all places must find a solution.[22] Within the practice of community organization, a pluralistic American society requires a special awareness of the cultural beliefs, values, and behaviors of the ethnic community and the adaptation to its cultural milieu. The major thesis is that individuals, families, and groups in the Chinese-American community have been subjected to negative valuations from the mainstream society to such an extent that powerlessness in the community is pervasive. Thus, when working with the Chinese-American community, consid-

eration must be given to the structure and process of service delivery systems that have the greatest potential for facilitating empowerment of minority groups.

## 2. Individual and Community World View

A community is said to exist when interaction between individuals has the purpose of meeting individual needs and obtaining group goals. In all societies physical, psychological, and social needs are met through the creation of social systems. Particular structures within systems are called institutions, and these become the basic features of a community. In a pluralistic society, both ethnic individuals and their community's world view need to be understood.

World view refers to the values and beliefs one holds about the world. These values and beliefs are manifested in actions and behaviors. For minority people and their communities, world view may include degree of acculturation, impact of social oppression on the group as well as the individual, and the extent of opportunities to interact with people from one's own culture as well as from the dominant culture.[23] Further, there are specific ways in which a client's world view may affect social services, such as help-seeking behaviors, formulations of problem assessment, and strategies for problem resolution.

## 3. Cultural Deprivation and Discrimination

Many empirical reports have generally portrayed ethnic minorities in a negative manner, regularly finding them disadvantaged or deficient in some way. This is the "cultural deficit model," which rests on the assumption that norms and cultural patterns of minority groups that vary from those of the majority culture are for the most part deviant and destructive and lead to a self-perpetuating "cycle of poverty and deprivation."[24] Ethnic minorities are kept in a subordinate and disadvantageous position because it serves the interests of the dominant groups to maintain such a stratified system. People of color come to believe misinformation about their particular ethnic group and thus believe that their mistreatment is justified. Racism, then, is a form of systematic, institutionalized mistreatment of one group of people by another based on racial heritage. Therefore, inequality is a result of a struggle or competition for resources, privileges, and rewards that are in short supply. The "deficit hypothesis" has increasingly been challenged, and serious question has been raised concerning the methodological adequacy of ethnic research in the United States.[25]

## 4. The Cultural Difference Model

Minority individuals, including Chinese Americans, must learn to function in two environments: their own culture and that of the mainstream society. The cultural difference model posited that each minority culture is unique and should be viewed as an independent and internally consistent system. Therefore, each minority culture can be understood in its own context rather than judged according to its similarity to or difference from the majority culture.[26] This perspective can become somewhat complicated in view of the fact that ethnic cultures, and indeed their communities, are contained in the majority culture. Further, the cultural difference model drew criticism based on its inability to explain how minority community members who were socialized within this totally distinct cultural context were able to function within the bounds of the majority society and its institutions.[27] The question is: according to which cultural standard ought ethnic communities be assessed? From the standpoint of community intervention, the answer is clear—the culture from which the community is an integral part must be seen in its own terms. What is important is the attempt to evaluate and understand ethnic community behavior in the social and cultural context in which it occurs.

### 5. The Model Minority Myth

The once predominant media caricatures of Chinese and Chinese Americans as inscrutable coolies, powerful kung fu masters, the effeminate Charlie Chan, the evil Dr. Fu Manchu, or the exotic Suzy Wong are gradually giving way to more subtle but equally damaging images and stereotypes. The emerging picture of Chinese-Americans, like other Asian groups, as hard-working, highly educated, family-oriented, and financially successful—in short, a "model minority"—appears benign at first, even beneficial. The pervasive perception that Asian-Americans are "making it," even surpassing whites despite their minority status, is resulting in a growing discriminatory backlash against their "model minority" status.

A closer examination of the facts, however, gives us a better picture of reality. For example, the higher figure of average family income for Asian Americans (and for Chinese Americans as well) in 1990 Census dramatically changes, however, if adjusted for the number of workers per family. As indicated above, because Asians generally have more workers per family, the total income of a family reflects less per individual. Further, nearly three-quarters of Asian Americans live in the urban areas of San Francisco, San Jose, Los Angeles, New York, and Honolulu, where the incomes and cost of living are correspondingly much higher.

Even though immigrants from Hong Kong, Japan, Korea, and Taiwan tend to come from wealthier and more educated backgrounds, the more recent immigrants from Southeast Asia do not mirror the image of instant success that the media and general public perpetuate. These hundreds of thousands of Southeast Asian refugees, many of them ethnic Chinese, suffer not only from language barriers and limited employment opportunities, but also from emotional and psychological trauma and disorders.

There is no denying that Asians often rise to the top of their college classes and then earn recognition on the job as diligent and dependable workers and professionals. But many Asian Americans hoping to climb the corporate ladder face an arduous ascent. Statistics reflect the difficulty that Asian Americans face in moving into the ranks of management.[28] They are frequently victims of lingering stereotypes that depict them as passive and self-effacing, with poor social and communications skills—traits that would rule them out for management.

### 6. The Cross-Cultural Perspective

There is growing evidence that human service interventions, when conceived in a cross-cultural framework, can be effective with minority clientele.[29] A cross-cultural approach can contribute a great deal to community organizing with minorities by providing another, potentially fruitful way of thinking about the practice of community organization. Basically, this model acknowledges cultural differences in social norms, behaviors, values, and traditions and promotes a more effective assessment and understanding of human services utilization and naturally occurring sociocultural forces (such as social support networks) within ethnic communities. Another realm in which a cross-cultural perspective is essential is in helping the community practitioner to be aware of both minority and majority cultures, points of contact between them, and the process by which cultural standards influence the community.

## Santa Clara County: A Case in Point

Asian and Pacific-Islander Americans comprise a significant portion of the population in Santa Clara County of the San Francisco Bay Area. Chinese Americans, who represent the largest Asian and Pacific-Islander group in the county, and their community organizing strategies and tactics are the main focus of our examination. Primarily by using secondary analysis, we will first provide a brief sociodemographic description of the county, followed by the assessment of issues and problems relative to the Chinese community organizations.

Located south of San Francisco, Santa Clara County, also known as "Silicon Valley," is a world-renowned center of the computer-electronics industry. Between 1980 and 1985, nearly half of all new jobs in the nine-county region of Northern California were created in Santa Clara County.[30] But economic success has its price, and the county budget is feeling the strain of growth and social change. It assumes one of the largest social welfare budgets of all California counties, partly because of the growing number of Asian immigrants and other poor people.[31] With the nation and especially the state of California becoming more culturally pluralist, it is important to examine and understand some of the significant factors that account for the Chinese community's organizing effort in interacting with mainstream society.

Santa Clara County is one of the fastest-growing counties in California. Since 1965, this high-tech-oriented county has experienced a large influx of Chinese professionals, immigrants, students, and business people. The Chinese population in Santa Clara County includes a broad range of socioeconomic levels and degrees of acculturation. Immigrants, refugees, and the American-born are all present in the

Chinese population of the county. In addition, some of the Indochinese refugees, although coming from Vietnam, Cambodia, and Laos, in fact are ethnic Chinese.

In Santa Clara County today, the Chinese population is largely integrated into the county, and there is no equivalent of the Chinatown of San Francisco. In 1980, almost three-quarters (71 percent) of the total county population was white, with Hispanics as the second-largest group, accounting for 17.5 percent of the total population. By 1990, the Census data indicated that whites accounted for far less than three-quarters (69.1 percent) of the total, while the Asian population increased dramatically from 8 percent in 1980 to 17.5 percent of all Santa Clara County residents (total county population = 1,497,577) over this time period.[32] Chinese Americans numbered 65,924 (4.4 percent) in 1990, which represented the largest Asian population in Santa Clara County.

Similar to national patterns, the Asian-American population is one of the most educated and economically advantaged groups in the county by virtually all objective indices of socioeconomic status. This condition is especially evident in terms of educational attainment: almost all of the Asian population (97.2 percent) twenty-five years old and over were at least high school graduates in 1990, significantly above the national rate.[33] Because of Silicon Valley's reputation as the world's center for high technology, it is not surprising that the Asian population as a group has the highest percentage of college graduates (50.2 percent). Asian Americans are among the highest-ranked county populations in terms of income. In 1989, for example, per capita income for Asian persons fifteen years of age and above was $21,218, compared with $28,333 for whites, $19,996 for blacks, and $15,247 for Hispanics, which is again distinctive among Asian Americans and the country as a whole.[34]

A notable aspect of the Chinese experience in Santa Clara County is the fact that some Chinese are descendants of one of the oldest immigrant groups in this area while other Chinese are among the newest immigrants to the area. The early Chinese worked in various industries in the valley as construction workers, miners, and agricultural laborers. Still, many were employed as domestics by wealthy families. During the labor struggles of the 1870s, state laws and local ordinances were passed prohibiting the employment of Chinese in various industries, forbidding them to buy land or to intermarry with whites. After the racial quotas were eliminated in the 1960s, a new wave of Chinese immigrants arrived, and for the first time intact Chinese families immigrated in large numbers. Because of the concentration of computer and allied high-technology industries in the Santa Clara County, more highly trained Chinese professionals have been drawn to this area since the 1970s.

With its diverse population and high-tech economic clout, Santa Clara County has become an area of great political importance. Generally, it has been faithfully Democratic, a reflection of its working-class history. But as home prices soar and more affluent people steadily move in, Santa Clara's changing sociopolitical environment will definitely shape the character of problems and issues in the Chinese-

American community. Continuing our focus on Santa Clara County, the next step of analysis is an examination of the scope and nature of organizing strategies relevant for Chinese-American community.

## Organizing Strategies: Discussion and Assessment

### Community Organizations and Community Organizing

A total of twenty-five community organizations in Santa Clara County, ranging from service-oriented to social and recreational, were identified. In order to further understand organizing strategies and tactics of the Chinese community fully, it is necessary to analyze the several types of community organizations and activities as they are practiced in Santa Clara County. In so doing, it should be noted that organizational characteristics serve as the classificatory basis.

**1.** First there are clan associations, or "family associations." Originally, these clan associations derived from the lineage communities so prevalent in China, and ideally unite all persons who bear the same surname. In the early days of Chinese immigration, the clan associations became a special kind of immigrant aid society, providing the newcomer with food, shelter, protection, advice, even employment.[35] Furthermore, the clan leaders often assumed an authoritative role, settling disputes, arbitrating disagreements, and in general containing interclan differences within the kinship fold. Until the recent arrival of large number of immigrants, the Chinatown clan associations, still prevalent in the New York, Oakland, and San Francisco areas, had been declining in power and authority because of the aging of their members and the acculturation of the younger American-born Chinese. Santa Clara did not have a single clan association.

**2.** A functionally similar but structurally different type of association based on a common dialect or the same district is found in mainland China and Taiwan. This is the community organization generally called *tong xiang hui* (same village/township/province association), or *hui guan* (society or club). The two terms are used interchangeably, except that the latter usually applies when the organization has its own building.

In many ways, these community organizations are similar to those immigrant aid and benevolent societies established by Germans, Irish, Jews, and other Europeans in America. In fact, a coordinating organization of all these district-oriented associations came into being about 1850 with the name of "Zhong Hua Hui Guan" (Chinese Society). In 1901, this organization was incorporated under the California state law as the Chinese Consolidated Benevolent Association in San Francisco.[36]

Traditionally, the *hui guan,* like the clan association, exercised community leadership by conducting arbitration, mediating disputes, managing and collecting debts of its members, including charging various fees for its services. With membership exceeding 3,000 recent refugees from Southeast Asia, the Chinese Mutual Assistance Association of Santa Clara County is a good example of such an organization. However, all other like-minded community organizations, such as San-Dong Association, San Francisco Tung-Pei Association, Hu-Nan Association, Hakkas Association, and Taiwan Association, are organized primarily for the purpose of social networking only. Their memberships ranged from a few hundred to a few thousand as well.

**3.** The third type is the human service–oriented organization, which is devoted to providing socioculturally sensitive services in meeting the needs of the Asian community. This is primarily an ethnic-sensitive practice approach, which includes community organizations such as the Asian Law Alliance (ALA), the American Cancer Society's Asian task force, the Center for Southeast Asia Refugee Resettlement, the South Bay Charity Cultural Services Center (CCSC), and Asian Americans for Community Involvement, Inc. (AACI).

As Chinese-American community workers deal with problems in their own community, they are becoming increasingly aware of the shared needs and problems with other Asian and Pacific-Islander communities. This critical factor is the major moving force that led to the creation of Asian Americans for Community Involvement, Inc., which was officially incorporated on November 27, 1973. Founded on the basis of the importance of solidarity in a common struggle for social justice, AACI has become the largest nonprofit advocacy, education, health, and human service organization dedicated to the welfare of Asian-Pacific Americans in Santa Clara County. Providing more than 45,000 client visits annually, AACI has over eighty professionals and paraprofessionals who provide human services to nine Asian ethnic communities, including the Chinese community. AACI has actively engaged in organizing the Asian-American community to support its human services, health and mental health programs for the American-born as well as for new immigrants from China, Hong Kong, Indochina, Southeast Asia, and Taiwan.

Many of the AACI's board members and professional social work staff are known Chinese-American community leaders, whose knowledge and skills in organizational development, community outreach, coalition formulation, networking, fund-raising, and interorganizational planning were effectively utilized in organizing local and statewide campaigns. For example, one of AACI's major advocacy efforts was to eliminate stereotyping of Asian Americans in textbooks and to promote a new commitment toward an accurate presentation of the Asian-American contribution. In cooperation with school boards and the state Department of Education, AACI operated on both local and state levels to create the Textbook Screening Committee, an organization that actively screens for overt and subtle racism and sexism. When this state committee faced the threat of elimination in 1980, AACI took a leadership role first in forewarning the community and later in rallying a unified voice of eighty-two groups statewide to preserve the committee. This coalition later evolved to become the Asian Pacific American Coalition, USA (APAC), a national organization aimed at producing a united voice to articulate common concerns and to effectively advocate on behalf of Asian-Pacific Americans.[37]

**4.** The diversity of Asian-Pacific elders is also apparent in contrasting the extent to which Asian-Pacific populations in the United States consist of the foreign-born. When the proportion of foreign-born Asian elders is further assessed, ranked at the high end was the Chinese elderly population in the county, which was more than 80 percent foreign-born.[38] It is not surprising therefore that the fourth type is target population–oriented community organizations such as Self-Help for the Elderly, the Taiwanese Elderly Association, and the Chinese Senior Club of Santa Clara County. With the exception of the Taiwanese Elderly Association, whose primary function is social and recreational, the other two organizations arise on a temporally limited basis and frequently require and enlist the intervention of professional social workers. In such circumstances, the community organizer is expected to play many different practice roles, particularly since these elderly self-help oriented community groups lack organizational skills, influence, human service technical expertise, and money. Much of the organizer's time may be devoted to rectifying this imbalance through education and advocacy. And the lack of funding is often made up through the concerted use of community members, including family and volunteers.

**5.** The Chinese written and spoken language continues to be of importance especially among Chinatown-centered Chinese in urban areas and among first-generation Chinese Americans. Skillful community organizational strategies among Chinese Americans are specifically reflected in their effort to establish bilingual/bicultural education for their children. Almost entirely carried out by volunteer efforts, parents and teachers devote considerable time and resources to a frantic expansion of Chinese schools and classes. The results are impressive. Established in 1978, a coordinating organization—Association of Northern California Chinese Schools—is by far the largest community organization in the county and currently includes sixty member schools with a total of 12,000 students.[39] Among them, eighteen schools are located within the boundary of Santa Clara County.

The Chinese schools, like the church before them, have played and will continue to play a significant role in helping to bring different groups and individuals within the Chinese community together.

**6.** Known for being the world's computer-electronics industry capital, Santa Clara County is home to many Chinese-American engineers and scientists who play significant roles in the rapid growth of the technology in the professional and business community. Naturally, a few Chinese organizations have taken on new purposes and functions to provide a forum for exchange and networking, and above all, to promote cooperation among sociopolitically concerned Chinese-American engineers to enhance their image in and contribute to the American society.[40] Examples of such community-oriented nonprofit organizations include the Chinese Institute of Engineers, USA; the Monte Jade Science and Technology Association; and the Chinese American Economic and Technology Development Association. In addition to sponsoring annual conferences, these socially sensitive organizations also work closely with other Asian-American organizations for social welfare and political fundraisers, as well as providing scholarship for Chinese-American high school and college students.

7. Since the 1980s, new political action was taking place in the Chinese-American community in the county. Chinese Americans began to mobilize resources in supporting Chinese and other Asian-American candidates for local political offices and succeeded in electing a number of members of local county boards, city councils, and school boards.

In addition to promoting and exercising electoral rights, direct representation of Asian Americans in government agencies ensures political participation. Along with other Asian community leaders, many members of the Chinese community have been appointed to city and county commissions on Human Relations, Status of Women, Juvenile Justice, Library, and Drug Abuse Coordination. Others have served on the state-level Board of Education, Council on Mental Health, and Equal Educational Opportunities Commission. The list of involvement is extensive and continues to grow as more members of the community are encouraged to pursue these important posts. Asian Americans for Community Involvement (AACI) and the Chinese American Voters Education and Promotion Council are two prime community organizations that provide the basis for advocacy and coalitions in the political arena.

## Analysis and Assessment

The Chinese in America are learning how to pool their considerable resources for a common goal, something many see as quite atypical of Chinese in general. It is a commonly shared opinion among the Chinese that they are not a cooperative people among themselves. A closer look at their community organizations appears to support this view. For example, in the Los Angeles area alone, there are more than 300 different Chinese organizations, organized primarily based on differences in political views, places of origin, family clan, professions, and so on.[41]

Traditionally, Chinese immigrant elites have managed to establish a kind of added legitimacy to their leadership and control by winning unofficial but practically useful recognition from white civic elites. However, the old order must contend not only with the mounting opposition of the community's respectable professionals and American-born younger and middle-aged Chinese Americans, but also with the new breed of more socially concerned community leaderships.

## 1. Organizational Characteristics and Functions

Our purpose is to examine Chinese community organizations' characteristics and patterns of behavior in contrast to their American counterparts and to show how those patterns have fared in the Chinese-American community.

The community organizations illustrated here were all private and nonprofit. Nearly all were found to be delivering services to Chinese Americans and have extensive involvement with the Chinese community (i.e., serving Chinese-American elderly, having Chinese-American staff and board members). In fact, among the twenty-five community organizations, Chinese board members were in the majority, comprising more than 90 percent of the boards' membership. It should be noted that the idea of kinshiplike solidarity is still important among Chinese Americans, for alleged local origin, kinship, and quasi-kinship are obviously prevalent bases for many of their community organizations.

The aims and activities of these community organizations in Santa Clara County mostly differ from the past, although some of their functions remain similar. For example, some of the current Chinese organizations' services included outreach programs and aggressive publicity regarding available services to the Chinese as well as to the other Asian groups, as in the case of South Bay Charity Cultural Services Center. With the exception of Chinese schools, most of these community agencies were not located near the ethnic neighborhoods of the Chinese community, reflecting the fact that accessibility is not a major issue because of the marked increase of mobility among the Chinese Americans in the county. The newer organizations developed by the Chinese in Santa Clara County are therefore neither extensions of traditional ones (except in the case of the Chinese Mutual Assistance Association of Santa Clara County, which is entirely composed of ethnic Chinese from Southeast Asia) nor reactions to those of the white majority.

Thus in Santa Clara County, for instance, the newer community organizations such as the Taiwanese Association and Chinese American Economic and Technology Development Association are not managed in the traditional Chinatown-connected style. The same is true of the Taiwanese Chamber of Commerce and Chinese American Culture Center, which contributed much to social welfare and to the interorganizational planning and networking.

## 2. The Strategies and Tactics Underlying Practice

Organizers in Santa Clara County choose to work with the Chinese-American community based on several criteria: common cultural patterns (such as speaking the same Chinese dialect or coming from the same place of origin); specific issues or concerns (for instance, new immigrants, youth employment, and voter registration); targeted population (elderly people); business associations and mutual support; or the objectives of a social movement (i.e., Asian Americans for Community Involvement). Social movements are increasingly of interest to the Chinese community because their concerns transcend the boundaries of the ethnic community and because the nature of their advocacy and the solidarity they engender bring them increasingly to public attention. They often face the dilemma common to most organizing strategies—the need to produce tangible results while promising deferred social betterment. As in the case of AACI, social movements combine cause orientation with service orientation. For these reasons, agencies like AACI must constantly guard against goal displacement.

The Chinese community organizations presented were concerned with improving sociopolitical conditions, the delivery of needed services, enhancement of the coping mechanisms of target populations, and strengthening community participation and integration. These objectives, however, frequently conflict with one another. The establishment of a multiservice center, for example, may be achieved much more effectively without resorting to broad community involvement. There is also an underlying tension between the advocacy of the service-oriented approach and a political or action orientation. For this reason, action-oriented organizations—AACI, for example—have added a multitude of services as supports to their action platforms.

### 2. The Organizer's Roles
One of the critical skills of an organizer is the capacity to build effective relationships with the Chinese community, whether it is the task of developing community cohesiveness or the task to develop new services. Without attempting to be exhaustive, and at risk of omission or distortion, we list the roles that are readily identifiable in the above-mentioned case illustrations.

Communicator
Cultural broker
Advocate
Educator
Community Leader
Interpreter
Expert
Enabler
Activist
Developer

The most impressive feature of our observation is that a social developer role of the organizer has already begun to exist in the Chinese community organizations. The role assumes, first, not only that the problems of people are imbedded in social structural arrangements but that a rational, problem-solving framework is necessary to community intervention. Second, the role is founded on knowledge of social change and commitment to cultural values, which generate expectations that community involvement needs to be created. Third, in the case of these community organizations such as AACI, elderly associations, and Chinese schools, the role performed by the worker was generally carried out in some integrated way. The techniques and strategies of various traditional macro roles, for example, administrator, community organizer, planner, even the policy developer, were viewed as similar to, or at least complementary or integrated with, one another. Essentially, the orientation of the social developer is working toward adaptation and culture building rather than contest or conflict.

### 3. Acculturation Issues

Another issue relevant to organizing strategies is the level of acculturation. In community organization, the enormous variation associated with differences in environmental context, geographic region, or acculturation is often underestimated. As the time goes on, the Chinese in America will undoubtedly develop more community organizations based on ties other than kinship and local origin. But three observations are in order. First, the Chinese kinship and locality organizations will persist for a long time to come. Second, in spite of finding little attraction in such organizations, the newer generations of American-born Chinese will be positive in initiating or joining cause-oriented activities, especially if the causes are politically correct. Finally, more Chinese Americans are ready to associate with non-Chinese groups on the basis of social, political, or professional interest.

### 4. Bilingual/Bicultural Services

Over the last decade and a half, we have seen an emerging need for bilingual/bicultural services and socioculturally sensitive care for the elderly. It is particularly critical and stressful for the Chinese elderly immigrants whose productive lives were lived in their native land and who have maintained familial and social networks in a traditional Chinese cultural environment. Although the recent upsurge of interest in the health and social problems experienced by the Asian elderly population has been evident, services available to Chinese elders and their needs in Santa Clara County are sparse. An examination of the elderly's perceptions of the social environment and the processes through which Chinese elderly attain the necessary kinds of social network may lead us to a better understanding of the consequences of coping mechanism on health, quality of life, and general well-being.

As can be seen, many of the Chinese community organizations in the county are so-called indigenous organizations and have become diversified and broad-based. Some groups are easily distinguished by their political alliance with different political parties in Taiwan and mainland China; others are oriented toward local, state, and national politics in this country. Still, some organizations are geared to the interests of first-generation immigrants, others to the service needs and problems of the American-born Chinese. However, one thing seems to stand out clearly: the human service needs of the Chinese Americans are largely unmet. As mentioned earlier, Chinese Americans do not utilize services as much as might be expected based on the size of the Chinese community. Further, our survey of Chinese community organizations in the county indicates that underutilization is due partly to the lack of responsiveness of the human service delivery system to provide culturally sensitive and bilingual services.

## Conclusion and Implications

When the first Chinese arrived in America to labor as railroad workers and miners, little did they know that they would stay. They had come to make better lives and then to return home to China. For many years, the Chinese were a silent and invisible minority in the United States. For the rest of America, they were a mysterious people on the fringes of society, living secret lives behind the walls of Chinatown. Today, more than a century later, their descendants, as well as more recent waves of Chinese immigrants, constitute a dynamic and creative force in the pluralistic American society. Their contributions in scientific research and business are well-known, and now their influence is growing in other fields as well. There is no doubt that Chinese Americans have overcome many barriers, but the final stumbling block on the road to complete citizenship is politics. Long hesitant to assert their voice in government, the Chinese have been reluctant to get involved in politics. As their voice begins to be heard, they will have more freedom to forge a new and different image for themselves, without the burden of stereotypes, new and old.

Beyond the issues and problems of the Chinatown itself—some of which are typical of all poor ethnic enclaves in American cities, others of which are peculiarly Chinese—loom the attitudes and actions of the larger society. The Chinese community's myth of social propriety, communal self-help, familiar solidarity, and a low crime rate was a carefully nurtured mystique, prepared to counteract the vicious stereotype of coolie laborers, immoral practices, and inscrutable cunning that characterized American racism. Discrimination and prejudice are still kindled in America. Thus Chinese Americans are constantly reminded that all their efforts at convincing mainstream America that they are a peaceable, law-abiding, family-minded, and docile people who have contributed much and asked little in return might be for naught. In time of crisis they too might suffer the same fate that overtook the highly acculturated Japanese-Americans during World War II: incarceration. History, however, does not repeat itself. As illustrated in our analysis, a new "Chinatown" community is emerging, as well as new sorts of Chinese-Americans who bid fair to supplant them and try new solutions to old problems. Attention shifted from factors within the individual to those of the social system.

While valuable ideas have emerged from this chapter, we also see as fruitful two major themes that are relevant to strategies of community organizing in the Chinese-American community. On the one hand, there is a "social development orientation," which takes as its basic tenet that an ethnic minority's social and economic status, personal and group dignity, political power, and well-being of minority group members depends on the capacity building of the people involved. In working with Chinese-American community, we would also propose using a "cross-cultural" perspective, which begins from the assumption that there are indeed differences among all groups in U.S. society, each has its own unique tradition, culture, ways of living, and, in some cases, language. The cross-cultural perspective can foster a greater sensitivity to the role that culture and values play in community organization of ethnic peoples.

## *The Social Development Perspective*

In the social development perspective, the community organizer's primary role is to seek qualitative growth and to that extent the remedial task is secondary. The primary base, then, is on conditions conducive to qualitative growth, with greater emphasis on how social structures are related to better human functioning. Therefore, in the context of community organization practice with Chinese-Americans, political, social, economic, and technological structures of society are studied with a view to channeling their contribution to human betterment and quality of life.

**1.** From the social development point of view, the element within the community organization that appears to have the greatest potential for being an organizing strategy is the concept of community control. In the social development model, citizen involvement is essential to achieve a solution to problems in the Chinese-American community. This perspective further stresses that human services delivery systems should function as social action programs, as in the case of AACI in the county. Therefore, efforts at social change or institution building should reflect the priorities and sense of urgency of the ethnic community served, and the system should take an active, aggressive role in that changing process. In order to achieve this, control should be taken out of the hands of the professional community worker and invested in a community representative. A perhaps more potent force is the recognition that a sense of empowerment, of group effort and belonging, and of being able to take greater control over one's destiny is an important source for further community solidarity and development, as well reflected in the organizing effort of the Chinese schools.

**2.** A related issue is the problem of short-term strategies. While the ultimate goal for ethnic minorities in America is large-scale social development, experience suggests that this will require unremitting effort over an extended period of time, perhaps even generations. To begin with, we need more research, for example, in almost all areas involving the Chinese community: essential demographic data, needs assessments, intergenerational relations, culture, and ethnic identity, mental health, community functioning, discrimination, the cost of racism to Chinese-Americans and all other Americans, family structure, human service delivery system, and ethnic resources, to name a few. Further, a group of concepts might be selected relevant to important practice issues, such as effective community-base networkings, organizational development techniques, the use of grass-roots staff, client and community participation, leadership skills, public speaking skills, as well as conflict management.

**3.** For the Chinese-American community at the current stage of development, the integration of leadership between first and second generations, between the grass-roots and professionals, and between the social and political groups must be made to form a solid foundation for positive ethnic identity and all necessary social action programs. While the ultimate goal of leadership development is to effect positive social changes in the Chinese community, both older and younger generations of Chinese Americans must learn to respect each other, taking account of their differences in language abilities, political orientations, sociocultural values, and mentality.

In leadership development, a new awareness of our own diversity as a people must be the acknowledged reality of the Chinese community in the 1990s. In particular, the newly arrived immigrants must recognize that Chinese-Americans, along with all other ethnic minority groups, have experienced a painful history of oppression in this country. For this reason, Chinese-American community leadership must be given the opportunity to explore and understand the complexity of American multicultural society and its historic, social, and economic makeup. They too need to have a better understanding of their own Chinese diversity before they can begin to understand and effectively interact with other cultures.

**4.** In the Chinese community, there will continue to be problems associated with the gradual decline of the informal, indigenous natural resources and support network that have traditionally taken care of many community problems. Realistically, the Chinese-American community will have to develop professional systems of services as alternative forms of community-based service organizations. During this transitional phase, professional social workers with extensive experiences in the Chinese-American community can assume a special role of responsibility and leadership. For example, community organizers can serve as social developers to find ways to provide alternative services that are socioculturally sensitive and appropriate. Since many Chinese-specific community organizations are often linked in unstructured and ad hoc ways, a great deal of attention must also be directed to the management of relationships between and among organizations.

**5.** Philosophy and method, objective and technique have to be joined. The social development framework in community organizing requires not only a social change perspective and integrated strategies, but interrelationships between these factors. The social developer must employ a variety of techniques or skills and generally be concerned with accountability, including cost-efficiency and coordination. The role of the social developer is essentially concerned with the impact of social policies, programs, interorganizational relations, and administrative procedures on meeting the social needs of the ethnic community.

## *The Cross-Cultural Perspective*

Within the cross-cultural framework proposed here, the crucial issue is to understand functioning or particular behaviors of the Chinese community in the context of American society, though with a readiness to evaluate and propose change in terms of more universal standards.

**1.** A "cross-cultural perspective" views the behavior and problems of minority persons as expressions of their history and life conditions and can best be understood in terms of the customs and values of each of their cultures in a contemporary American pluralistic society. From a community practice standpoint, this conceptual model has important heuristic promise. Given the complexities of defining culture, the hypothesis that ethnic minority groups in American society have separate and distinct cultures is, given the historical, anthropological, and sociological data, a tenable hypothesis. Although the case for the Chinese-American group is perhaps more readily apparent, culture-bound community variables or categories must be modified until they are truly descriptive of the behaviors of the Chinese community. In community organization, there may be some categories that are in fact universal, or at least equivalently descriptive across cultures. But some basic categories, such as notions of roles and relationships, deviance, power, and empowerment, may require substantial thinking and modification.

**2.** The cultural adaptiveness of the Chinese-American community must be investigated. A beginning step in this direction requires deep sensitivity to the Chinese community's cultural beliefs, values, and behaviors. Further, the community organizer needs to understand the Chinese-American's, regardless whether American-born or foreign-born, adaptation to his or her own cultural milieu. In short, the community organizer must first assume a nonjudgmental attitude when working with the Chinese community, one that allows an empathetic grasp of how Chinese culture and social position influence their phenomenology in the community. In addition, bilinguality is clearly preferred, although supportive roles for English-speaking monolinguals may well emerge.

**3.** Human service programs aimed at the Chinese community have to take into account the crucial role of stigma and shame associated with problems such as cancer and mental illness, as indicated by community investigations.[42] Such shame may lead to denying the seriousness and prevalence of problems in the community. To address this issue effectively, community and other human service professionals must begin by working in institutional and community settings, developing programs with, for example, Chinese schools and other community centers, and establishing regular meetings (preferably in the hub of the Chinese community like the Chinese American Culture Center in Santa Clara County) where an exchange of information and a sharing of perspectives can take place.

From the foregoing discussion, it is clear that those who are committed to the field of community organization, especially in working with ethnic minority groups, must continue to contend with these perspectives and dilemmas. This chapter has simply attempted to address the integrated sociocultural approach to community organization practice in social work. Nevertheless, this work must remain highly attuned to the political and social change context in which it is carried out.

## *Endnotes*

1. U.S. Bureau of the Census, *Statistical Abstract of the United States* (Washington D.C.: U.S. Government Printing Office, 1993).
2. Ibid.
3. U.S. Bureau of the Census, *U.S. Census of Population: 1990, General Population Characteristics* (Washington D.C.: U.S. Government Printing Office, 1993).
4. Wen Lang Li, "The Changing Patterns of Overseas Chinese in the United States," *World Journal,* March 21, 1993.
5. Karen Huang, "Chinese Americans," in N. Mokuau, ed. *Handbook of Social Services for Asian and Pacific Islanders* (New York: Greenwood Press, 1991), 79–96.
6. Ibid.
7. L. Mangiafico, *Contemporary American Immigrants: Patterns of Filipino, Korean, and Chinese Settlement in the United States* (New York: Praeger, 1988).
8. Selma Taffel, "Characteristics of Asian Births: United States," *Monthly Vital Statistics Report,* 32:10 (1984), 1–16. Also see U.S. Bureau of the Census, Statistical Abstract of the United States.
9. Ibid.
10. Francis L. K. Hsu, *Americans and Chinese: Passage to Differences* (Honolulu: University Press of Hawaii, 1981); Peter C. Lee et al., "Group Work Practice with Asian Clients: A Sociocultural Approach," in Larry E. Davis, ed., *Ethnicity in Social Group Work Practice* (New York: Haworth Press, 1984), 37–48; Huang, "Chinese Americans," 79–96.
11. Hans Kung and Julia Ching, *Christianity and Chinese Religions* (New York: Doubleday, 1989).
12. Huang, "Chinese Americans."
13. Winnie Chang, "No Longer Silent," *Free China Review,* 41:12 (1991), 5–18.
14. Ibid.
15. W. S. Tseng and D. Y. H. Wu, eds., *Chinese Culture and Mental Health* (San Diego: Academic Press, 1985); Betty Lee Sung, *The Story of the Chinese in America* (New York: Collier Books, 1967).
16. Bay Area Social Planning Council, *Chinese Newcomer in San Francisco: A Report and Recommendation* (San Francisco: Author, 1971).
17. Bok-Lim C. Kim, "Asian Americans: No Model Minority," *Social Work,* 18 (1973), 157–169.
18. S. M. Lyman, *Chinese Americans* (New York: Random House, 1974).
19. Mokuau, *Handbook of Social Services for Asian and Pacific Islanders.*

20. S. S. H. Tsai, *The Chinese Experience in America* (Bloomington: Indiana University Press, 1986).

21. Peter C. Y. Lee, *Little Overseas Student: Needs Assessment in Santa Clara County* (a research report submitted to the Coordinating Council for North American Affairs, San Francisco, 1991).; Helena T. Hwang and Terri H. Watanabe, Little Overseas Students from Taiwan: A Look at the Psychosocial Adjustment Issues (master's thesis, University of California, Los Angeles, 1990); Teresa Watanabe, "Child Dumping: Taiwan Teens Left to Struggle in U.S," *San Jose Mercury News,* March 26, 1989.

22. Florence R. Kluckhohn, "Dominant and Variant Value Orientations," in Clyde Kluckhohn and Henry A. Murray, eds., *Personality in Nature, Society, and Culture* (New York: Alfred A. Knopf, Inc., 1967), 342–357.

23. Noreen Mokuau, "Social Work Practice with Individuals and Families in a Cross-Cultural Perspective," in Daniel S. Sanders and Joel Fischer, eds., *Visions for the Future: Social Work and Pacific-Asian Perspectives* (Honolulu: University of Hawaii School of Social Work, 1988).

24. Daniel P. Moynihan, *The Negro Family: The Case for National Action* (Washington D.C.: U.S. Department of Labor, 1965); Diane de Anda, "Bicultural Socialization: Factors Affecting the Minority Experience," *Social Work* (March–April 1984), 101–107.

25. William T. Liu, ed., *Methodological Problems in Minority Research* (Chicago: Pacific/Asian American Mental Health Research Center, 1982).

26. de Anda, "Bicultural Socialization."

27. Charles A. Valentine, "Deficit, Difference, and Bicultural Models of Afro-American Behavior," *Harvard Educational Review,* 41 (1971), 137–157.

28. Winifred Yu, "Asian Americans Charge Prejudice Slows Climb to Management Ranks," *Wall Street Journal,* September 11, 1985; James C. Ma and Peter C. Y. Lee, "Asian Americans Climbing the Executive Ladder Need Feedback," *San Jose Business Journal,* July 7, 1986.

29. Enrico E. Jones and Sheldon J. Korchin, eds., *Minority Mental Health* (New York: Praeger Publishers, 1982); Davis, *Ethnicity in Social Group Work Practice;* Doman Lum, *Social Work Practice & People of Color: A Process-Stage Approach* (Monterey, Calif.: Brooks/Cole Publishing Company, 1986); Mokuau, *Handbook of Social Services for Asian and Pacific Islanders.*

30. Stephen Green, ed., *California Political Almanac* (Sacramento: Information for Public Affairs, Inc., 1993).

31. Ibid.

32. ABAG Regional Data Center, *Santa Clara: San Francisco Bay Area Census Tracts* (San Francisco: Association of Bay Area Governments, 1992).

33. Ibid.

34. *A Community Challenged: A Public Report on Human Needs in Santa Clara County* (United Way of Santa Clara County, 1989).

35. Hsu, *Americans and Chinese.*

36. Francis L. K. Hsu, *The Challenge of the American Dream: The Chinese in the United States* (Belmont, Calif.: Wadsworth Publishing Company, Inc., 1971).

37. Asian Americans for Community Involvement, Inc., *Annual Report* (San Jose: author, 1993); APAC-USA, *Achievements and Activities* (Sacramento: Asian Pacific American Coalition, USA, 1986).

38. Mokuau, ed., *Handbook of Social Services for Asian and Pacific Islanders.*

39. J. L. Lee, "Association of Northern California Chinese Schools: An Organizational Analysis," *World Journal,* February 19, 1994, B5.

40. Chinese American Economic and Technology Development Association, "New Development Prospect of the Pacific Rim Nations in the 21st Century" (1993 Annual Conference, Burlingame, California, November 27, 1993); Chinese Institute of Engineers, USA, "The Role of Technology for the Common Growth of the U.S. and the Pacific Rim Countries" (2nd National Convention, San Francisco Airport Hotel, California, January 25, 1992).

41. Isaiah C. Lee (1992). "The Chinese Americans—Community Organizing Strategies and Tactics," in Felix G. Rivera and John L. Erlich, ed., *Community Organizing in a Diverse Society* (Boston: Allyn and Bacon, 1992), 133–158.

42. Hector B. Garcia and Peter C. Y. Lee, "Knowledge about Cancer and Use of Health Care Services Among Hispanic and Asian American Older Adults," *Journal of Psychosocial Oncology,* 6, 3/4 (1988), 157–177; Roger G. Lum, "Mental Health Attitudes and Opinions of Chinese," in Jones and Korchin, eds., *Minority Mental Health,* 165–189.

## *References*

Patrick J. Burkhart and Suzanne Reuss. *Successful Strategic Planning: A Guide for Nonprofit Agencies and Organizations.* Thousand Oaks, Calif.: Sage Publications, Inc., 1993.

Fred M. Cox, John L. Erlich, John E. Tropman, and Jack Rothman. *Strategies of Community Organization.* Itasca, Ill.: F. E. Peacock Publishers, Inc., 1987.

Virginia Cyrus (ed.). *Experiencing Race, Class, and Gender in the United States.* Mountain View, Calif.: Mayfield Publishing Company, 1993.

Roger Daniels. *Asian America: Chinese and Japanese in the United States Since 1850.* Seattle: University of Washington Press, 1988.

Eileen Gambrill and Robert Pruger (ed.). *Controversial Issues in Social Work.* Boston: Allyn and Bacon, 1992.

Francis L. K. Hsu. *Americans and Chinese: Passage to Differences.* Honolulu: University Press of Hawaii, 1981.

Peter C. Lee, Gordon Juan, and Art B. Hom. "Group Work Practice with Asian Clients: A Sociocultural Approach," in Larry E. Davis (ed.), *Ethnicity in Social Group Work Practice,* 37–48. New York: Haworth Press, 1984.

Don C. Locke. *Increasing Mutual Understanding: A Comprehensive Model.* Thousand Oaks, Calif.: Sage Publications, Inc., 1992.

Noreen Mokuau (ed.). *Handbook of Social Services for Asian and Pacific Islanders.* New York: Greenwood Press, 1991.

Armando T. Morales and Bradford W. Sheafor. *Social Work: A Profession of Many Faces.* Boston: Allyn and Bacon, 1992.

Daniel S. Sanders (ed.). *The Developmental Perspective in Social Work.* Honolulu: University of Hawaii Press, 1982.

# 8

# *Organizing in the Japanese-American Community*

*KENJI MURASE*

This chapter on the status and role of community organizations and community organizing among Japanese Americans will be divided into two historical periods: pre–World War II and post–World War II. World War II was the turning point in the history of the Japanese in the United States. The World War II evacuation of Japanese Americans from the West Coast and their internment in concentration camps was a cataclysmic event that profoundly influenced the future course of their lives. Historically, the internment experience served as the basis for the development of two major community organizing campaigns by Japanese Americans: the campaign to repeal the Internal Security Act of 1950 and the campaign to secure redress and reparations. These campaigns will be analyzed in terms of the conceptual framework set forth by Rivera and Erlich in the opening chapter.

## *Definition of Terms*

In the discussion to follow, frequent references will be made to the terms used by Japanese Americans in identifying themselves: Issei (first generation), Nisei (second generation), Sansei (third generation), and Yonsei (fourth generation). Montero (1980) points out that the Japanese are the only ethnic group to emphasize generational distinctions by a separate designation and belief in the unique character of each generational group.

The Issei consist of immigrants who arrived in the early 1900s; the Nisei, their children born between 1910 and 1940; the Sansei, born between 1940 and 1970; and the Yonsei, born after 1970, became reference groups for individual Japanese-Americans, as each generation established its own rules of status and definition of behavioral boundaries. Accordingly, in this chapter, the terms Issei, Nisei, Sansei, and Yonsei will refer to each of the respective generations of Japanese Americans.

## Sociodemographic Profile

Unlike other Asian Americans, the population of Japanese Americans has remained relatively stable over the past several decades. In the ten-year period 1980–1990 the number of Japanese Americans increased by only 21 percent to a total of 847,562 (Bureau of the Census, 1991). In the same period, Pilipino Americans increased by 82 percent, Chinese Americans by 104 percent, Korean Americans by 125 percent, and Vietnamese Americans by 135 percent. These differences in population growth reflect a marked decline in immigration from Japan at a time of rapidly increasing immigration from other Asian countries.

Of the total number of Japanese Americans, the 1990 Census reports that the states with the largest concentration are: California (312,989), Hawaii (247,486), New York (35,281), Washington (34,366), and Illinois (21,831). Other states with substantial populations of Japanese Americans are New Jersey, Texas, Oregon, and Colorado. In Hawaii, Japanese Americans comprise almost one-fourth of the state population.

Of all Asian Americans, Japanese Americans have the highest median age (33.5), compared to Asian Indians (30.1), Chinese (29.6), Pilipinos (28.5), and Koreans (26.0). With an average of 2.7 persons per household, Japanese Americans have the smallest household among all Asian Americans (Gardner, Roby & Smith, 1985).

In the 25–29 age group, the 1980 Census reported that Japanese Americans have the highest proportion of high school graduates of all Asian Americans, with 96.4 percent high school graduates among males and 96.3 percent among females. In comparison, the proportion of high school graduates in the white population was 87.0 percent among males and 87.2 percent among females.

Family poverty levels reported for 1979 reveal that Japanese Americans had the lowest proportion among all major ethnic groups, with 4.2 percent compared with 7.0 percent for whites, 26.5 percent for blacks, and 21.3 percent for Hispanics. Among other Asian Americans the poverty level was 6.2 percent for Pilipinos, 7.4 percent for Asian Indians, 10.5 percent for Chinese, 13.1 percent for Koreans, and 35.1 percent for Vietnamese (Bureau of the Census, 1983).

## The Pre–World War II Period

### Origins—The Issei Immigrants

The initial period of Japanese immigration to the United States was from 1880 to 1924, when some 400,000 were admitted as an alternative supply of labor to the Chinese, whose entry was sharply restricted by the Chinese Exclusion Act of 1882.[1] The Issei immigrants answered the need for a steady supply of cheap and reliable labor by the agricultural, railroad, lumber, and mining industries that flourished in the American West. It was also a time of political and economic upheaval in Japan, and most of the immigrants were lured by the enticement of fortunes to be made in America. They were the *watari dori* (birds of flight) who would return with riches (Ichioka, 1988).

Despite their significant role in the development of rail transportation, mining, agriculture, lumber, and other industries, the Japanese, along with other Asian immigrants, were subjected to humiliating acts of racial discrimination and even mob violence. There were, for example, segregated schools for Japanese children in San Francisco, laws prohibiting interracial marriage, antialien land laws prohibiting ownership of property, trade union restrictions on entry into skilled crafts, and diversion into employment that was noncompetitive with white workers.[2]

Moreover, as Asians the Issei were barred from U.S. citizenship, which meant that they were excluded from the American political process and left defenseless against discriminatory legislation. In 1924 the U.S. Immigration Act shut the door on Japanese immigration completely.

Racism led to the emergence and institutionalization of a self-contained parallel community (Fugita & O'Brien, 1991). An extensive ethnic community infrastructure consisting of protective mutual aid associations, rotating credit unions, religious institutions, newspapers, language schools, and cultural and recreational groups evolved. This community structure was to continue the socialization of members in traditional Japanese ways and to maintain ethnic cohesion in the face of external threats. It remained largely intact and served to nurture the American-born Nisei generation until the outbreak of World War II.

### Early Community Organizing

Historically, the Japanese in America have a tradition of organizing formal associations for the purpose of taking collective action to protect or advance their interests.[3] Early immigrants in agriculture formed unions and engaged in work stoppages and boycotts as leverage to gain improved wages and working and living conditions. As early as 1907, Japanese and Chinese coal miners participated in collective action against coal mine operators in Wyoming (Ichioka, 1988). Soon after their arrival in this country, Japanese immigrants formed associations for mutual aid and support, such as rotating credit unions and burial societies. Through their hard work, perseverance, and personal sacrifices, the Issei generation was able to send its children, the Nisei generation, to colleges and other institutions of learning. It was education that became the foundation to secure their future and the future of succeeding generations.

The early community organizations of the Issei generation were formed primarily to serve economic and sociocultural interests rather than political purposes. Not until the Nisei generation reached adulthood did community organizations serve political ends. For example, the Japanese American Citizens League (JACL), founded in 1930, petitioned Congress to amend the Cable Act to permit Nisei women, who had married alien Japanese, to regain their citizenship, and to permit Asian-born men who had served in the U.S. armed forces in World War I to be granted citizenship. Increasingly, the JACL entered the political arena and began making representations on behalf of Japanese Americans before various governmental agencies and the legal system. In the period before the outbreak of World War II, the JACL was engaged in strenuous efforts to mitigate the rising anti-Japanese hostility that resulted from rapidly deteriorating U.S.-Japan relations. However, after the Japanese attack on Pearl Harbor, the JACL could do little to stem the tide of hysteria and hate that would engulf the country and lead to the eventual exclusion of Japanese Americans from the West Coast and to their internment in concentration camps.

## Exclusion and Internment

For Japanese Americans their internment in concentration camps during World War II is without question the defining historical event of the Japanese-American experience. At the time of the outbreak of war, some 125,000 persons of Japanese ancestry lived along the Pacific Coast. Approximately two-thirds were American citizens. Despite assurances from military intelligence and the Federal Bureau of Investigation that there was no danger of subversion by Japanese Americans, President Franklin Roosevelt acceded to the demands of the military, powerful agricultural and commercial interests, and racial bigots and issued an Executive Order authorizing the removal of all Japanese Americans from the West Coast.[4] Although the United States was also at war with Germany and Italy, no similar order was applied to German or Italian Americans.

"Internment" is perhaps the one word that best evokes an understanding of what it is like to be a Japanese American. Whether internment was personally experienced by the Issei and Nisei generations or retold and learned by the Sansei and Yonsei generations, all Japanese Americans have been profoundly affected by what happened to America's Japanese during World War II. The shared experience of being uprooted and removed to concentration camps left among Japanese Americans a deep sense of collective identity that persists regardless of their subsequent geographic dispersion to all parts of the country. The kinship of experiencing a common tragedy for an immutable physical trait, that of bearing the face of the enemy, and the humiliation and hardships endured during internment contributed to their sense of group identity, which would survive throughout the remaining years of their lives.

The internment of Japanese Americans is perhaps the bitterest national shame of World War II. It represented the mass incarceration on racial grounds alone, on false evidence of military necessity and in contempt of supposedly inalienable rights, of an entire class of American citizens with their parents who were not citizens of the country of their choice, only because that country had denied them the right to become naturalized citizens on the basis of race (U.S. Commission on Wartime Relocation and Internment of Civilians, 1982).

## The Concentration Camps

Between March 1942 and March 1946 approximately 110,000 Japanese Americans, two-thirds of whom were American citizens, were evacuated from the West Coast and interned in ten concentration camps located on deserts and wastelands in Arizona, Arkansas, California, Colorado, Idaho, Utah, and Wyoming. Each camp held from 7,600 to 18,800 residents, housed in tar-paper covered barracks, which, according to military regulations, were suitable only for combat-trained troops and then only on a temporary basis. For Japanese Americans, these barracks served as long-term housing for a period of close to four years. An average of eight people were assigned to a twenty-by-twenty-five-foot "apartment." Communal kitchens, dining halls, and bath houses provided little or no privacy. The camps were surrounded by armed guard towers and barbed wires. At one camp, several internees were shot and killed, though not during attempted escapes; they died when guards fired into unarmed public demonstrations (Daniels, 1971).

Psychologically, the internment was a devastating experience (Mass, 1986). To the Issei the forced evacuation and detention symbolized a repudiation of their years of toil and sacrifice for their children. For the Nisei the internment meant rejection by a nation to which they had pledged allegiance. Repression of the painful internment experience was a common reaction. It was not until their children, the Sansei, gave legitimacy to expressions of outrage and indignation about the injustice of the internment that the Nisei could confront and come to terms with their own deeply buried emotions. Only then could they join in the movement with the Sansei to seek redress and reparations for the physical and psychological damages inflicted by the internment.

## The Post–World War II Period

### Rebuilding the Community

The end of World War II and the closing of the concentration camps in 1946 signalled the beginning of a new era in Japanese-American history. Upon their release from the camps, Japanese Americans had to recreate their former communities, which had been destroyed by their removal and internment. There followed a difficult process of recovery and rebuilding of their economic base, their social institutions, and their network of relationships to restore a viable community life (Zich, 1986).

With an economic base reestablished primarily in small businesses, the professions, and service occupations, Japanese-American community workers were soon able to address emerging community concerns such as poverty, employment, housing, health care, crime, and delinquency. Over time a network of indigenous community-based services and support systems developed that served to meet the economic, social, and psychological needs of the community (Murase, 1985). This indigenous community care/support system was composed of: (1) institutions, such as local churches, prefectural associations, credit unions, social and fraternal organizations; and (2) individuals, such as ministers, priests, doctors, lawyers, teachers, shopkeepers, bartenders, and others who had gained a measure of respect in the community. Their role as community caretakers represented an extension of the traditional attitude and practice of collective responsibility derived from old world values and customs.

In the process of community rebuilding, the leadership was taken by the Nisei and Sansei generation as the aging Issei generation withdrew. In dealing with problems in their own community, Japanese-American community workers soon became aware of the commonality of their problems with those in other Asian-American communities. This awareness lead increasingly to collaboration with Chinese, Pilipino, Korean, and other Asian communities in a common struggle to secure equity of resources from public and private funding sources. The United Way was a primary target for intensive organizing efforts in many Asian communities in the effort to gain recognition in the allocation of funding for social programs. Urban renewal also became a battleground for Japanese and other Asian community activists for the preservation and extension of low-income housing in the face of fierce resistance from city redevelopment agencies and corporate interests (Tatsuno, 1971). This experience of collaborating with the leadership of other ethnic communities in various common causes led to an interethnic network that was to provide the basis for future coalitions in the political arena.

## The Resurgence of Community Organizing

The heightened militancy and demand for redefinition by minorities of color that characterized the civil rights movement of the 1960s had a powerful impact upon the Sansei generation of community leaders. The struggles of African Americans, Hispanic Americans, and other minorities of color provided Japanese-American community activists with a new social context, which spawned an awareness of the broader legal and social relevancy of their historical internment legacy to the current state of race relations.

The newly awakened awareness of the significance of the internment experience may be seen as exemplifying Freire's concept of "critical consciousness," or how personal and political factors interact with each other and with one's personal role and responsibility (Freire, 1973). The task of community organizing, then, was to engage the Japanese-American community in a process of "conscientization"; i.e., to educate the Japanese-American community to recognize the linkage between the internment, its portent for other minorities of color, and one's personal responsibility to act. The "conscientization" process is illustrated by the organizing campaign led by Japanese Americans to repeal the Internal Security Act of 1950.

## Repeal of the Internal Security Act of 1950

The Internal Security Act of 1950 was enacted at the beginning of the infamous McCarthy era, when a hysterical fear of subversion by domestic Communists was whipped up. Its Title II, or Emergency Detention Act, authorized the imprisonment, without trial, of persons regarded as security risks in times of national emergency. Six sites for detention camps were actually designated by the Department of Justice to carry out the provisions of Title II. The Emergency Detention Act might well have become another obsolete and unenforced law but for the black power movement, the ghetto riots of the late 1960s, and the anti–Vietnam War movement. As the country became swept up in the civil rights and the antiwar protest demonstrations, the power structure reacted with police violence and increasingly repressive countermeasures. Rumors of imminent incarceration of dissenters, under the Emergency Detention Act, spread across the land.

Japanese-American community leaders responded to the alarms sounded by African-American leaders who warned about the existence and potential use of the concentration camps under the Emergency Detention Act (Okamura, 1974). Their response was linked to the deeply imbedded Japanese cultural values of *giri* (an obligation to be fulfilled) and *on* (a debt of gratitude to be returned in the future) in relation to their role as beneficiaries of the civil rights movement. In their view, the Japanese-American community had a special obligation to take the leadership in the removal of a law that threatened to abridge the civil rights of other Americans. As the past and only victims of American concentration camps, Japanese Americans were in a strategic position to lead such a campaign.

Accordingly, Japanese-American activists initiated the formation in 1968 of a National Ad Hoc Committee for Repeal of the Emergency Detention Act. The singular role of Japanese Americans as the first and only group to be interned in American concentration camps became the basis for wide support of the campaign. During its three-year campaign, the committee mobilized the support of civil rights groups, labor unions, religious organizations, governmental bodies, and the media. Two Japanese-American members of Congress, Senator Daniel Inouye and Representative Spark Matsunaga, introduced bills in their respective chambers, and on

September 25, 1971, President Richard Nixon signed the bill into law, which would henceforth prohibit the detention or imprisonment of citizens without due process of law.

## Redress and Reparations

Unquestionably the most significant community organizing effort among Japanese Americans was their national campaign to secure redress and reparations for their internment during World War II. This campaign involved all segments of the Japanese-American community, and the unified support it commanded was without historical precedent. From the original formal approval in 1978 by the Japanese American Citizens League for a national campaign to take the Japanese-American case to the American public, to the signing of the redress bill, the Civil Liberties Act of 1988, took ten long years of persistent, unflagging effort.

The initial organizing activities of the redress campaign concentrated upon sensitizing awareness of the redress issue among Japanese Americans. A major obstacle to the community workers intent on raising the consciousness of Japanese Americans to the injustice of their internment was the abiding influence of such cultural values as *gaman* (perseverance, enduring of pain or difficulties), *enryo* (not to be a burden to others), and *haji* (shame to family honor). The common reaction among Japanese Americans to having the internment issue raised anew was to say it was *shikataganai* (it can't be helped, nothing can be done about it) and to accept it as their fate with uncomplaining stoicism. To counteract the cultural resistance to seeking redress, the campaign organizers seized upon another important cultural value, that of the authority of elders to sanction behavior that might otherwise be disapproved. The endorsement of the campaign by elders in the community, ministers and priests, and other authority figures in support of redress was an important element in the strategy for gaining wide acceptance by the Japanese-American community.

A variety of vehicles were utilized by the redress campaign organizers. In many cities "Days of Remembrance" events were held to commemorate the internment experience. Pilgrimages were organized to visit former sites of concentration camps to recall and revive memories of the internment years. For many Sansei and Yonsei, it was a voyage of discovery and illumination of the dark years that their parents had withheld from them.

During this period the campaign organizers effectively utilized the available media and mass communications techniques to bring the redress issue before the larger American public. Five Japanese-American members of Congress (Senators Daniel Inouye, Spark Matsunaga, and S. I. Hayakawa, and Representatives Norman Mineta and Robert Matsui) performed a pivotal role in the passage of a bill in 1980 that established a Commission on Wartime Relocation and Internment of Civilians. The commission's charge was to conduct public hearings to determine whether any wrong had been committed by the U.S. government when it interned

Japanese Americans, and to recommend to the Congress remedies for any wrongful act.

Japanese-American community leaders astutely recognized in the commission hearings a golden opportunity for media attention and public education. They mobilized a massive campaign to publicize the hearings and to disseminate the hearing testimonies to the general public. In February 1983 the commission issued its report, which concluded that the internment of Japanese Americans had not been justified by military necessity, as claimed by the government in 1942 (U.S. Commission on Wartime Relocation and Internment of Civilians, 1982). It recommended to the Congress that the government make a one-time compensatory payment of $20,000 to each of the approximately 60,000 surviving former internees.

The campaign for enabling legislation to implement the commission's recommendations took four additional years of sustained effort. After numerous bills were introduced and had failed, an all-out national campaign was mounted by the Japanese-American community leadership, targeting the 1987 congressional session, in which both houses were controlled by Democrats. A massive letter writing and lobbying effort was launched in which hundreds of supporters visited their congressional representatives. Especially effective in the lobbying role were veterans of the celebrated 442nd Regimental Combat Team made up entirely of Japanese Americans, which was the most decorated unit of World War II. They in turn enlisted the support of veterans of other military units that had fought alongside them.

Endorsement of support for the redress bill was secured from hundreds of influential organizations, ranging from American Legion Posts, the national Veterans of Foreign Wars, American Jewish Committee, Leadership Conference of Civil Rights, and city and county councils or boards of supervisors throughout California, Oregon, and Washington. The key players in the drama, however, were the Japanese-American members of Congress—Senators Inouye and Matsunaga and Representatives Mineta and Matsui. Even the most conservative members of Congress were won over by their persistent lobbying efforts, and H.R. 442 was finally enacted in April 1988. However, the hurdle remained of securing President Ronald Reagan's signature, and every indication at the time was that he would veto the bill.

The redress campaign then shifted to the White House and lobbying efforts focused upon contacts with the highest levels of government. Although thousands of letters and telegrams had deluged the White House, the redress leadership was aware that the mail would not weigh heavily in the president's decision. The lobbying efforts would have to reach the very inner circle of the president's staff. Representative Matsui was prevailed upon to make personal contact with the White House deputy chief of staff, who was then persuaded to intervene with his superior, the president's chief of staff. To offset opposition from the Justice Department, Grant Ujifusa, the JACL legislative strategist, entreated two Cabinet secretaries, whose conservative credentials were impeccable, to support the president's signing of the redress bill. The stage was set for a direct approach to the president himself.

According to one account, the foundation for the president's support of the redress legislation was laid by the Republican governor of New Jersey, Thomas A. Kean (Stokes, 1988). It was known that the president would visit New Jersey and that the governor would accompany him. It also happened that Ujifusa had edited a book written by Kean and knew of his personal conviction that the internment of Japanese Americans was a blot on American history. Ujifusa convinced Governor Kean that this was an opportunity to remove the stain. At an opportune moment, the governor urged the president to do just that by providing restitution to Japanese Americans who had been interned during World War II. He then reminded the president that in 1945, when the city of Santa Ana, California, would not allow a Japanese-American soldier, heroically killed in action, to be buried at the local cemetery, a young actor named Ronald Reagan had had the courage to participate in a ceremony awarding the Distinguished Service Cross to the dead soldier's family. In a follow-up letter to the president, Governor Kean enclosed a note from the soldier's sister and snapshots of the award ceremony. He also pursued the matter further in a telephone conversation with the White House deputy chief of staff.

The president, faced with a mass of input from his own staff and Cabinet secretaries, as well as the prospect of a divisive veto override battle just before the coming presidential election in which the California vote would be critical, relented and signed the redress bill, the Civil Rights Act of 1988, on August 10, 1988. At the signing ceremony the president recounted his 1945 participation at the posthumous award ceremony for the Japanese-American soldier killed in battle, and he commented that the blood soaked into the sands of a beach is all of one color. Had not Governor Kean reminded the president of his earlier personal involvement with a dead Japanese-American soldier, the episode might have been easily forgotten. Perhaps the reminder of his personal connection with the Japanese-American soldier was more influential in persuading the president to sign the redress bill than any rational argument. To Washington insiders, this episode was the crowning touch to a classic political lobbying effort.

## Analysis and Assessment of the Japanese-American Community Organizing Experience

### Styles of Response

A review of the Japanese-American experience in community organizing reveals a clear pattern of distinct styles of response to ethnic group issues and community problems, differentiated generationally. The Issei, preoccupied by survival concerns, directed their efforts primarily to building indigenous community institutions and strengthening their family and community networks to provide a haven within their ethnic enclaves against the hostile world outside. They had neither the necessary resources nor the will to seek the overturn of discriminatory laws or judicial decisions or to confront the forces of racial bigotry and oppression. Their destiny was to endure hardships and make sacrifices for the sake of their children's education and economic future. They accepted the internment mostly with characteristic stoicism and quiet dignity.

For the Nisei, World War II was a turning point. They first had to rebuild the shattered communities that they had left behind upon their internment. In time their educational achievement brought economic rewards and the security to deal with community problems. They could then begin to confront the injustices of discriminatory laws and to right the wrongs inflicted against Japanese Americans in World War II. However, it was not until the coming of age of the Sansei that there was a resurgence of community activism and direct confrontation of issues of concern not only to Japanese Americans but also to all minorities of color. This was the phase when Sansei youth began to challenge the legitimacy of the Nisei community leadership and the authority of American political and judicial institutions. In addition to seeking redress and reparations for the internment of Japanese Americans, the Sansei spearheaded efforts to challenge the underlying legality of the exclusion and imprisonment (Irons, 1983). Notable was the case of *Korematsu* v. *the United States* in which a U.S. District Court vacated the conviction forty years earlier of Fred Korematsu, who had refused to abide by the Executive Order authorizing the removal of Japanese Americans from the West Coast.

**Accommodation.**   The style of both the Issei and Nisei generations may be characterized as essentially that of conservatism and accommodation. The accommodationist approach, as postulated by Maykovich (1972), describes the behavioral mode of minority group members who accept their segregated role while attempting to integrate into the larger society wherever possible. While they do not submit passively to an underprivileged situation, neither do they contend militantly against it. They adopt the values and norms of the dominant group, yet are not accepted into equal personal and social relationships with members of the dominant group. The accommodationist style is typified by the response of some of the Nisei leadership, who advocated cooperation with the exclusion and internment order of the government in order to demonstrate their loyalty as American citizens (Daniels, 1971).

The degree of one's accommodation was related to the issue of ethnic identity. In contrast to the Issei, who were secure in their identity, the Nisei were torn between their marginal status as American citizens and their heritage of traditional Japanese cultural values transmitted by their Issei parents. For the Nisei there existed no clearly defined reference group to counteract their feelings of insecurity and marginality. Although the Issei functioned as a normative reference group, the Nisei also sought the approval of their white peers who rejected them on racial grounds. This identity dilemma led to pressures on the Nisei to disavow their ethnic heritage, to embrace Americanism and to behave as super-patriots. They believed that acceptance of the norms and values of the dominant white society, plus hard work, discipline, and education would be the way to overcome racial barriers.

The Sansei, on the other hand, did not experience the same degree of conflict between their cultural heritage and the need for white peer approval. Their Nisei parents, unlike the Issei, were less bound by traditional Japanese values and exerted fewer controls on their Sansei children. More Americanized than their Nisei parents, the Sansei could more openly challenge adult authority and interact more freely with white society. At the same time, the Sansei, many of whom were born in the concentration camps, learned about the history of the Japanese in America. They saw that complete racial equality and integration was a myth and that Japanese Americans are basically only tolerated rather than fully accepted by white society.

The awakening of the Sansei to their past history compelled them to question the accommodationist orientation of their parents and to seek a redefinition of their own identity. Their quest led them to other Asian Americans who were similarly concerned about issues of ethnicity. Their associations with the broader Asian-American community then became the basis for a new reference group. Whereas for the Nisei the major referent was their white peers, the key reference point among the Sansei became other community activists of Asian ancestry. This development was an outcome of the Sansei involvement in the racial and political turmoil of the 1960s and 1970s related to ethnic studies programs, broad-based community action on social issues, and activities directed to institutional change (Espiritu, 1992).

**Exceptionalism.**  In contrast to many other ethnic groups, Japanese Americans have been characterized as a "model minority" because of their low rates of poverty, crime, delinquency, and mental illness, and their high educational achievement (Petersen, 1971). Their transcending of racial barriers and their upward mobility have been attributed to the compatibility of their cultural values with those of the American middle class. The implication that follows is that other racial groups, who lack similar cultural compatibility, will continue to be confined to the lower levels of the social order. Therefore, in order for minorities to emulate Japanese Americans, they must somehow modify their "inferior" culture to make it more compatible with white middle-class values. For example, Light (1972) in his comparative analysis of Asian and black enterprise implies that lower-class urban blacks must develop a more "moral" community and a sense of "ethnic honor" if they are to be successful in the manner of the Chinese and Japanese. This notion of exceptionalism, however, is seriously flawed because it ignores the historical conditions responsible for the status of racial groups and overlooks the racial structure that restricted the development of "moral" communities for blacks and not for Asians.

**Racial Subordination.**  An alternative view is to emphasize the impact of the political and economic context upon the changing behavior of the Japanese in American society (Takahashi, 1980). According to Takahashi, the notion of racial subordination offers a historical point of departure for defining the economic and political context in which Japanese Americans struggled to better their lives and strive for equality with other Americans. The status of the Issei, for example, as migratory cheap labor limited their organizing capabilities to alter their abject conditions of living. Their energies and resources had to be channeled into the development and maintenance of stable communities in order to secure their children's future. The racial structure thus restricted their economic development and their social mobility and undermined their ability to develop the power necessary to combat their subjugation. Denied such assets as citizenship, land ownership, employment opportunities, political office, and access to the media, the Issei had no means to influence the political system.

The Nisei, though citizens by birth, were still segregated from the social and economic life of the larger society. Despite their educational achievement, their college degrees failed initially to provide access to the more desirable white-collar jobs, and they were essentially dependent upon the local Issei-controlled economy for their primary source of employment. Like the Issei the Nisei also found few options for participation in the political structure of the wider community, and their focus was directed to internal community affairs, which had little or no impact upon their status of racial subordination. With the coming of age of the Sansei and the birth of the Yonsei generation, large-scale societal changes occurred, such as greater public acceptance of ethnic and cultural diversity, which reduced the racial subordination of Japanese Americans. The Sansei and Yonsei could then capitalize on their educational achievement to derive the economic benefits that would expand their choices in life.

**The Political Context.**    Changes in the status of the Japanese in American life were also related to major changes in the American political economy. For example, the renewal and intensification of racial hostility that erupted in the 1930s may be traced to the Great Depression and the deterioration of U.S.-Japanese relations of that period. At that time Japanese Americans were compelled to distinguish themselves from Japanese nationals for fear that they would be lumped together as potential subversive agents of Japan. Since any expression of ethnic identity would have made their loyalty suspect, identification with Japanese cultural traditions had to be suppressed. Again, as in their early history of discriminatory legislation, Japanese Americans lacked the power and the capacity to mobilize external support to combat the prevailing public anti-Japanese hysteria. The passive acceptance of internment by Japanese Americans may be understood within the context of a dominant ideology of loyalty and patriotism that called for their obedience to the government's order for exclusion and internment. Rather than generate mass protest and public indignation, the internment process led to the stigmatizing of those few who actually protested the incarceration (Okihiro, 1973).

As relations between the United States and Japan improved in the 1950s, the international context created a more favorable climate of race relations for Japanese Americans. The political conservatism of the cold war period and the expansion of the economy during the Korean War were other factors in the political economy that improved their position. Then came the cultural crisis and racial turmoil of the

1960s, which had a profound impact upon the Sansei youth. Their involvement in the student and third world movements on college campuses resulted in a new political consciousness, reflected in actions patterned after the characteristic protest style of that period.

## Community Organizing Practice Knowledge and Skills

Assessing the community organizing experience of Japanese Americans also shows generational differences in the character of community organizing and the use of community organization practice knowledge and skills. During the ascendence of the Issei generation, the level and quality of the organizers' contacts in the Japanese-American community were essentially primary, internal, and wholly concerned with indigenous community issues. While still limited largely to primary-level contacts, organizers of the Nisei generation engaged in some contacts on the secondary level, that is, functioning as liaisons with the external community and institutions such as the courts, governmental agencies, educational establishment, and the social services.

It was not until the Sansei and Yonsei generations came of age that contacts extended to the tertiary level of community organizing, where the community organizers were involved with the external infrastructure as advocates and brokers for the community, to provide technical expertise in approaching or confronting external systems and structures. Community organizing at all three levels of contact is well illustrated by the activities generated in relation to the national campaign to secure redress and reparations for the internment of Japanese Americans.

A review of the redress and reparations campaign also illustrates community organizers' use of specific community organization knowledge and skills. They include: (1) familiarity with and use of a constituency's cultural traditions and values; (2) ability to work with and involve existing community leadership to build a strong base of support; (3) knowledge of the political system and how to access and leverage its center of power; (4) skill in involving the constituency in a process leading to its conscientization and empowerment; (5) knowledge of organizational behavior and decision-making in the operations of a large-scale enterprise such as a national campaign; and (6) knowledge about and skills in planning, program development, and administration of a complex project that involves participation by multiple interest groups and organizations.

## Problems and Prospects for the Future

### Trends

Two countervailing trends are emerging that will shape the future character of problems and issues in the Japanese-American community. On the one hand is a continuing and accelerating dispersal of Japanese Americans into the wider main-stream society, not only geographically but also economically and socially (O'Brien and Fugita, 1991). This trend toward greater structural assimilation of Japanese-Americans will occur as a function of several factors: (1) an increasingly higher rate of intermarriage, now close to 60 percent of all new marriages (Kitano, Yeung, Chai, and Hatanaka, 1984); (2) the career-related movement of highly educated profes-sionals and managers to cities away from Hawaii and the West Coast; and (3) the consequent increase in their contacts with Caucasians as well as other minorities.

At the same time, as Japanese Americans become more structurally assimilated, they, like Americans of European origin, will also become more sensitive to the im-portance of heightening and preserving a sense of symbolic ethnicity. This trend will be reflected in a renewed interest in language study and traditional cultural arts and a desire to learn about the history of the Japanese in America. The possible impli-cations of these trends will be discussed in terms of the community problems and issues, the response of community organizations, and the role of community organ-izers in the future.

## Problems and Issues

There will continue to be problems related to family breakdown, drug and alcohol abuse, long-term health care, services for the elderly, equal opportunity in employ-ment, and affordable housing. Compounding the solution to these problems is the gradual decline of the informal support network that has traditionally taken care of many community problems. Increasingly, Japanese Americans will have to turn to the established system of services as the alternative forms of community-based services founded in the 1960s and 1970s will have difficulty surviving. In this transition the challenge to Japanese-American community organizers is to find ways to preserve the benefits of improved accessibility and relevance of services demon-strated by community-based social services.

Earlier it was noted that historically the nature of U.S.-Japanese relations has affected perceptions of Japanese Americans. If the current trade imbalance with Asian countries continues and grows, anti-Asian hostility is likely to be exacerbated further (U.S. Commission on Civil Rights, 1992). The massacre of Southeast Asian refugee children in Stockton, California, by a mentally deranged Vietnam War veteran may be seen as an expression of the pent-up hostility and frustration engendered by the trade imbalance. Fueling the fires of hostility is the mass media's interpretation of the trade imbalance issue. Japanese Americans and other Asian Americans need to take a much more active role in countering the media's influence in creating negative images about Asian countries and their role as trading partners in the global economy.

The perception of the success of Japanese Americans, particularly in higher education, is also a source of the growing anti-Asian sentiment and discriminatory backlash (Orlans, 1992). Perhaps more insidious is the way that the media denigrate other minorities of color by attributing Japanese-American educational achievement and upward mobility to a family system that emphasizes the virtues of hard work, sacrifice, and reverence for learning. Such praise for the Japanese-American family appears to be part of a broader ideological perspective that blames educational deficits of other minorities on the deterioration of the family. The political implication is that the cultural system of other minorities is somehow defective and that they, and not societal factors, are to blame for their inequality.

The new emerging Japanese-American leadership now rejects the model minority myth and views the future of Japanese Americans as bound up with the fortunes of all Asian Americans and other people of color. They now recognize that they must move beyond their own community and respond to the problems and issues common to all minority communities (Asian Pacific American Public Policy Institute, 1993).

## Role of Community Organizations

To counteract the trend toward the physical dispersal of their community and the diminution of ties to their ethnic heritage, Japanese-American community organizations and community workers must seek ways to perpetuate and strengthen their collective identity. The internment experience remains a dominant element of their heritage and a compelling reason to maintain group identity as Japanese Americans (Nakanishi, 1993). Not to be forgotten is the singularly distinctive nature of their collective experience as survivors of the internment. Japanese Americans must continue to bear witness to the larger society whenever and wherever civil rights are being threatened and when other minorities are being invidiously scapegoated during periods of war, economic distress, or profound social change. As Nakanishi (1993) notes, to share the collective memory of being a Japanese American is to be alert to future situations that could repeat their tragic past, to accept an obligation to come to the aid and defense, even in direct opposition to popular opinion, of other groups such as Arab Americans during the Persian Gulf War, whose loyalties to this country were questioned and who became victims of public hostility and violence.

With respect to relationships with other Asian Americans, organizations like the Japanese American Citizens League have a special role to play. With its history of successful national campaigns, the JACL may well serve as a model for other Asian-American organizations. Because it has the largest national membership of any Asian-American organization and a proven record of legislative and legal accomplishments, the JACL has the resources and the experience to affect that national political and legal process on behalf of other Asian-American communities. The time may be propitious for the JACL to expand its base beyond the Japanese-American community and to merge with other Asian-American organizations to make the Asian-American presence felt on the national scene. Such a development would symbolize the political maturity of an ethnic group that was once singled out by the government as potentially subversive and required to be confined to concentration camps. Japanese Americans are now presented with a new opportunity to justify the trust and faith of their immigrant Issei forebears and the sacrifices they made for the generations to follow.

## Endnotes

1. For a comprehensive history of Japanese immigrants, see Ichioka, 1988; see also Conroy and Miyakawa, 1972.
2. For a history of discriminatory acts against Japanese Americans, see Chuman, 1976; also Daniels, 1962.
3. The history of Japanese-American participation in organized labor is chronicled in Ichioka, 1988; for a personal account, see Yoneda, 1983.
4. An extensive literature is available on the exclusion and internment of Japanese Americans, including: Bosworth, 1967; Daniels, Taylor, and Kitano, 1986); Grodzins, 1949; and TenBroek, Barnhart, and Matson, 1954.

## References

Asian Pacific American Public Policy Institute. (1993). *The state of Asian Pacific America: A public policy report.* Los Angeles: Asian Pacific American Public Policy Institute, Asian American Studies Center, University of California at Los Angeles.

Bosworth, A R. (1967). *America's Concentration Camps.* New York: Norton.

Bureau of the Census. (1983). *1980 Census of population, detailed population characteristics.* PC80-1-D1-A, Tables 148, 149, 158, 159, 164, 165. Washington, D.C.: Government Printing Office.

Bureau of the Census. (1991, June). Race and Hispanic origin. *1990 Census Profile,* no. 2.

Chuman, F. F. (1976). *The Bamboo People: The Law and Japanese Americans.* Del Mar, Calif.: Publisher's Inc.

Conroy, H., and Miyakawa, T. S. (1972). *East Across the Pacific: Historical and Sociological Studies of Japanese Immigration and Assimilation.* Santa Barbara, Calif.: Clio.

Daniels, R. (1971). *Concentration Camps U.S.A.: Japanese Americans and World War II.* Hinsdale, Ill.: Dryden Press.

Daniels, R. (1962). *The Politics of Prejudice: The Anti-Japanese Movement in California and the Struggle for Japanese Exclusion.* Berkeley: University of California Press.

Daniels, R., Taylor, S. C., and Kitano, H. H. L. (1986). *Japanese American: From Relocation to Redress.* Salt Lake City: University of Utah Press.

Espiritu, Y. L. (1992). *Asian American pan-ethnicity: Bridging institutions and identities.* Philadelphia: Temple University Press.

Freire, P. (1973). *Education for critical consciousness.* New York: Seabury.

Fugita, S. S., and O'Brien, D. J. (1991). *Japanese American ethnicity: The persistence of ethnicity.* Seattle: University of Washington Press.

Gardner, R., Robey, B., & Smith, P. C. (1985, October). Asian Americans: Growth, change and diversity. *Population Bulletin,* 40(4). Washington, D.C.: Population Reference Bureau.

Grodzins, M. (1949). *Americans Betrayed: Politics and the Japanese Evacuation.* Chicago: University of Chicago Press.

Ichioka, Y. (1988). *The Issei: The World of the first generation Japanese immigrants, 1885–1924.* New York: Free Press.

Irons, P. (1983). *Justice at war.* New York: Oxford University Press.

Kitano, H. H. L., Yeung, W. T., Chai, L., & Hatanaka, H. (1984). Asian American interracial marriage. *Journal of Marriage and the Family,* 46:179–190.

Light, I. (1972). *Ethnic enterprise in America.* Berkeley: University of California Press.

Mass, A. I. (1986). Psychological effects of camp on Japanese Americans. In Daniels, Taylor, & Kitano, pp. 159–163.

Maykovich, M. K. (1972). *Japanese American identity dilemma.* Tokyo: Waseda University Press.

Montero, D. (1980). *Japanese Americans: Changing patterns of ethnic affiliation over three generations.* Boulder: Westview Press.

Murase, K. (1986). Alternative mental health service models in Asian Pacific communities. In T. C. Owan (ed.), *Southeast Asian mental health: Treatment, prevention, service, training and research,* pp. 229–260. Washington, D.C.: Government Printing Office.

Nakanishi, D. T. (1993). Surviving democracy's "mistake": Japanese Americans and the enduring legacy of Executive Order 9066. *Amerasia Journal,* 19(1), pp. 7–35.

O'Brien, D. J. & Fugita, S. E. (1991). *The Japanese American experience.* Indianapolis: Indiana University Press.

Okamura, R. (1974). Campaign to repeal the Emergency Detention Act. *Amerasia Journal,* 2(2), pp. 74–111.

Okihiro, G. Y. (1973). Japanese resistance in America's concentration camps: A re-evaluation. *Amerasia Journal,* 2(1), pp. 20–34.

Orlans, H. (1992). Affirmative action in higher education. *Annals of the American Academy of Political and Social Science,* 523: 144–158.

Petersen, W. (1971). *Japanese Americans: Oppression and success.* New York: Random House.

Stokes, B. (1988, October 22). Behind the scenes: Dynamics of redress. *National Journal.*

Takahashi, J. H. (1980). Changing responses to racial subordination: An exploratory study of Japanese American political styles. Ph.D. dissertation, University of California, Berkeley.

Tatsuno, S. (1971). The political and economic effects of urban renewal on ethnic communities: A case study of San Francisco's Japantown. *Amerasia Journal,* 1: (1), pp. 33–51.

TenBroek, J., Barnhart, E. N., and Matson, F. W. (1954). *Prejudice, War and the Constitution.* Berkeley: University of California Press.

U.S. Commission on Civil Rights. (1992). *Civil rights issues facing Asian Americans in the 1990's.* Washington, D.C.: Government Printing Office.

U.S. Commission on Wartime Relocation and Internment of Civilians. (1982). *Personal justice denied.* Washington, D.C.: Government Printing Office.

Yoneda, K. (1983). *Ganbatte.* Los Angeles: Asian American Studies Center, University of California at Los Angeles.

Zich, A. (1986, April). Japanese Americans: Home at last. *National Geographic,* 169, pp. 512–539.

# 9

Pilipino-American
Community: Organizing
for Change

ROYAL F. MORALES

This chapter is on community organizing in the Pilipino-American community in the context of the purpose, objectives, framework, and premises of this book.[1] In reviewing the literature, one finds very few articles on community organizing and development, perhaps because the few Pilipino and non-Pilipino organizers do not consider this area interesting despite the many activities of "social work organizations." Maybe it is also because the schools of social work and other institutions are not targeting the Pilipino community, which is often identified as a "model minority" and is not seen as needing organization and mobilization.

This chapter presents some community organizing experiences and observations and discusses and explores some tools, strategies, and principles utilized and suggested to respond to the various human service needs of the community. Based on my professional and personal experiences as a social worker and community activist in Los Angeles, I see the areas to be covered as: demographic growth pattern and profile of Pilipino Americans; human service needs and problems; waves of immigration and history; and some community organizing issues, concerns, and recommendations.

## Community Profile and Problems

The Pilipino-American community, like other groups, is rapidly growing and is confronted with social, health, economic, and welfare problems that are symptomatic of those faced by the greater society. Often denied, hidden, and pushed aside by the community itself and by the mainstream health and welfare institutions, these difficulties are further complicated by negative stereotypes, the "model minority" myth, and the "glass ceiling."

In Los Angeles, the United Way conducted a study of several Asian and Pacific-Islander groups, including Pilipino Americans. Summarizing its findings, the report on the Specific Service Needs of Each Asian Pacific Community listed priority needs and recommendations in terms of the following categories:

- Community resource development and advocacy
- Health and mental health services
- Services for the elderly
- Family services
- Services for youth
- Employment and language education

The specific needs and service recommendations for Pilipino Americans were:

*Among youth, identified needs include delinquency prevention programs, gang outreach, recreational activities and stay-in-school efforts. Pilipino elderly need social recreation services, transportation, health and nutritional counseling. Also important are job retraining, legal aid, single parent counseling, shelter for abused women, low-cost housing and child care. Military wives and mail-order brides of interacial marriages may also experience social adjustment problems. New immigrants and undocumented aliens are in need of legal assistance.*

*All four identified priority needs would be most effective if delivered from agencies with a Pilipino focus, from a multi-service center within the community. Youth centers similar to Search to Involve Pilipino Americans (SIPA) in Central Los Angeles are needed in other areas of high Pilipino population. Increased bilingual staffing is also important.*[2]

The 1960s marked the beginning of dramatic population growth of Pilipinos in America. Thus the reference to the Pilipino-American experience "from colonials to immigrants to citizens." The growth is closely tied to several historical events: population explosion and implosion in the Philippines; the "push-pull forces" of people immigrating to other countries; and the impact and influence of the U.S. Immigration Act of 1965. The act 1) redefined and broadened the various categories of immigrants focusing primarily on professionals ("brain drain") and family reunification; 2) shifted the geographic source of new immigrants to Asia and Latin America; and 3) increased the quota of immigrants from the Philippines to a maximum of 20,000.

For the Philippines, the quota increase, from 100 (1946) to 20,000 led a flood of people to apply for immigration to the United States and other parts of the world, and the "push-pull forces of immigration" caused the population shift to be quick and dramatic. Consider the following growth pattern of Pilipino Americans for three decades in Los Angeles, California, and the United States:

|      | LA City | LA County | California | USA |
|------|---------|-----------|------------|-----|
| 1970 | 18,625  | 33,459    | 138,859    | 344,060 |
| 1980 | 43,713  | 100,849   | 357,492    | 744,690 |
| 1990 | 88,889  | 223,276   | 731,585    | 1,406,770 |

Given this trend, the Asian American Health Forum, Inc., of San Francisco projected that by the year 2020, the population of Pilipinos in the United States will be 3,354,990.[3] If this projection is startling, so is the dramatic growth of Pilipinos throughout the United States, as of 1989 and compared with 1980 census data, of selected states:[4]

| | | | |
|---|---|---|---|
| Hawaii     | 168,682 | Washington | 43,799 |
| Illinois   | 64,224  | Virginia   | 35,067 |
| New York   | 62,259  | Texas      | 34,350 |
| New Jersey | 53,146  | Maryland   | 19,376 |

A population breakdown of selected areas of California reveals the following areas with a Pilipino-American population of more than 20,000.

| | | | |
|---|---|---|---|
| San Diego   | 95,945 | San Francisco | 42,652 |
| Santa Clara | 61,518 | Orange        | 30,356 |
| Alameda     | 52,535 | Vallejo       | 28,368 |
| San Mateo   | 44,732 | Contra Costa  | 24,663 |
|             |        | Carson        | 18,318 |

The trend reflects related causes: escalating "push-pull" forces of immigration. (Bill Tamayo indicated that the visa waiting list in the Philippines as of January 1992 was 472,714, much more than in Mexico)[5] that over 60,000 immigrated to America in 1992; and the other cause is 5.0 fertility rate of Pilipino Americans between 1986 and 1990. In addition, it is clear that the population distribution of Pilipino Americans can be characterized as concentrating in the urban-inner city enclaves and dispersed into the suburban areas of the various states. Over 70 percent are foreign-born and primarily speak Pilipino (Tagalog), which is the third most spoken language in California, and in the top six in the United States.[6]

Some preliminary but significant social, economic, and education data from the 1990 census are:

*Poverty: 9 percent, as compared with 7.1 percent in 1980*
*Unemployment: 8 percent in 1989 as compared with 4.8 percent in 1980*
*Median household income (2 or more workers): $25,696, compared with*
*$21,926 in 1980, and the Asian Pacific Islander MHI of $36,100, in 1989*
*Education: High college education, next to the Japanese and Chinese-*
*American educational levels*

The lack of current data and the delay in reporting by the Census Bureau is unfortunate and detrimental to the needed response for human services and related socioeconomic needs of Pilipino Americans. As in the past, by the time census reports are out the problems have multiplied and the planning and organizing are delayed and useless, since they are obsolete.

## Overview of the Waves of Immigration

Fully understanding the Pilipino-American experience requires a brief overview of U.S.-Philippine history and relations. Often unknown and misunderstood by the greater society, the Pilipino-American experience and community is about struggles, survival, and victory. It is a story that has to be told and told again as a significant and important part of the American history of multiculturalism.

At the conclusion of the Spanish American War and the defeat of the Spanish Armada at Manila Bay in 1898, the United States cheaply "acquired" the Philippines from Spain as provided for in the Treaty of Paris. In addition, another provision of the treaty was for the victor, the United States, to decide the political fate and future of the new colony. Thus began the U.S.-Philippine "special and unique relationship" that lasted for almost a century.[7] To Pilipino nationalists and historians, the "sealed fate" handed down by Spain was detrimental to the social, economic, and political well-being of the country.

The first wave were the colonial workers, recruited and imported between 1900 and 1934 under the Sacada system, a replica of the eighteenth-century "indentured servitude" applied to Europeans. During this period strong anti-Japanese feelings and attitudes resulted in laws decreasing the immigration of this Asian people. Their absence left a need for replacements—the Pilipinos filled the requirement for young, single, able-bodied, non-educated workers for the plantations of Hawaii and the vegetable-citrus farms of California and other Western states. Over 100,000 were imported as the "brawn power" in addition to the thousands of students and government-supported *pensionados* who while in America learned the skills of administering political and educational programs and services for their developing country.

Like their immigrant predecessors during the Depression years, the Pilipinos, limited in their use of English, "neither citizens nor aliens," faced racism, exploitation, and oppression. Faced with hard labor and low pay, they were unwanted by the labor organizations, and from one season to the next, they moved as contract laborers throughout the West coast. Perceived as competitors, they were threats to economic prosperity, as they were "taking away jobs" and were social threats for "marrying white women"; this translated into personal and institutional racism, which ended in bloody anti-Pilipino race riots. Having no civil rights, they were not allowed to own property, to marry white women, or to vote, and were ghettoized; in the end a law was passed repatriating the Pilipinos to the Philippines. Few Pilipinos took up the offer since it meant that their return to the United States would be foregone.

Carlos Bulosan's *America Is in the Heart* and Carey McWilliams's *Brothers Under the Skin* depict this part of the story of the Pilipino in America. This wave, through difficult times and sacrifices, contributed to America and the agribusiness and city entrepreneurs; they paid their taxes and shared their cultural values and traditions; with their hard-earned money, they educated relatives and helped their families build homes and start businesses.

The second wave started after Philippine Independence (1964) and into the cold war of the 1950s, and as a result of U.S.-Philippine military and economic agreements. Each year, according to the agreement, thousands of young, able-bodied males were recruited into the armed forces, especially the Navy, to serve on ships, at various military academies, and naval installations throughout the world. Known as "brawn military power," their job classifications qualified them for menial jobs—in the galleys, in the cabins, and in the kitchen and yard of the White House. Other types of jobs and upward mobility were slow in coming.

Timothy Ingram's October 1970 article in *Washington Monthly,* "The Floating Plantation," presents the hard struggles and condition of life of the Pilipino in the Navy.

Like the old timers and pioneers, the Pilipinos in the armed forces contributed to the mission of America, "making the world safer" and enhancing the status of the country as a military power. They also established community enclaves on various military installations and bases, thus keeping their value of "family togetherness" for support. They also sent money to those left behind for their education and related family needs. The sons and daughters of this wave are now filling up colleges and universities. Moreover, they pay their taxes and enhance the multiculturalism of the country.

A third parallel wave of immigrants started in the late 1950s, and escalated dramatically and rapidly in the 1960s. As indicated above, the "push-pull forces" included the socioeconomic and political turmoil in the country during this period: poverty, high unemployment, Vietnam War, Martial Law, and the unprecedented impact of the U.S. Immigration Act of 1965. The "professional immigrants"— medical doctors, Ph.Ds. in the social sciences, dentists, engineers, accountants, pharmacists, lawyers—contributed to the "brain drain" of the country while it was developing.

This wave provided yet another dimension to the multiculturalism of the United States and the Pilipino-American community. Rich in education, talent, and youth, they are contributing to the development of the country—taxes, community enclaves, and organizations, business development, and in political activities. Their children are in universities and are making their presence known with their money and status.

The fourth wave is known as the "political exiles and asylees," referring to the impact of the ten-year Martial Law under the presidential administration of the late Ferdinand E. Marcos. This occurred during the 1970s and 1980s as thousands (15,000+) left the Philippines or were forced out because of the imposition of Martial Law. This wave included politicians, military, intellectuals, teachers, students, and community activists against the new order. With their political perspectives, resources, connections, and resolutions, they organized and developed organizations with a primary goal: to topple Marcos and bring democracy back to the Philippines. This segment of the Pilipino-American community educated and enlightened America to the economic and political plight of Pilipinos, articulated issues, established businesses, and paid their taxes.

## 1970s: Decade of Events

In the late 1960s and into the 1970s, after the LA Watts riots and the refreshing movement for civil rights, ethnic studies, and affirmative action, our involvement began with community organizing in response to community conflicts and problems. Facing up to the challenges of the time as a social worker for a youth agency supported by the United Way, I joined the ranks of the "activists" whose watchwords and slogans were: eliminate ghettoism, racism, alienation, violence, and economic poverty; and end the Vietnam War. It was an era of trying to win two wars: the war in Vietnam and the war on poverty in America—both great dilemmas, unsatisfactorily resolved.

Targeting South Central Los Angeles, the focus of community organizing was to resolve and respond to age-old community problems: economic and educational disparities, institutional racism, ethnic relationships, and structural and organizational changes toward community empowerment. One-to-one approaches and segmented methods of human service were insufficient, we later found out. The combination of macro and micro approaches—community organizing and empowerment of the community—would have lasting results.

Personally and professionally, I found a gap and a weakness. My social work preparation and training in community organizing was limited and lacking in experience. After so many years in the community, I used the fruitful and practical experiences in community collaboration and interethnic relationships as a basis for work with the Asian and Pacific-Islander and the Pilipino-American community.

The search for answers, approaches, and community support in the Asian and Pacific-Islander communities was assisted by a conference held at UCLA in the early 1970s, called ACT I, Asians Coming Together. The conference brought together human service workers, students, community representatives, teachers, and other observers from the various Asian-American communities. Participants at this gathering, including myself, started with questions, suspicions, and guarded confrontations. Fortunately, with patience and understanding, ACT I ended as a community vehicle for constructive dialogue on common problems, issues, and program development. For me it was the beginning of ethnic awareness and interaction with the greater Asian-American community.

It was the turning point of my lasting associational and organizational involvement with the minority movement, leading to social activism among the Pilipino-American community. The experience and feelings associated with ACT I were summarized by one of the Pilipino-American leaders: "Ang pagsasabing tapat ay pagsasamang maluat" (a sincere dialogue guarantees a lasting association).

Immediately after ACT I, another conference was held in Seattle—the Pilipino Far West Convention—with an exhaustive agenda including Pilipino-American history, search for roots and cultural consciousness, discussions on Pilipino-American studies, activism, youth and elderly problems, and the role of community-based programs and human services. Speeches, workshops, skits, songs, poetry, and "community demands" merged with Pilipino-American activism—as the anger, tears, laughter, and noisy rhetoric shifted to united and collective efforts, later to be translated into community-oriented projects, and ethnic studies at several colleges on the West Coast. We joined in a ritualistic hand clasp, a gesture of unity and pride in a movement relevant to the times, as the students, social workers, teachers, and community people became involved with their respective local projects guided by the principle of self-determination and the commitment to "serve the people."

A decade of "happenings," the 1970s were also a time of lasting contributions: of strong bonds between the campus and the community in organizing for responsive leadership and cooperative activities. For me, the promise, dreams, and visions were translated into the thrust and challenges of organizing, developing organizations, and serving on boards or in leadership positions of the Council of Oriental Organizations (COO, later to be renamed Council of Asian Pacific Organizations) and its service arm, the Oriental Service Center (currently headed by a Pilipino American); the Asian American Education Commission of the Los Angeles Unified School District (currently headed by a Pilipino-American); the Los Angeles Day of the Lotus Festival (still being celebrated); the Asian American Community Mental Health Training Center (now defunct because of Reaganomics); the Search to Involve Pilipino Americans (SIPA, currently headed by a Pilipino American); a now-defunct Pacific Asian Coalition, headed by a Pilipino American; and the currently active Asian Pacific Planning Council (APPCON).

Additional experiences in involvement and as "training grounds" in leadership were the countless hours of activities and continuing education through the National Institute of Mental Health, the National Association of Social Workers, and the

Council on Social Work Education. Although these mainstream organizations provided me with an opportunity to learn skills and techniques in organizing, planning, and development of programs, they also gained by my information, knowledge, cultural values, and way of working with various ethnic minorities.

Through the years, other involvement and activities led us to assist educational groups in the development of Asian-American studies and the writing of syllabi and ethnic/culture-sensitive materials for elementary and college levels. In 1974, *Makibaka: The Pilipino American Struggle,* which I authored, was published as an introductory book on the Pilipino-American experience and history. It served as a reference to contemporary community problems, and it encouraged other Pilipino Americans to write their experiences and related stories.

Related organizing/learning activities include the directing of the Asian American Community Mental Health Training Center (AMTRAC), which was established through the collaboration of the Asian American Social Workers, community members of the Asian-American communities, students, and faculty members of the local School of Social Work, which was funded by the National Institute of Mental Health (NIMH). The center provided needed scholarships, training, mentoring, field work placement, and supervision of over 180 students of Asian and Pacific-Islander heritage, for a decade. The center, as a community-based organization (CBO), was a base for networking between the campus and the community; a forum for discussing issues and related social work and community concerns, for activism and advocacy; and leadership development, both for students and community representatives.

Much of the coactivities were directed at the development of Pilipino-American studies, advocating for the inclusion of relevant education that reflected the historical and cultural perspectives of a Pilipino American, and the recruitment and hiring of bilingual and bicultural personnel. Accordingly, within the framework of the campus community connection (3Cs) we/I played the "mentor/role model" in leadership development and training. Easily forgotten and even taken for granted, the "role models" inspire, catalyze, lead, and make things happen—at times in the forefront and other times in the background. Activists and advocates, they establish the contacts and attract others to join in the spirit of *bayanihan*—collective efforts— for worthy community causes. In the 1970s, the impact of the role models was felt far and wide—locally, regionally, and nationally. They created a basis for some noteworthy united fronts, building coalitions and making use of their own resources (self-help) and "piggy backing" on regional/national conferences held by mainstream organizations.

## *1980s: Responding to the Retrenchment*

If the 1970s were a decade of promise, the 1980s were a time of retreat, retrenchment, and curtailment tied to the social, political, and ideological climate of conservatism. It was characterized by the chipping away and dismantling of minority programs on campus and in the community. There was the false and misleading assumption that the problems of racism, poverty, and education had been resolved and that minorities and people of color had gained enough and no longer needed assistance. Funds for poverty programs decreased, affirmative action and minority scholarships diminished, and ethnic studies were curtailed, almost to a halt. And the list goes on.

As the priorities of the 1980s shifted, so did the push and significance of social action and the activism of community organizing. Deeply affected, some of us scrambled for whatever jobs were to be had, and joined unemployment lines with the nagging feeling of "betrayal" and being left out in the cold. However, the spirit, the dreams for social change, and the visions continued, perhaps at a slower pace, but still daring to move on and push for the efforts already started. By the middle of the 1980s, concerned Pilipino Americans and new faces renewed their spirit to organize the conference "Pilipino Americans: Facing Up to Our Challenges," held in Wilmington, CA. The issues and concerns included problems associated with youth and their growing up, the elderly, the new immigrants, the college students, and community organizing. The spirited conference ended with a list of recommendations.[8]

## *Barriers to Organizing*

The workshop on Community Organizing resolved that the community, which is now deluged with hundreds of organizations, *must* organize, pro-actively, and face the socioeconomic problems faced by youth, the elderly, and immigrants. Understandably, organizing is a difficult but a challenging task in a community that has overcome mistakes and failures because of unresolved conflicting agendas, uncompromising "personalities," and the negative side of *pakikisama* and other related cultural practices by Pilipinos. Deeply rooted in aged traditions and culture of the MA-I people based on such codes as the *Maragtas* and *Kalantiaw, pakikisama* is neatly intertwined with the basic and encompassing value *bayanihan* (collective spirit of togetherness). Values are practiced within the circles of loyalties—firstly, serving and protecting the immediate family circle; secondly, the extended family of relatives; thirdly, the compadre and comadre circle (Spanish influence) and finally, the outer circle, neighbors and community residents of the *barangay* (village/neighborhood).

The misuse of *pakikisama* is further complicated when it is operationalized by someone or a group who supports or promotes a person, a group, or a cause based on a particular loyalty regardless of a predictable negative outcome. In an attempt to explain the Pilipino values—conflicts and dilemmas—writers make reference to the Pilipino's "desire for smooth interpersonal relations" (SIR) in conjunction with such related values as *utang na loob* (debt of gratitude or obligation); *amor propio* (being extra nice and self-esteem); *hiya* (shame and face saving); and *bahalana* (fatalism) attitudes and behaviors.[9]

Other barriers to organizing include the numerous languages or dialects, over eighty-seven; while Tagalog is the national language as the medium of communication, Pilipinos prefer to speak what is familiar and, when appropriate, sharply shift to the popular use of "Taglish," a mixture of Tagalog and English. Non-Pilipinos find this amusingly smart. If the values and cultural traditions are in conflict with each other so are the American values of individualism, assertiveness and out-right competition affecting the organizing processes. Moreover, there is the long-term negative impact of foreign domination and colonization—over 350 years of Spanish rule; almost 100 years by the United States; 3 years by the English, and 4 years by the Japanese. As a result the colonization, oppression, and exploitation transformed the Pilipino psyche, emotion, and behavior, typically described by sociologists, historians, and writers as "colonial mentality," "crab mentality," and *ningas cogon* (easy to ignite, quick to disintegrate, or no follow-through). These kept the Pilipino disunited and slow to progress and engendered low self-esteem. During the workshop, community organizing and development were recognized as efforts to identify problems, needs, and solutions, however limited, short-sighted, or short-lived. To the questions of how efficient previous attempts have been; who was organizing; and what are the basic knowledge base and experiences, the recommendations and answers to the questions were:

*Very few social workers are focusing on Pilipino concerns, and fewer still are trained community organizers;*

*A handful of organizers must deal with a wide range of ethnic and regional perspectives; do routine and patch-up job; disappears or "burns out" rapidly;*

*The efforts of the non-Pilipino professionals and volunteers serving the community need to be coordinated.*

Some pro-active recommendations included:

- A need to establish services with accountability, credibility, and primary responsibility to the community;
- Pilipino Americans must organize by building linkages and bridges with other ethnic communities, accepting differences, and recognizing commonalities and approaches to organizing.

In response to the question of barriers to effective community organizing, the participants acknowledged these:

- Regionalism and diversity based on geography/languages and place of birth in the Philippines.

- Ego-pride, social status consciousness; individual quests for power, praise seeking rather than promoting collective community power;
- Inability to identify and capture resources, political, social, economic and educational information;
- Lack of communication and linkage among leaders, which allows self-interest to supercede community efforts;
- Stereotype of a divided community and disunity among groups: among the various groups of seniors, students, immigrants, professionals, and the American-born vs. the Philippine-born.

"In a very negative way, the 'colonial mentality' and 'crab mentality' have been identified as the core of the problem around organizing. They came about as a result of centuries of colonization, by Spain, America, and Japan, and through exploitation and suppression which created self-depreciation and disharmonious relationships among the people, between regions, and in the leadership hierarchy. The colonial mentality disregarded the historical relevance of ethnicity and pride, and devalued traditional cultures and history," the report concluded.

## *Qualities of an Organizer*

In view of the difficult tasks in organizing, a good organizer should have several critical qualities to organize successfully. In no particular order, the report enumerated the following:

- Recognize cultural and individual differences, minimizing their impact and emphasizing similarities;
- Tolerance, sensitivity, and an open mind, to allow for better communication;
- An ability to cope with fragmentation and frustration, and confidently pursue objectives despite obstacles and disappointments;
- Be a motivator listener, and be pro-active and creative;
- Personal knowledge and familiarity of issues; understanding and learning the history and roots of the problems or the group;
- Taking the initiative to develop a person-to-person approach to constituency building.

Other lists in the report include sustaining and maintaining interest in the organizing process and recommendations for the participants, as action-oriented challenges after the conference. Some significant recommendations:

- Round table discussions to create common goals and objectives;
- Issues and problems should be brought to a body where ideas and changes can occur, based on self-determination, consensus, and democratic process;

- Outreach to other organizations is encouraged between Pilipino-American and other ethnic groups;
- A working definition of community organizing should be developed and long-range goals established;
- A political force and new leaders should be developed.

Full assessment and evaluation of the results of the recommendations are not available. However, it is clear that a body or an organization, named Pilipino American Network and Advocacy (PANA), was formally established immediately following the conference. As an organization, it was structured with a CO-coordinator with various committees, focusing on human services, health, welfare, civil rights, educational, and socioeconomic issues. Currently, it is led by a chair and a coordinator, meets monthly, and holds conferences every two years; has an official logo and set of bylaws; and is financed partly through membership dues, as of 1993.

It is worth noting that following the 1985 conference, two politically oriented organizations were established—Republican and Democratic in affiliation—which were active in local, statewide, and national partisan politics. Successes and failures of these groups have not been assessed.

If there are community organizing skills and experiences to be learned and if there are groups of significance to be studied, researchers and students should look into some local and national organizations—some of which are fraternal associations; historical societies, some youth groups in San Francisco and Los Angeles, medical and nurses associations, and some veterans groups. These groups have gone through some ups and downs in their organizational formation and development, according to media reports and through the Pilipino "bamboo telegraph," *tsismis* (gossips).

Further studies should focus on the role of Pilipinos in labor/union organizing (such as Larry Itliong and Phil Vera Cruz, Pilipino Organizing Committee) activities of the farmers, later to be known as the United Farm Workers; the Alaskan fisheries (Wards Cove case); and the union organizing in the cities where there are many Pilipino Americans. Similarly, there are related areas to explore: organizing efforts and dynamics in related nonprofit groups; the church/clergy community; and informal networks, "Bagoong Connection," *kapihan* (coffee meetings) and "breakfast meetings," college and university student groups and movements.

## Future Challenges

The future of community organizing in the Pilipino-American community and the involvement of Pilipino Americans in the process is more than just a concept. As long as problems and issues confront the elderly, youth, women, the physically challenged, the undocumented, the at-risks or the healthy, and the victims of wars— the Amerasian (Pilipino) children and the veterans of World War II—community organizing will be a relevant strategy toward a healthier and stronger society. What then are the challenges?

- For the Schools of Social Work, Council of Social Work Education, and under-graduate schools to fully address the community organizing needs; do research, gather data, and develop basic knowledge base that reflects community needs; and recruit, support, and challenge students to be COs;
- For the mainstream social work agencies and the community-based agencies to creatively utilize the experiences and expertise of the few Pilipino-American organizers, as consultants, volunteers, and mentors;
- For the schools and community-based organizations (CBOs) to develop and implement a basic curriculum (campus community connection) with the following content:

  1. Pilipino Americans: from colonials to immigrants to citizens; experiences in racism, civil rights, cultural pluralism, and acculturation processes; conflicts and confrontation; Pilipino values vs. American trations, finding the balance;
  2. Contemporary problems: community, family, individual; micro and macro levels; strength, contributors, resources, community networks, and related organizations;
  3. Profile of the community: waves and patterns of immigrations, the Sacada "brawn power" workers; the military "brawn stewards and cabin boys"; the "professional brain drain"; and the Martial Law "political exiles and refugees"; impact of colonization by Spain, the United States, Japan; the MA-I people and culture and history; and the demographic, socioeconomic characteristics and related data.

- For the schools, organizations, students, and practitioners to operationalize the "paradigm shift" and incorporate in theory, knowledge, and practice such concepts as multiculturalism, bilingual and bicultural competency; ethnicity and identity empowerment of the community through justice, peace, self-determination; and civil rights.

Readings and references should be supplemented with anecdotes by guest speakers and lecturers to speak on current issues and subjects that are of historical importance to the Pilipino-American community and in the Philippines.

In retrospect, what facilitated my role as community organizer within the Pilipino-American community and in the Asian-Pacific community in general included:

1. Past involvement and historical presence in the community, being actively engaged in community events and cause-oriented movements through the

years, day in and day out; and weekend visibility and accessibility when needed;

2. Being bilingual and bicultural, having had the experiences of two worlds—the United States and the Philippines—and in touch with historical and cultural issues, problems, and conflicts;
3. Development and maintenance of social and political contacts and continued networking with various ethnic and mainstream organizations and individuals;
4. Educational, theoretical, and experiential background, identification with values and the field of social work and community organizing.
5. Application and utilization of learned skills and techniques of organizing and working with other ethnic people of color, levels of education, and economic strata;
6. Planning and developing, designing and evaluating programs relevant to individual and community needs;
7. Hands-on sharing, learning, teaching of practical approaches, as well as doing fun things, like kite making and flying and related arts and crafts of Pilipino origin.

In conclusion, it is very apparent that the Pilipino-American community and population will dramatically expand, and in the process of transition and Americanization, their lives will be affected by social, labor, economic, political, civil rights, health, and welfare issues. If the indicators are correct there are unending and unfinished agendas; challenges, and opportunities for community organizing. In such a state of affairs, necessity dictates the need to train and develop responsive and pro-active community organizers, social workers, advocates, and policymakers, and to join hands to deliver direct services, organize strategies, evaluate the processes and products, research the experience, and support worthwhile causes.

## *Endnotes*

1. The term "Pilipino-American" is used rather "Filipino-American" because it is related to the ethnic consciousness that emerged in the 1960s and 1970s during the civil rights movement. The spelling "Pilipino" is associated with ethnic pride and the discovery of ethnic roots and heritage, like the terms black, Chicano, and Asian. Activists further asserted that this spelling should be used because there was no "F" in the alphabets/languages of the MA-I people, before Spain colonized the islands.

2. United Way, Needs Assessment on the Asian Pacific Islander Communities (Los Angeles, 1988).

3. Asian American/Health Forum, Inc., "Population Projections for API" (San Francisco, April 1989).

4. Asian Week, "Asian Pacifics in America" (San Francisco: Grant Printing House, August 1991).

5. Bill Tamayo, "Legal and Civil Rights Issues in 2020: Civil Rights Policy," *The State of Asian Pacific America,* LEAP Asian Pacific American Public Policy Institute and UCLA Asian American Studies Center, Leadership Education for Asian Pacifics, 1993.

6. Los Angeles *Times,* "Land of Language," July 5, 1993, Sec. E.

7. Walter LaFeber, *The New Empire: An Interpretation of American Expansion, 1860–1989* (Ithaca: Cornell University Press, 1963).

8. PANA, "Facing Up to Our Challenges," Los Angeles, March 1985.

9. Pal Hunt et al., *Sociology in the Philippine Setting* (Quezon City, Philippines: Phoenix Publishing House, 1971).

## Suggested Readings

Barrugh, Herbert, Robert W. Gardner, and Michael I. Levin. *Asian Pacific Islanders in the U.S.* New York: Russell Sage, 1993.

Boradus, Emory S. "Anti-Pilipino Race Riots." In *Letters in Exile: An Introductory Reader in the History of Pilipinos in America,* pp. 51–62. Los Angeles: Asian American Studies Center, 1976.

Buaken, Manuel. *I Have Lived with the American People.* Caldwell, Idaho: Caxton, 1948.

Bulosan, Carlos, *America Is in the Heart.* Seattle: University of Washington Press, 1947.

Clifford, Sister Mary Dorita. "The Hawaiian Sugar Planters' Association and Filipino Exclusion." In *Letters in Exile,* pp. 74–89.

Corpuz, Onofre D. *The Philippines.* Englewood Cliffs, N.J.: Prentice-Hall, 1965.

Friend, Theodore. *Between Two Empires: The Ordeal of the Philippines, 1926–1946.* New Haven: Yale University Press, 1965.

Gall, Susan B. and Timothy L., eds. *Statistical Record of Asian Americans.* Detroit: Gale Research, 1993.

Lasker, Bruno. *Filipino Immigration to the Continental U.S. and Hawaii.* Chicago: University of Chicago Press, 1993.

McWilliams, Carey. *Brothers under the Skin.* Rev. ed. Boston: Little, Brown, 1946.

———. *Factories in the Field.* Boston: Little, Brown, 1940.

Melendy, H. Brett. "California's Discrimination Against Pilipinos." In *Letters in Exile,* pp. 35–43.

Morales, Royal F. *Makibaka: The Pilipino American Struggle.* Los Angeles: Mountainview, 1974.

Poole, Fred and Vanzi, Max. *Revolution in the Philippines: The U.S. in a Hall of Cracked Mirrors.* New York: McGraw-Hill, 1984.

# 10

*Organizing with Central-American Immigrants in the United States*

CARLOS B. CÓRDOBA

## Central-American Migrations to the United States

Central Americans have a long-standing tradition of migrating to the United States that dates back to the early 1900s. Central Americans have migrated to the United States as a result of political and economic factors that have affected their countries throughout the years. Economic and political instability have created the right conditions for Central Americans to migrate to this country. Many of the early immigrants arrived during the 1930s–1940s and settled in San Francisco, Los Angeles, Houston, and New Orleans to escape their failing economies, political persecution, and lack of personal freedom. This migration network established the social and economic foundations of the ethnic immigrant community for future generations of Central Americans who would arrive later in the United States.

During the 1960s, Central-American immigration to the United States increased as a direct result of the Immigration Act of 1965, which allowed immigrant quotas to be granted to countries that historically had not been included in U.S. immigration policies. The 1965 law encouraged professionals and skilled laborers to migrate to the United States and permitted the resettlement of large numbers of young working-class and middle-class Central-American families. Many U.S. cities had Latin-American immigrant neighborhoods that attracted Central Americans to their communities. Newcomers settled in the Latin-American neighborhoods because of already established ethnic networks, familiar cultural traditions, and support systems that were maintained there. The new Central-American arrivals further developed the economic, social, and cultural foundations of the Latin-American ethnic networks and economic enclaves in San Francisco, Los Angeles, Houston, New York, and Washington. The impact of the new immigrants to the already established Latin-American communities was clearly discernible during the mid-1960s.

The influx of Central-American immigrants to this country has sharply increased since the late 1970s. Presently, Central America ranks as the second Latin-American region contributing migrations to the United States. Before the 1970s, most Central-American immigrants arrived with legal immigration status as permanent residents or with student visas. In the 1980s the migration patterns changed as a result of the sociopolitical and economic conditions present in Central America, which led large numbers of Salvadorans, Guatemalans, and Nicaraguans to enter the United States without legal documentation or as political asylum applicants. The pre-1979 migrations were mostly economic in nature, while the post-1979 migrations were generated by the economic and political realities faced by the nations in the region (ACLU, 1984; Córdoba, 1986, 1987).

## Demographic Characteristics of 1970–1994 Central-American Immigrants to the United States

The Latin American population in the United States has increased to more than 20 million people in 1989, an increase of 5.5 million people since the 1980 census. The fastest-growing population are Central and South Americans, together 2,545,000 people. These demographic statistics reflecting the Central-American population appear to be a low estimate as they do not include the figures of undocumented people residing in the United States.

The actual number of legal and undocumented Central-American immigrants are not available. The demographic statistics calculated by the Immigration and Naturalization Service (INS) estimate that only 2 million Central Americans are in this country. These figures are not accurate because the majority of Central Americans in the post-1979 migration waves entered the country as undocumented workers or as political asylum seekers, and have not been included in the demographic surveys conducted by the U.S. government (ACLU, 1984). While I was conducting field research among Central-American immigrants, many families told me that they had not filled out the census questionnaires. Some of the reasons given included the fact that even though they had legal immigration status, they did not understand the significance and importance of the census and were afraid of having interactions with the INS or any other governmental agencies.

Sociopolitical and economic crises are the most important determinants for the present Central-American migrations to the United States. Guatemala, El Salvador, and Nicaragua have been affected by armed insurgency against the established sociopolitical systems. Since 1980, more than 200,000 people have been assassinated by right-wing paramilitary death squads and the armed forces in El Salvador and Guatemala. During this time of war and persecution the most common targets for assassination were labor leaders, Indian leaders, intellectuals, community organizers, Catholic priests, lay preachers, catechizers, agricultural workers, and students. The Sandinista revolution and the contra war also claimed more than 200,000 victims in Nicaragua.

It is important to consider the entire spectrum of cultural, social, and political factors in an analysis of the demographic makeup and social organization of Central-American communities in the United States. One should not attempt to generalize the demographic, political, or socioeconomic characteristics of this population because of the complex nature of the Central-American population and their migration determinants. It is imperative to look at the conditions of the various countries to avoid creating stereotypes or generalized characterizations of the different Central-American nationalities. Central-American communities have divergent political ideologies ranging from conservative right-wing views to orthodox Marxist orientation. A community in a specific geographical location may manifest a wide diversity of political views such as in San Francisco or Los Angeles. On the other hand, the Central-American immigrant community may hold a unified political position, as it does in Miami. There are more similarities present across socioeconomic class status rather than in national identity issues among the different Central-American populations. The majority of Central Americans in the United States are middle-class or working-class individuals. They were teachers, high school and university students, secretaries, accountants, housewives, domestic workers, office workers, and skilled factory workers in their countries.

## *Guatemalans*

During the early 1980s numerous Mayan-Indian communities in Guatemala were systematically destroyed. Entire populations were involuntarily relocated in strategic villages or forced to migrate to Mexico or the United States as part of a program of intensive military repression and anti-insurgency campaigns carried out by the armed forces. The refugees have been subjected to government military actions resulting in the massacres of the elderly, women, and children, who make up the vast majority of the refugee population (ACLU, 1984; Amnesty International, 1983; Camarda, 1985; Manz, 1988).

In rural areas in the U.S. Southwest, the Central-American population is composed mostly of indigenous rural people who made a living from traditional agricultural activities in Central America. The indigenous culture is governed by the rhythm of corn agriculture and the seasons, and people prefer rural over urban lifestyles. The majority of Guatemalan-Mayan immigrants are unskilled young males with low educational backgrounds, who are employed as seasonal migrant workers in the agricultural farms throughout the Sunbelt. Numerous Guatemalan-Mayan people work in the agricultural fields of Florida, Texas, Arizona, Oregon, Washington state, and California.

The situation of Guatemalan Mayans in the United States is difficult because they hold non-Western cultural values and are often monolingual in their Mayan languages. The majority of Guatemalans working in Florida are Kanjobal-speaking people who originate from the town of San Miguel Acatlan located in the northern province of Huehuetenango. Mayan people have encountered major cultural problems that disrupt their culture and religion and forced the discontinuation of their rituals and cultural traditions related to the cultivation of corn. The Mayan refugees in Florida work in the harvesting of the citrus fields and no longer are engaged in the cycle of corn agriculture.

One case that illustrates the complexity of the Mayan acculturation experience in this country took place in San Francisco. A Mayan couple had a serious run in with the authorities when their neighbors noticed that the young teenage girl was pregnant. The neighbors reported the young man to the police and to social services, and he was arrested and accused of child molestation. They spent more than six months in a legal battle to get married and to keep their child, and as soon as the man was released from custody they fled California and resettled in Florida. They could not understand why the local authorities would interfere in their own personal affairs. It is common in Mayan communities for a man in his mid-twenties to marry a young teenage girl. The common belief is that a man at that age will be more experienced and will have saved enough money to support a family. That practice is not accepted in the United States.

In U.S. urban centers, the majority of Guatemalans are of urban backgrounds and originate from middle- and working-class backgrounds in Guatemala. This population is mostly mestizo and Spanish-speaking and has higher levels of education and is more skilled and better prepared to cope with the U.S. culture and society than are the Mayans.

## Salvadorans

The Salvadoran immigrant population in the United States is not a homogeneous group: it originates in different socioeconomic and cultural backgrounds. In the 1970s and 1980s members of the ruling classes could foresee the developing political crisis, left El Salvador and resettled in Florida and California. They had economic, cultural and political ties in the United States. For decades, the Salvadoran upper class removed its assets from Central America and deposited them in U.S. banks. Many of them were educated in U.S. universities, and their economic and educational status, bilingual skills, and their legal residency or U.S. citizenship helped them to readily adjust to their new life in this country. This phenomenon is characteristic of Latin American revolutions as it was observable in the case of Cuba and Nicaragua.

On the other hand, the more recent Salvadoran immigrants arriving in the United States are undocumented and come from middle- and lower-class backgrounds lacking the economic and social support available to upper-class Salvadorans. They do not have the educational, occupational, and language skills needed to succeed in this country. The working-class populations in Central America have strong similarities in their social and cultural experiences and have little in common with the upper-class social and cultural experiences.

As in the case of Guatemalan immigrants, the majority of Salvadorans have left their country to escape the civil war and to search for personal safety and a new life. Salvadoran society has been severely affected by a long history of political corruption and the impact of the civil war has been multidimensional. The judicial system does not offer protection to civilians, and threats and intimidation prevent justice and freedom in El Salvador (ACLU, 1984). Many Central-American immigrants bring with them those fears. They project those fears on their social experiences while living in this country and are extremely apprehensive about interacting with governmental agencies and the authorities.

Since the early 1980s Salvadorans have comprised the largest Central-American group in the United States, but the actual demographic figures are not readily available because of the undocumented immigration status of a large percentage of this population (Córdoba, 1992; Melville, 1988). These new immigrants arrived in this country as a result of already established ethnic and family networks such as in the case of San Francisco, Los Angeles, Houston, and Washington, D.C. Migrations to the United States are a social process that is mediated by long-standing family, friendship, and community ties that facilitate moving and ease the immigrant's integration into the new environment (Portes and Bach, 1985).

## Nicaraguans

The Nicaraguan migrations to the United States began in the 1930s and were characterized by a flow of people escaping the Somoza government, many of whom settled in San Francisco and Los Angeles. During the 1940s Nicaraguans entered the United States in search of economic opportunities; many of them eventually returned to their country to become part of a new entrepreneurial class. During the 1960s the Nicaraguan population in the United States was the largest Central-American group. The political situation in the 1970s escalated to armed conflict and Nicaraguans sought refuge in the United States. After the fall of Somoza and the Sandinista victory, many of the original immigrants or their descendants returned to Nicaragua.

At the same time other Nicaraguans associated with the former government arrived in the United States. Some of the first Nicaraguans to arrive in the United States during the early 1980s were members of the upper class fleeing the country because of their ties with the former Somoza dictatorship and their disagreements with the Sandinista government. Some were businessmen who had direct economic ties to Somoza and his government, while others were former members of the National Guard who escaped from the wrath of the Sandinista army. The majority of Nicaraguans settled in Florida and California and brought with them their wealth and their conservative political ideology. More recently, Nicaraguan immigrants were young working-class people who left to escape the contra war and the military draft.

## Hondurans and Costa Ricans

Academic studies of the Honduran and Costa-Rican immigrant communities in the United States are scarce since their populations are not very large. The majority of Hondurans reside on the East Coast from Florida to New York. Their social and cultural experience has not been studied in depth. One can assume that not many Costa Ricans live in the United States or have left their country because of a long history of political stability and democratic traditions in that Central-American country.

## The Structure of Central-American Communities in the United States

Central Americans arrive in U.S. metropolitan centers following already established ethnic and family networks. Newcomers use ethnic or family contacts to secure employment or housing or to meet immediate needs. After one person is settled and able to save money, other relatives begin to arrive. After a few years of living in the Latin-American neighborhoods, many Central-American immigrants socially adapt to the new environment and acquire the necessary employment skills and education to participate fully in mainstream economic life. Many relocate in other ethnically mixed neighborhoods or suburban cities. Others take advantage of economic opportunities and develop business enterprises in the Latin-American neighborhoods and utilize the immigrant labor force to maximize their profits.

The ethnic enclave is where the new immigrant becomes familiarized with a new social environment as it provides the proper mechanisms and institutions to gradually introduce new arrivals to U.S. society. Latin American enclaves maintain the culture, language, religion, foods, and traditional festivities. Concrete features illustrate the clear distinctions between an ethnic enclave and ethnic immigrant communities. As a rule, immigrants initially relocate in ethnic communities while developing a few small business enterprises to meet local consumption demands.

However, ethnic neighborhoods lack the sophisticated economic structure and the extensive division of labor of the enclave (Portes and Bach, 1985). The Central American enclaves in San Francisco, Los Angeles, Washington, and Houston, among others, demonstrate a well-diversified economic base and division of labor.

The economic structure of the enclave provides for bilingual professional services to the community. The ethnic enclave allows the immigrant to receive legal, educational, immigration, medical, dental, accounting, income tax consulting, counseling, employment training and referrals, food services, and so on. This sector is made up not only of immigrants but first- and second-generation Central Americans and Latin Americans providing professional services. Other bilingual ethnic and mainstream professionals and merchants also provide services in Spanish within the enclave.

The enclave provides familiar settings by allowing the development of regional associations that support the immigrant with cultural, social, and recreational activities. Regional associations and the enclave provide new immigrants with support structures and resources that develop cultural identification, security, and a sense of belonging in the host society. Regional associations allow the preservation of cultural traditions and the retention of a strong cultural and national identification as a Central American. Many regional associations are named after towns, cities, states, or regions where the immigrant populations originate in Central America. Some organizations are affiliated with religious societies, sports clubs, artistic or cultural organizations, or social service organizations as they exist in Central America. Some of the most popular regional associations are identified with soccer or baseball clubs that participate in Latin-American or mainstream sports leagues. These associations have well-structured organizations, large memberships; their members pay dues and usually rent a small place as a recreation center. Other regional associations are dedicated to religious worship to a patron saint or a special Catholic deity. Such are the examples in the Nicaraguan community with groups dedicated to the worship of Our Lady of the Conception (La Purísima) or Saint Dominic (Santo Domingo). Salvadorans have regional associations dedicated to El Salvador del Mundo.

The study of Central-American enclaves and the immigrant's social interaction in the community may be analyzed under the Neo-Gemeinschaft Model developed by Rivera and Erlich (1981). This model is based on Toennie's (1957) concepts of Gemeinschaft, or community, where the primary relationships are conducted and involve intimacy and privacy; and Gesselschaft, or society, which represents the individual's public life or the pursuance of secondary relationships for utilitarian and survival reasons. Rivera and Erlich expanded Toennie's model to explain the formation and interaction dynamics of ethnic groups in this country. Ethnic enclaves develop as subgroups within society as a result of an antagonistic social environment where the members of the immigrant or minority group are not totally functional in mainstream society and thus become victims of discrimination and economic exploitation.

According to this framework, the immigrants will only develop secondary relationships at the societal level (Gesselschaft), while the individual experiences discrimination as a result of racial, cultural, and linguistic differences. Primary relationships (Gemeinschaft) are restricted to members of the same national or ethnic group. This model also applies to analysis of the religious views and preferences of Central-American immigrants since they often attend religious services in Spanish in their own ethnic neighborhoods. This is an important fact to consider since the church is one of the primary social institutions in the life of an immigrant or refugee, and it is often regarded by them as the most important institution other than the family.

## The Emergence of Political Power and Influence in Central-American Communities

Because of the socioeconomic and political diversity observed in Central-American communities, they have limited political power and influence within the United States political structure. The Central-American communities are divided on issues related to national identity and origin, political affiliations in Central America and the United States, ethnicity, religion, and socioeconomic status. These divisions do not allow the social cohesion needed to transform this population into a strong political body that will be able to seek viable political solutions to the problems and realities that they encounter in this society. There is a need to develop responsible and accountable political and social activists within the Central-American community in order to critically affront the wide range of problems that they face in this country.

Another obstacle to empowerment in Central-American communities is the common belief on the part of the immigrants that their stay of residence in the United States will be of a temporary nature. Therefore, immigrants become isolated and neglect to participate in political affairs at the community, municipal, state, or national levels. Unless individuals have some degree of political sophistication, most Central Americans show apathy toward U.S. political and social issues. Community activists have attempted to persuade Latin-American immigrants to become U.S. citizens and to register to vote. These efforts have been fruitless because many Latin Americans believe that if they become U.S. citizens, they are betraying their national identity and citizenship. Some organizations in the Central-American communities strive to achieve political power, a few closely associated to political parties or organizations in Central America. Casa El Salvador, Casa Nicaragua, and Guatemalan organizations have close ties with Central-American popular revolutionary movements.

In California, the popular revolutionary groups have been successful in their actions against U.S. policies in Central America. They have been successful because they have not limited their activities to the Latin-American communities. They have reached out to the mainstream and have created multiethnic coalitions by working closely with international solidarity coalitions and networks such as CISPES, Amnesty International, or the Emergency Response Network. Their main objectives deal with issues that directly affect the Central-American region, but do not place their main emphasis on empowerment efforts within the local communities.

On the other hand, organizations such as the Coalition for Immigrant and Refugee Rights and Services have worked within the local community structure to advocate for immigrant issues, especially abuses against immigrant women. Their efforts have been successful in organizing within the local immigrant community by creating bridges between different immigrant communities.

## *The Paulo Freire Model of Community Empowerment*

The Freire method of community empowerment is based on pedagogical and organizational strategies that bring about critical consciousness in individuals and the community. Paulo Freire's methodology has been widely used in Latin America by the Catholic base communities in the empowerment of political activists, union leaders, lay preachers, campesinos, and students. Freire's methodology teaches basic literacy skills to adults while providing the students with basic notions of political awareness to develop praxis and community social action.

These pedagogical strategies have been implemented by base community organizations and educational centers in the United States while teaching English language skills to Spanish monolinguals. This pedagogy introduces basic concepts of social and political awareness in language lessons as the means of empowering new immigrants. In San Francisco, the Mission Reading Clinic, Project Literacy, and the High School Step to College Program at San Francisco State University have accomplished great successes in their educational efforts while utilizing the critical education methodology.

Other successful organizations include the refugee self-help committees located in various U.S. cities such as San Francisco, Los Angeles, and Washington, D.C., have been successful in the implementation of these methodologies. Three refugee organizations have been particularly effective at representing the refugees in the mainstream society and local political structures. They are (1) the Comité de Refugiados Centro Americanos (CRECE), which provides refugees with social services; (2) the Central American Refugee Center (CARECEN), the legal and immigration services and advocacy agency of refugee organizations in San Francisco and Los Angeles; and (3) El Rescate in Los Angeles.

In these organizations, the refugees themselves empower other refugees. They are designed following the organizational models of Freire's critical consciousness and the Central-American Catholic base communities. Because of their organizational structure, history, philosophy, and empowerment efforts, these community groups are recognized to represent the leadership in the Central-American refugee community. They address issues affecting the social experiences and cultural adaptation of Guatemalan and Salvadoran immigrants and refugees.

CRECE provides the refugee community with basic survival services such as food and clothes distribution, emergency housing, medical services, job referrals, cultural survival skills, and employment skills development workshops. They provide educational information to the mainstream communities by making presentations at schools, universities, churches, and home meetings where they give testimonies of their experiences in Central America. CRECE is an active advocate of refugee rights in Central America, and is actively involved in the repatriation of refugees in El Salvador.

CARECEN provides legal representation to refugees in political asylum hearings, gives health referral services, trains health promoters, and produces literature for the Central-American refugee community. CARECEN played an important role in the formation of the Central American National Network (CARNET), which includes 38 refugee agencies and grass-roots organizations in the United States. CARECEN and CRECE demonstrate a strong commitment to empowering the Central-American community. The development of local leadership is an important priority in their selection and training of low-income refugees who work as refugee rights promoters and refugee advocates. The promoters provide services to the refugee community, speak in public forums, monitor and attempt to influence legislation affecting the Central-American refugee community at the municipal, state, and national levels. Their achievements include the declaration of cities of refuge in which local governments and law enforcement agencies would not cooperate in INS raids against undocumented workers. Unfortunately, in San Francisco, the City of Sanctuary ordinance was repealed because of legislation passed by the mayor and the state governor declaring the ordinance illegal.

These organizations work closely with the religious organizations, network of churches associated with the Sanctuary movement, Catholic charities, the Baptist ministries, Quakers, and others. They receive funds and direct services from religious organizations and private foundations. One successful model can be seen in the work done by St. Peter's Church in the heart of San Francisco 's Mission District. Led by the efforts of refugees working side by side with the local pastor, they have created a Central American refugee program that provides a wide variety of services such as long-term shelter for homeless men, mental health counseling, rights advocacy, and day laborer advocacy.

## What Needs to Be Done in the near Future

### The Need for More Research Studies

Further theoretical and practical research studies are necessary to fully comprehend and resolve the acculturation issues faced by Central-American immigrants in the

United States. The specific areas in need of greater examination are legal, medical, psychological, educational, professional and occupational skills retraining, nutrition, counseling, and religious issues affecting this population. There is a need for studies in the major metropolitan and rural centers where the Central-American populations are settling. It is imperative for mainstream professionals, researchers, and religious organizations to develop critical awareness to effectively address the needs of Central Americans in the United States.

Institutions of higher education must implement broad curricular offerings across the various disciplines addressing the cultural, socioeconomic and historical backgrounds, and the basic needs of this rapidly growing population. In cities with high numbers of Central Americans, universities must include specific curricular offerings and training programs for students enrolled in undergraduate and graduate studies. Course offerings must develop in students a critical understanding of the ethnic, cultural, economic, religious, and sociopolitical backgrounds of Central Americans residing in their geographical areas.

A number of studies recently conducted on why Latin-American immigrants converting from Catholicism to Protestantism show interesting findings that could help in organizing with Central-American communities (Deck, 1985, 1988, 1989; Greeley, 1988; Vilar, 1989; Marin and Gamba, 1990). These studies analyze the immigrant's expectations of the church, the role of the priests, and the nature and structure of religious services. Marin and Gamba (1990) find of particular significance the high degree of dissatisfaction with U.S. Catholicism expressed by recent Latin-American immigrants. Furthermore, they found that the lower the level of acculturation to U.S. culture, the higher the level of dissatisfaction.

Protestant ministers take very seriously their role as missionaries by actively walking and targeting the Latino barrios and ethnic immigrant communities. They also place a high degree of importance on their work among the youth by taking on challenging issues such as drug abuse, gang violence, and education among young Latin American immigrants. In most cases, these ministers, who are recruited from the ranks of the local populations, are fluent in Spanish and are competent in the immigrant's cultural experience. Protestant churches provide a feeling of family and community and are sensitive to the immigrant's cultural experiences (Deck, 1985).

## The Need for Immigration Changes

In the present anti-immigrant climate, undocumented immigration status is the most serious problem faced by the majority of Central Americans in this country. There is a great urgency to modify the governmental policies and practices at the macro level in order to have a positive impact on the economic, social, and cultural experience of this population. Extensive work must be done to stop the wave of anti-immigrant attitudes and violence that has recently escalated. Many government officials are engaging in immigrant bashing to account for the ills of our society, while ignoring numerous studies indicating that immigrants do not depress the local economies but stimulate growth and stability.

The American Civil Liberties Union and the United Nations High Commission on Refugees have declared that Salvadorans and Guatemalans in the United States are prima facie refugees and should not be deported or forced to return to their countries of origin. Temporary refuge and extended voluntary departure status has been granted to Salvadorans but not to Guatemalans as an attempt to solve this complex problem. It must be noted that extended voluntary departure has been granted in the past to other refugee populations. Extended voluntary departure should be granted on a temporary basis until the U.S. Congress determines that hostilities have ended and personal safety has been restored in Guatemala.

Central-American activists and refugees strongly believe that when individuals escaping the terror and political violence of the civil war arrive in this country, the U.S. government has a legal and moral obligation to treat them in a humane manner consistent with U.S. and international laws. If Central Americans were granted refugee status, their most difficult acculturation problem would be resolved thus resulting in their gradual adaptation and incorporation into U.S. society. The immigration status of these individuals prevents their adaptation and incorporation into U.S. society and culture. Undocumented Central Americans have a difficult time finding employment because of their immigration status. This creates an underclass of workers who can find only subminimum wage employment in the ethnic enclave, the domestic, and secondary labor sectors.

## The Need for Counseling Services

It is important to reframe the immigrants' perceptions regarding counseling and social services. In Latin America, the extended family and the church provide economic, emotional, spiritual, and social support to individuals. Family cohesion and support are strong, providing security and stability to the individual and the community. Social services are seen as charity in the traditional Central-American culture, and to receive charity is not considered a positive communal action. People must work to make a living; only the lazy or disabled are expected to receive charity. This attitude may create complications for them in the United States. For instance, individuals may not seek medical help until an illness or problem becomes life-threatening. It is a common belief that if an able-bodied individual cannot afford to pay for a medical service then one seeks home remedies or assistance from family or friends but not from the government or the church.

Undocumented Central Americans need to be informed about available social services. They must know their legal rights as well as the legal implications of their undocumented status. Although there are community agencies providing information and referral services, organizations need budget increases to provide more efficient services. Financial support is needed to expand available facilities and services, and effectively train their professional staff. There is a need to develop culturally sensitive counseling and social services at low cost or free of charge that provide support to Central Americans in their relocation and acculturation experiences. At the micro level, community organizers must offer classes or workshops that provide cultural, social, and political awareness as well as survival skills. Workshops must include an orientation to the U.S. cultural, legal, and social systems to ensure understanding and familiarity with societal dynamics of the United States.

Basic cultural differences must be explained to newcomers to develop a clear understanding of the host society. It is important for the newcomer to acquire an understanding of and competency in the cultural attitudes, values, and laws of the United States. For example, concepts of time and punctuality are themes to discuss with newly arrived immigrants. In Central America, the pace of life is slower and punctuality is not considered as important as it is in this country. Individuals need to be acquainted with proper procedures and expected behavior such as scheduling, punctuality, and canceling appointments, when they cannot attend interviews or meetings.

Other important subjects for community organizers and school professionals to discuss with recently arrived immigrants are the values, attitudes, and laws related to child-rearing practices and child abuse. It is common in Central-American culture to discipline children by using corporal punishment. What is accepted behavior in Central America, however, might be child abuse in this country. In the Central-American culture a parent may discipline a child with corporal punishment, which can range from spanking or belting, to forcing a child to kneel on the floor for prolonged periods of time. If a parent does not punish a child as expected, people might feel that the parents are too permissive and are allowing the children to run their lives. In the United States, corporal punishment is not a widely accepted child-rearing practice; spanking a child on the buttocks may be accepted only in extreme situations.

A high incidence of child abuse by undocumented Central Americans is reported by community agencies, clinics, hospitals, and schools. Parents must be aware of the different values, attitudes, and laws dealing with child-rearing to prevent any legal problems for the family. It is imperative to develop cultural awareness and sensitivity among school administrators and teachers, community organizers, doctors, and other professionals who frequently interact and treat Central Americans. A problem was brought to my attention by a high school counselor in San Francisco when a Salvadoran father had belted a young teen student in the legs. The child showed several bruises from the punishment, and the school administrators called the father to a meeting to discuss the problem. The father was upset at the school administrators for threatening to report him to the authorities for child abuse. In anger the father told the principal that if he was expected not to discipline the child in the traditional ways, then the child would be the responsibility of the school officials and they would have to assume the expense of bringing up the son. There are also instances in which the children begin to threaten to report the parents to the authorities for child abuse. This situation creates discord within the family because the parents see their traditional roles challenged by what they consider disrespectful children.

The majority of family problems encountered by this population arise from the conflicts between the values and cultural systems held in the U.S. society and the contrasting nature of Central-American values and traditions. Children and adolescents, especially girls, are given more rights and privileges in this country. When teenagers begin to date, problems may arise as a result of interethnic or interracial prejudices, freedom to go out with friends, and sexual attitudes and practices. The cultural values held in this society are considerably different from the traditional family values held in Central-American society. I encountered one Salvadoran family whose young teenage daughter started to date a young African-American man. When the young woman became pregnant, the father was deeply disturbed because of racial prejudice to the point of throwing her out; for more than three years, the father refused to see her or talk to her. It was not until the family received counseling and became critically aware of ethnic issues in this country that the father dropped his racist attitudes and the young couple were accepted into the family. The process took a great deal of intervention by community activists, teachers, and friends who were close to the family.

Problems often develop in the family resulting in intergenerational conflict between parents and their children. Conflicts develop when children and adolescents find part-time employment to help fulfill the family's financial responsibilities. Emotional problems are created for the father because of the disruption of the traditional image of the father as the financial provider for the family. Problems may arise because the young usually acculturate faster and learn English at a more rapid pace than the adult family members. Children become interpreters for the family when the parents interact with the mainstream society in family business affairs, including interactions with utility companies, school officials, and landlords. These interpreting responsibilities empower the children, placing them in a bargaining situation with the parents. Children begin to negotiate with parents for privileges as well as for access to more material things that they desire for their social activities.

## Educational Needs

Language acquisition is an important process of the acculturation experience faced by Central-American immigrants to the United States. Mastering the English language is necessary to improve the socioeconomic and cultural experience of recently arrived immigrants. Besides providing cultural awareness of the host society in the basic English language curriculum, educational programs must include counseling to newcomers. It is important to implement empowerment pedagogies like Freire's critical education to develop social and political awareness.

Professionals, university professors, and teachers encounter serious obstacles because they can not find employment in their areas of expertise. Many professionals experience downward social mobility and are often employed in menial occupations that generate frustrations and emotional and psychological problems. It is difficult for attorneys, architects, or professors to earn a living as dishwashers, janitors, or babysitters. Their high expectations of the opportunities available in the United States and the disappointment of not fulfilling their expectations creates a high level of stress.

Occupational retraining programs are needed for individuals employed outside their area of expertise. Professionals need to find employment in fields related to their area of expertise and should receive academic counseling and training to prepare them for accreditation by the appropriate professional qualifying boards. The development of English language courses designed for professionals is needed so that they can acquire the language proficiency to pass the accreditation examinations to practice their professions in this country.

## Medical and Mental Health Care Needs

Many of the medical and health services to immigrants and especially those offered to the undocumented are currently being threatened by the anti-immigrant histeria spreading in our government. Legislators have proposed the passage of restrictions that would not allow the undocumented or their U.S.-born children to receive any medical services. If such legislation is passed then the immigrant health crisis will escalate to serious proportions.

The Central-American population in the United States is in great need of culturally sensitive health-care services. They have special needs in the areas of health and nutrition as recent immigrants suffer from a variety of tropical diseases such as parasites as well as gastroenteritis, malnutrition, tuberculosis, and high mortality rates. Further academic research is needed on the incidence of psychosocial trauma and post-traumatic stress disorders (PTSD) among Central Americans in this country. Until recently only a few social workers, psychologists, and psychiatrists have studied the problem, and more scientific and psychological studies need to be conducted to understand and develop successful treatment for individuals affected by the various forms of psychosocial trauma and PTSD.

Many Central Americans are not familiar with Western mental health concepts and psychological treatment. It is a common belief in Central America that healthy and sane individuals do not need the services of psychologists and that only the mentally ill do. The incidence of mental health problems such as psychosocial trauma, PTSD, alcoholism, and abuse of pharmaceutical drugs is reportedly high among Central-American immigrants. Central Americans suffer psychological and physiological stresses created by the civil war and their relocation experiences. These stresses are categorized as various forms of psychosocial trauma by Latin American psychologists (Martín-Baró, 1987).

Psychological stresses common in political refugees are also manifested in Central Americans. Individuals may suffer from PTSD related to the environment of violence and the effects of the civil war. They are reported to suffer anxiety and acute depression, which may result in hospitalization and intensive psychiatric treatment. Individuals or their relatives who were victims of political violence in

Central America often manifest various forms of psychological problems upon their arrival and settlement in the United States. Torture victims suffer from PTSD symptoms exhibited as severe depression, guilt, nightmares, hyper alertness, insomnia, suicidal tendencies, and withdrawal. Psychiatric evaluations of Central Americans conducted by refugee centers in the San Francisco Bay Area have concluded that a significantly large number of their clients suffer from psychosocial trauma and PTSD. Reports documenting the impact of psychological disorders on the immigrants and their families suggest that marital and family relationships are negatively affected by these mental health problems. Conflicts, depression, alcohol and drug abuse, frustration, domestic violence, separation, and divorce are the recurring consequences.

At the macro level, the medical profession has the moral and social obligation to develop competency on the cultural perspectives of health and disease held by the Central-American population. Psychologists, psychiatrists, doctors, nurses, and hospital staff need to understand the traditional healing concepts and methodologies used by Central Americans to effectively treat the medical and mental health problems of this population. Workshops and curricular offerings need to be developed by universities, hospitals, and clinics to develop in their professionals a critical awareness of the socioeconomic, political, and cultural backgrounds of undocumented Central Americans.

Culture-bound diseases in Central-American patients are often reported by doctors in hospitals and clinics. Many illnesses are perceived to be of supernatural or magical origin. Patients usually do not respond to Western medical methodologies unless they undergo the necessary rituals or take remedies as determined by the traditional cultural beliefs in Central America. In California, efforts are being made to develop effective methodologies and programs to treat Central-American patients in hospitals and community agencies. Because of the high incidence of torture cases reported among recent Central-American immigrants and refugees, a national coalition of medical and mental health professionals and organizations was created to treat survivors of torture. Increased efforts need to provide adequate treatment to individuals who have suffered psychological and physical torture (Córdoba, 1986).

## Employment Needs

Employment is a major issue concerning the social adaptation and economic stability of Central-American immigrants in the United States. Employment opportunities are closely linked to the immigration status of the participants, a situation that forces the majority of undocumented individuals to find employment in the ethnic enclave, in the secondary labor sector, or in domestic labor.

Working conditions in the enclave appear more acceptable to newcomers and undocumented workers, because cash wages are often paid. Cash payments minimize the fears of disclosing a persons' immigration status to strangers and do not require documentation needed to work, as required by the Immigration Reform and

Control Act of 1986 (IRCA), that is, a social security number or an alien registration card.

## Conclusion

The spectrum of problems faced by Central Americans may dishearten many church leaders and community organizers in the United States. Their challenges and responsibilities are many and range from the development of a body of knowledge and understanding around immigration issues, educational concern, to housing and the broad dynamics of acculturation. Added to these responsibilities are the cultural sensitivity and critical awareness required for successful community action.

Since literature on organizing with Central Americans is scarce, community and religious organizers must modify and adapt existing methods of practice and strategies. Social action models, with the exception of the Sanctuary movement, the Freire model, and the Catholic base communities, are the least favored, because of the attention drawn to the people involved in the process. They usually have a negative outcome as police or immigration officials become aware of the individuals and their possible undocumented immigration status. Furthermore, since many Central Americans live marginally in our society, they are reluctant to engage in this level of social change and advocacy. Traditionally, the poor and disenfranchised are conservative in nature and are reluctant to engage in direct confrontation tactics.

Community and economic development models are more acceptable and effective in working with Central Americans in this country. They are more status quo in their orientations and offer more real material gains like employment, housing, and the development of an economic exchange market parallel to the traditional mainstream market systems. The utilization of Paulo Freire's methods for developing critical awareness and empowerment are especially relevant in organizing with Central Americans, since they do not posit false expectations and emphasize real material and educational rewards. Furthermore, many Central-American immigrants are already familiar with Freire's methods, as they were implemented in the Central-American Catholic base communities. These challenges are obvious; the strategies have to be determined on a day-by-day basis as we work with and learn to develop a critical understanding of the communities.

## Bibliography

American Civil Liberties Union. *Salvadorans in the United States: The Case for Extended Voluntary Departure.* (National Immigration and Alien Rights Project, Report No. 1). Washington, D.C., April 1984.

Amnesty International. *Annual Report.* Washington, D.C., 1983.

Burgos, Elisabeth. *I . . . Rigoberta Menchu.* New York: Schocken Books, 1984.

Camarda, Renato. *Forced to Move: Salvadoran Refugees in Honduras.* San Francisco: Solidarity Publications, 1985.

Chernow, Ron. "The Strange Death of Bill Woods: Did He Fly Too Far in the Zone of the Generals?" *Mother Jones,* 4, no. 4 (May 1979).

Córdoba, Carlos B. "Organizing in Central American Communities in the United States." In *Community Organizing in a Diverse Society,* edited by Felix G. Rivera and John L. Erlich. Boston: Allyn and Bacon, 1992.

―――. "The Mission District: The Ethnic Diversity of the Latin American Enclave in San Francisco, California." *Journal of La Raza Studies,* 2, no. 1 (summer/fall 1989): 21–32.

―――. "Undocumented Salvadorans in the San Francisco Bay Area: Migration and Adaptation Dynamics." *Journal of La Raza Studies,* 1, no. 1 (fall 1987): 9–37.

―――. "Migration and Acculturation Dynamics of Undocumented Salvadorans in the San Francisco Bay Area." Ph.D. dissertation, University of San Francisco, 1986.

Deck, A. F. "Fundamentalism and the Hispanic Catholic." *America,* January 25, 1985.

―――. "Proselytism and Hispanic Catholics: How Long Can We Cry Wolf." *America,* December 10, 1988.

―――. *The Second Wave: Hispanic Ministry and the Evangelization of Cultures.* New York: Paulist Press, 1989.

Fallows, James. "The New Immigrants: How New Citizens and Illegal Aliens Are Affecting the United States." *The Atlantic,* November 1983, pp. 45–106.

Freire, Paulo. *Pedagogy of the Oppressed.* New York: Seabury Press, 1970.

―――. *Education for Critical Consciousness.* New York: Seabury Press, 1973.

Greeley, A. M. "Defection Among Hispanics." *America,* July 30, 1988.

Manz, Beatriz. *Refugees of a Hidden War: The Aftermath of Counterinsurgency in Guatemala.* Albany: State University of New York Press, 1988.

Marin, Gerardo, and Gamba, Raymond. *Expectations and Experiences of Hispanic Catholics and Converts to Protestant Churches.* San Francisco: University of San Francisco, Social Psychology Laboratory, Hispanic Studies, February 1990.

Martín-Baró, Ignacio. "Political Violence and War as Causes of Psychosocial Trauma in El Salvador." *Journal of La Raza Studies,* 2, no. 1 (Summer/Fall 1989): 5–15.

Melville, Margarita. B. "Hispanics: Race, Class or Ethnicity." *Journal of Ethnic Studies,* 16, no. 1 (1988): 67–84.

Muller, T., and Espenshade, T. with Manson, D., de la Puente, M., Goldberg, M.; and Sanchez, J. *The Fourth Wave: California's Newest Immigrants.* Washington, D.C.: Urban Institute Press, 1985.

National Lawyers Guild. *Immigration Law and Defense.* New York: Clark Boardman Company, 1981.

Portes, A., Nash Parker, R., and Cobas, J. A. "Assimilation or Consciousness: Perceptions of United States Society by Recent Latin American Immigrants to the U.S." *Social Forces,* 59, no. 1 (September 1980): 200–224.

Portes, Alejandro, and Bach, Robert L. *Latin Journey: Cuban and Mexican Immigrants in the United States.* Berkeley: University of California Press, 1985.

Rivera, Felix G., and Erlich, John L. *Community Organizing in a Diverse Society.* Boston: Allyn and Bacon, 1992.

―――. "Neo-Gemeinschaft Minority Communities in the United States: Implications for Community Organizing." *Community Development Journal,* 16, no. 3 (October 1981): 189–200.

Toennies, Ferdinand. "Gemeinschaft and Gesellschaft." *Theories of Society,* Vol. 1, Talcott Patrsons, Edward Shils, Kaspar D. Naegele and Jesse R. Pitts, eds. New York: The Free Press, 1961, pp. 191–201.

United Nations Human Rights Commission. *Report on the Situation of Human Rights in El Salvador.* Washington, D.C., 1983.

Vilar, J. J. D. "The Success of the Sects Among Hispanics in the United States." *America,* February 25, 1989.

*11*

Southeast Asians in
the United States:
A Strategy for
Accelerated and
Balanced Integration

*VU-DUC VUONG*

April 1975 marked the end of U.S. military involvement in Cambodia, Laos, and Vietnam and at the same time opened a new chapter in the ongoing saga of immigration to the United States: the Southeast Asian wave.[1]

By the end of 1989, over a million Southeast Asians had migrated to the United States, as both refugees and immigrants. The Southeast Asian diaspora in the United States is thus the largest in the world and, thanks to the resources and circumstances in this country, potentially the most influential one as well.

This chapter briefly profiles this community, raises some critical issues for the 1990s and beyond, and advances a strategy to enable it to achieve its full potential in the twenty-first century.

## *Southeast Asians in the United States: A Profile*

When the Phnom Penh and Saigon regimes fell to the Communists in April 1975, no more than a few thousand Southeast Asians lived in the United States. Most were students at American universities; the rest were diplomats, bureaucrats serving in the United States, or military personnel in training. Virtually overnight the United States admitted over 130,000 refugees, mostly from Vietnam. This earliest group was dispersed throughout the country, from Duluth to New Orleans, and from Maine to Hawaii, in a deliberate policy of minimizing the impact on local communities and of accelerating the integration process.

During the following three years, 1976 to 1978, the refugee outflow from the three countries dwindled down to a trickle, to about 37,000. More than half came from Laos alone, while comparatively few escaped from either Cambodia or Vietnam. In Cambodia, the Khmer Rouge, under a reign of terror, massacred at least one million of their fellow countrymen, including the majority of the professional and educated class. In Vietnam, the incarceration of tens of thousands of former public servants and officers of the overthrown regime, and the initial, somewhat hopeful, "wait-and-see" attitude among many who did not escape in 1975, accounted for the reduced outflow of refugees.

By the end of 1978, and during 1979, two major events in Southeast Asia unleashed another exodus from that region. In the South, Vietnam invaded Cambodia, overthrew the Khmer Rouge, and set up a new Cambodian government under its protection. To the North, tensions between China and Vietnam, close allies during the war, led to harassment of the Chinese population in Vietnam and open warfare along the border.

Anti-Chinese policies in Vietnam caused a massive, unprecedented exodus of "boat people" from Vietnam that included both Chinese ethnics and Vietnamese who had given up on hope for a better Vietnam. Hundreds of thousands of new refugees from Vietnam braved high seas in their minuscule boats to reach Thailand, Malaysia, Indonesia, the Philippines, Hong Kong, and Japan. In Cambodia, by the time Vietnamese tanks rolled into Phnom Penh, they also awakened and unchained a population incapacitated by the Khmer Rouge's atrocities. Over a quarter of a million Cambodians made it across the border to Thailand within the following year; most of them would have to stay in makeshift camps for years before being resettled elsewhere. From Laos, the exodus also intensified; hundreds of thousands of Laotians, predominantly of the Hmong hill tribes, crossed over into Thailand. Like their Cambodian counterparts, they too would have to spend years in refugee camps in northern Thailand.

During the four year period from 1979 to 1982, the United States alone admitted well over 400,000 refugees from Southeast Asia. This group was often referred to as the "second wave" of Southeast Asian refugees. Since 1983, the level of Southeast Asians admitted to the United States as refugees has leveled off and hovers between 35,000 to 50,000 annually. The composition of refugees admitted to the United States changed significantly in 1989 when this country began accepting in large numbers two distinct groups with special claims: Amerasians and former political prisoners. From 1990 to 1993, nearly two-thirds of the annual quota of about 50,000 came from these two groups, mostly from Vietnam.

In terms of status, most Southeast Asians were admitted as refugees, but since 1990, an increasing proportion was admitted as immigrants, often sponsored by close relatives already in the United States. Both refugees and immigrants were allowed to seek work immediately but only refugees were eligible for government assistance, from English language and vocational classes to welfare benefits and Medicare. After residing in the United states for one year, a refugee became eligible for permanent residence status, and four years later, he or she was allowed to petition for citizenship. Immigrants were admitted as permanent residents upon arrival; they too would have to wait for five years to become citizens. By 1993, well over half of all Southeast Asians in the United States had become citizens.

In terms of procedures, most Southeast-Asian refugees and immigrants arrived in the United States in one of two ways: a smaller number directly from their home countries, usually under the auspices of the Orderly Departure Program (ODP), but the majority had to escape first to a neighboring country of asylum and from there were selected for resettlement elsewhere.

ODP essentially was an escape valve for people who had reason to leave Vietnam, (persecution, for instance), and who had been accepted for resettlement by another country, to leave Vietnam legally and safely. The procedure required two authorizations; from the Vietnamese side authorization to leave and from the recipient country authorization to immigrate. It was therefore susceptible to political caprice on either side, and indeed ODP had often been delayed, scaled down, or simply held hostage by one side or the other during the first ten years of operation following the 1979 agreement. Nevertheless, ODP provided safe passage for well over 100,000 Vietnamese during that period. Today, ODP remains a much more humane and effective alternative to clandestine escapes on land or by boat.

For the vast majority of Southeast-Asian refugees, however, clandestine escape was the only available means. In general, Laotians and Cambodians crossed the Thai border while the Vietnamese left by boats to a country of asylum. By the end of 1992, over 2 million Southeast-Asian refugees had reached a country of first asylum. The number of people who perished during these flights will never be known with certainty; they disappeared in the jungles or at sea.

First asylum countries provided shelter and basic needs with funds from the United Nations and contributions from developed nations. Under the best of circumstances, which almost never happened, refugee camps in these countries epitomized the welfare state that can cause debilitating dependence if continued too long. More frequently, however, most governments resorted to mistreatment of refugees to discourage more from coming. Thus, in 1981, for example, Thailand "pushed back" Cambodian refugees across the border into a mine field; in 1983 Hong

Kong established the "closed camp" system, a jail-like facility with little service beyond subsistence and little opportunity for resettlement elsewhere; in 1988, Thailand, Malaysia, and Indonesia pushed boats back out to sea often at great imminent risk.

Since 1989, Hong Kong, with approval from the United Nations, adopted an even more draconian policy to empty the camps and to discourage more from coming. It established a first-layer, stricter screening process even before a refugee can be consider for resettlement elsewhere. Under this plan, called the Comprehensive Action Plan (CAP) and subsequently adopted by other Southeast-Asian countries of asylum, everyone who landed in Hong Kong had first to be certified, by Hong Kong authorities and without effective, independent legal counsel, to be a bona fide political refugee—as opposed to an economic migrant—before he or she could be interviewed by a third country for possible admission as a refugee. In effect, over 90 percent of new arrivals from 1989 to 1992 have been "screened out," that is, declared economic migrants to be sent back to Vietnam. The next step after screening is repatriation. Beginning in 1989, Hong Kong began offering cash incentive for the "screened out" refugees to return to Vietnam. As expected, few took up the offer; so the authorities started using force to send them back. Hunger strikes, riots, self-immolations ensued in many camps from 1990 through 1992, but the cause of the later refugees was a lost one. Under a combination of harsher living conditions in camps, virtually no hope of resettlement elsewhere, and some modest enticement to return, refugees accepted their fate and complied with repatriation. By the end of 1993, it was anticipated that most of the "screened out" refugees in Hong Kong, and around Southeast Asia, would have been repatriated within a year. A few days after the lifting of the trade embargo against Vietnam on February 3, 1994, the United Nations High Commissioner for Refugees (UNHCR) simply declared the Southeast-Asian refugee exodus to be over.

Of the more than 2 million who made it to a country of first asylum since 1975, most were able to petition a third country to accept them as refugees. The potential recipient country set up interviews and from that point on, procedures varied from country to country as to eligibility criteria and preparation for resettlement. Australia, Canada, and France, for instance, provided orientation and language instruction to refugees after their arrival in the respective country of destination. Australia and Canada also used the applicants' language ability, education level, and skills as criteria of selection. The United States, on the other hand, accepted refugees on broader, and more humane criteria of family ties, previous association with the United States or the former Vietnamese regime, or reasonable fear of persecution. It then sent most of the admissible refugees to one of the three refugee processing centers for some cultural orientation and some rudimentary English instruction before allowing them into this country for resettlement. In reality, however, the actual orientation, language, and vocational training took place in the United States, after arrival, through a network of agencies and community-based organizations, and with federal funds.

Overall, the developed world has admitted some 1.7 million refugees worldwide, with Australia, Canada, China, France, and Germany as major resettlement countries after the United States.

## *Similarities and Differences*

Numbers and circumstances aside, Southeast-Asian refugees in the United States make up a very complex community in virtually every aspect. Beyond the fact that they come from three different countries, and thus speak at least three separate languages, Laos and Vietnam also contain linguistic minorities. The Hmong and Iu Mien, two primary hill tribes resettled in the United States, speak two different languages from each other and from the mainstream "low-land" Lao language. In Vietnam, many ethnic Chinese still cannot read or write Vietnamese. In each country, there are sufficient numbers of illiterates in their own language, making English instruction a Herculean task.

Their respective pasts also vary greatly. Cambodians have suffered the most—physically, emotionally, psychologically—under the genocidal Khmer Rouge. It is safe to say that no Cambodian family, from the royal down to the poorest, was left untouched by tragedy during that brief but atavistic reign. Before the war, however, Cambodian life was easy, with ample food and a leisurely lifestyle. Many believe that the Khmer (another name for Cambodia) empire peaked in the twelfth century as illustrated by their sophisticated waterworks and celebrated temples of Angkor Wat. The Khmer empire encompassed much of today's South Vietnam and the eastern part of Thailand.

Vietnam had been at war almost constantly since the 1930s, first against the French, then against the Japanese, then the French again, then the Americans, and most recently against the Chinese and Khmer Rouge, and almost always against one another. Instead of genocide, Vietnam suffered a half century of steady hemorrhaging of its best and brightest youths.

Even Laos, though not completely embroiled in the recent wars, was not spared from the fighting. During the American phase of the Vietnam War, Laos provided cover for the Ho Chi Minh Trail, a major supply route, and the Hmong tribesmen were recruited, paid, and trained by the CIA to assist the American war effort.

Vietnam was the most urbanized of the three countries, although agriculture remained the backbone of all three economies. Constant warfare in Vietnam had driven many people from the countryside to cities in search of some measure of security. In 1954, when the country was divided, nearly one million Northerners moved South and often were resettled on the outskirts of major towns. In Laos and Cambodia, by contrast, a more agricultural way of life prevailed until very near the end of the war, thus people were still able to live on their lands and the hill tribes were still able to practice slash-and-burn farming.

Education levels also vary. At the risk of gross generalization, it can be said that the majority of Vietnamese and Chinese Vietnamese were literate in some language, having received some form of formal education. The proportion goes down in Cambodia—particularly Laos, where some hill tribes did not have a written language until a few decades ago. Urbanization would most likely have played a role as well, at least to the extent that one would have to rely more on literacy to function in urban settings.

The predominant—and in a sense unifying—religion in all three countries was Buddhism. Only in Vietnam was there a significant minority of Catholics and Protestants. Since Buddhism was not a highly structured religion, such as Christianity, Islam, or Judaism, most people believed in their hearts and seldom displayed their faith with outward practices or observances.

Because the war was protracted and several million Americans supported the war effort in-country, many Vietnamese had ties to the defeated regime, either as government officials, armed forces personnel, or support personnel for the Americans. Likewise, the Hmong in Laos who fought alongside the Americans during the war found themselves in the same situation. In Cambodia, unfortunately, most of the former government officials, most of the educated class, and most of the trained professionals had been decimated by Pol Pot's Khmer Rouge.

After 1975, instead of the blood bath that many had feared, the Communist regimes in Laos and Vietnam incarcerated the people from the "old regime" in re-education camps where they were usually put to hard labor during the day, indoctrinated at night, kept isolated from their families except for an annual or occasional visits, fed at subsistence levels, and generally tortured mentally. These people—estimated at over 100,000—would qualify as political refugees under both the United Nations and the U.S. standards. But it took until September 1989 for the United States and Vietnam to agree on their fate. By this time, most had been released from re-education camps but were not allowed to resume a normal life; they were denied job opportunities and food rations. The United States agreed to accelerate these refugees' and their families' resettlement in the United States while Vietnam agreed to let them go.

Another vestige of the war with an even more direct link to the United States was the Amerasians, literally the common children of Vietnam and the United States. Estimated at between 7,000 and 15,000 these children were fathered by American servicemen while serving in Vietnam, and in most cases were abandoned after they returned home. The children, now adults, and their mothers and often their siblings survived as best they could in a society that, for the most part, refused to accept them. After 1975, they also became the living reminders of the defeated enemy.

Congress passed a bill in 1982 giving preference to the admission of these children and their families, but it took until 1989 for them to begin to arrive in any significant numbers. They too are an integral part of the Southeast-Asian community in the United States, and perhaps particularly in the United States where they function as natural bridges.

## *Southeast Asians in the United States: Critical Issues*

Issues that are of critical importance to Southeast Asians in America in the 1990s and beyond can be roughly separated into two categories: issues that are particular to Southeast Asians, or adaptation issues, and those that they share with other populations in this country, or maintenance issues. These categories are merely conceptual tools; they are neither mutually exclusive nor exhaustive.

Issues specific to Southeast Asians range from the obvious ones like language, acculturation, and employment to the more subtle ones like overcoming trauma, regaining a sense of stability, of security, and of order, to name a few.

The English language is a barrier for virtually all Southeast Asians who did not attend grade school in the United States. To the extent that one overcomes that barrier, by learning and practicing, the issue recedes. However, for many adult Southeast Asians, effective mastery of English remains an elusive goal. The chance to become fluent in English becomes even less attainable for the small segment of the population who did not have any formal education, thus lacking even the fundamental building blocks of learning. Moreover, there are levels of fluency appropriate for different lines of work or positions in society; the level that enables a shopkeeper or keypunch operator to function often is not adequate for a loan officer or a software engineer. It becomes therefore an almost unending process of self-improvement if one wants to progress and move up.

But far more intractable than the language issue is acculturation, in the sense that one not only understands what surrounds him or her, but also that one can take part and function well in that environment. In this context, the newcomers essentially must be able to build their own support networks and to be at ease in whatever circumstances, from the lunch counter to the boardroom, from the ballpark to church pews, to be able to function effectively.

If language is the prerequisite for basic communication, then social skills are the prerequisites of acculturation. Sometimes, there are elementary skills such as the ability to strike up new friendships, to express displeasure, or to make oneself heard, to cite a few examples. But at times these skills can also be quite sophisticated and complex, such as playing the corporate culture and dynamics to one's own advantage, or competing openly, successfully, in the electoral process.

By this standard, Southeast Asians still have a long way to go before achieving sufficient acculturation, as illustrated by the following situations. In schools, it is true that many Southeast-Asian students excel academically, but often glossed over is the fact that many of the same students are quite isolated from the rest of the student body, unable to cross over the invisible walls that separate them. Many simply hang out with fellow Southeast Asians only. When does a support network become a crutch? How does a student balance his or her need for a secure identity and the need to participate fully in school activities, to build up new friendships that will carry on into their future?

At the workplace, few Southeast Asians have developed lasting, trusting friendships with their coworkers. While many have managed to move up to skilled professional levels, Southeast-Asian professionals rarely function as effectively in social settings as in their respective assigned duties, or perform public duties as easily as their secluded tasks. At first glance, it may seem irrelevant. The passive mentality of "as long as I do my job well, it will be recognized" still prevails among Southeast Asians. Unfortunately, recognition seldom comes automatically, and in the workplace, racial stereotypes and outright prejudice are still facts of life.

Thus, the deadly combination of corporate discrimination against minorities in general, on the one hand, and our own inability to build allies, on the other, can and does lead to untold numbers of blocked career paths in the Asian and Southeast-Asian communities. It is not a coincidence that in the electronic industry, where Asians provide a disproportionate range of engineering skills, yet attain very few leadership, decision-making positions, the frustration has led to very high incidence of job switches and the growth of small, privately owned firms. Many of these engineers and entrepreneurs realize that they cannot win the corporate battle and so opt for independence and more risk, but situations where they can exercise both skills and leadership.

In the political arena, Asians contribute a disproportionately high amount of money to candidates, yet very few win political appointments and fewer still see their issues seriously considered. As for elected positions, they are still rare. For Southeast Asians, by and large, the situation is even bleaker; they are still well outside the arena.

There is therefore a long and difficult road ahead before Southeast Asians—and to a lesser extent other minorities—can truly achieve full acculturation, full integration. As with most problems, the sooner they can recognize them and find ways to remedy them, the easier it will be for them to cope.

In addition to language difficulty and acculturation, Southeast Asians in America also face many other collective and individual road blocks. On the collective side, the lack of a democratic tradition in all three countries becomes an impediment to efforts at organizing the community in the United States. From the lack of basic practices such as a tradition of open debate, open disagreement without becoming enemies, to more fundamental dynamics such as a peaceful, honorable way to retire the old leadership to make room for a new one, Southeast Asians often are unable to tolerate different points of view that can move the community forward.

Compounding the lack of a democratic tradition is the half century of warfare, of clandestine operation, of deceit and betrayal, of corruption and incompetence that make many in the Southeast-Asian community unable to function in the broad daylight of public scrutiny. And without public scrutiny and debate, allegiance and loyalty must be based on factors other than the intellectual, moral correctness of the cause or the capacity and character of individuals. To this day, Southeast Asians, and Vietnamese in particular, tend to take things or people seriously only if they have a few layers of secrecy around them.

The protracted war left another piece of luggage: distrust of one another and the facility with which one labels one's enemy. Factionalism and the "us versus them" mentality might have been necessary and useful to protect war secrets; in the open, democratic society they greatly hinder our efforts to integrate and build bridges with other people, including our former enemies. During colonial times, many people lost their lives after having been fingered as "collaborators" with the French, even if the proof was unconvincing, or many others also lost their lives on the mere suspicion of being a resistance fighter. In our times, being labeled "Communist" carries the same stigma and danger. Unfortunately, the tradition is alive and well in the United States and at times still practiced with gusto, at least within the Vietnamese community.

This inability to tolerate differing opinions, to accept others as they are, and to respect majority rule has prevented the Vietnamese community in the United States from effectively organizing itself over the last two decades. It has even cut off all useful debate among members of the community, stifled the development and nurturing of emerging leaders, and refused to acknowledge that the war has ended and life goes on. The consequence of this collective deficiency has been both damaging and ironic. Damaging because nearly twenty years after their arrival in this country, Vietnamese Americans still lack a national leadership generally recognized by both the American mainstream and the majority of its own community. They still do not have a consensus on how to deal with Vietnam: is it still an enemy to pursue to the bitter end, by all available means? or is it a country of origin, to be helped as necessary and to take pride in as appropriate? Despite countless individual achievements in many fields, the Vietnamese-American community, as late as the end of 1993, is still unable to show one single collective achievement, in domestic or foreign policy, that the community identified as important and advocated for.

It is also ironic because members of the same community can be their own worst enemies; and nothing illustrates this situation better than the joint issue of freedom and democracy. By definition, all refugees from Cambodia, Laos, and Vietnam fled communism to seek individual freedoms and a democratic society. No doubt, many have lost everything they had—status, wealth, power, land, even loved ones—but the principal criterion is the search for freedom. Yet, once arrived in a Western country, Vietnamese refugees tend to impose on themselves the strictest orthodoxies and flagrant abuses of personal opinions and freedoms. For the first ten years, 1975–85, understandably with the losses still recent and the emotions still raw, anticommunism was the order of the day. In those early years, the most popular cause to champion, the easiest fundraising to organize, and the most ready emotions to fan, all involved in one way or another, a call to arms to return, fight the Communists and retake the country. After most of these movements were exposed as no more than fraudulent exploitation of refugees' emotion, around the mid-1980s, the anticommunist orthodoxy and its heavy-handed implementation took hold in the community. Scores of journalists, community organizers, and others who spoke up from a more moderate platform were threatened, abused, vilified, and even killed. At least half a dozen murders remain unsolved to this day.

This orthodoxy within the community had devastating consequences. On one level, it maintained in leadership and opinion-forming positions the same group of people who fought, and lost, the last war. This generation of leadership cannot function in the relatively peaceful and open American democracy; yet it effectively blocked off any challenges or diverging viewpoints from younger, potential leaders, less scarred by the war. On a second level, the forced uniformity, and at times strong-arm fundraising tactics, drained the meager resources away from long-term community building, and wasted them on political or personal dreams. On a third level, this self-imposed orthodoxy perpetuated the worst characteristics of the Vietnamese behavior of the twentieth century: mistrust, deceit, jealousy, corruption, and suppression of ideas, and if possible people, not from the same mold. It effectively left the Vietnamese American without a political or social agenda, either on domestic resettlement issues or in international treatment of refugees. By February 1994, when President Bill Clinton lifted the trade embargo against Vietnam and paved the way for renewed diplomatic relations shortly afterward, the Vietnamese-American community was still without a recognized leadership, without a consensus or coordinated agenda, and without the resources either to organize itself or to interact with its former enemy, the authorities in Vietnam.

On the individual side, let us first consider the issues that were caused by circumstances. The most obvious one is the assault on one's status, sense of dignity, sense of security, and the ability—however limited—to control one's own life and destiny. When one becomes a refugee, by definition, one loses everything: job, status, wealth, friends, even family members. Some may be replaceable, some are not. Refugees know that they will carry these physical and emotional scars for the rest of their lives. But they lost more than wealth and loved ones, they lost something deep inside themselves: the security and the ability to control their own lives. During the escape, they were at the mercy of traffickers, of pirates, of bandits, of troops from several governments, all of whom acted swiftly and often mercilessly. In camps, they were at the mercy of the soldiers who ran the camps, at the mercy of the United Nations that fed, clothed, and took care of them. When applying to a country for resettlement, they were completely at the mercy of immigration officers. Along the way, there was no reconsideration, no appeal. It is this sense of helplessness that they must overcome, and the only way to do it is to regain some sense that they are back in control of their own lives, and if nothing else, that they finally found a place where they belong.

Depending on the specifics of the escape and conditions in camps, some of them may have to recover from survivor's guilt; from atrocities inflicted upon them, upon their families, or merely witnessed; from rape, robbery, beatings, or starvation.

And the list goes on. It will be a long time, if ever, before some of us will not jump at the sound of a car backfiring, before some of us will forget the rapes and beatings suffered, or for that matter, that some of us will accept that earthquakes are only natural phenomenons and not the expression of some supernatural discontent.

The same traumas of escape, and the ability to escape itself, often cause other types of dysfunctions within the family as well. Many families are divided, many children are separated from their parents and must fend for themselves. While separation is usually a burden, sometimes even being reunited causes other tensions that are no less serious; one of the spouses, for instance, has moved on with life since being separated, and the spouses' mutual expectations are no longer valid. How to restore harmony, mutual respect, and love? How to avoid dwelling on the past traumas, to avoid becoming bitter or paranoid?

Even under the best of circumstances—a rare painless escape and resettlement, for example—external changes in the new society can cause serious disruptions in the family life of most refugees. Spousal roles often have to be readjusted where life requires two or more breadwinners instead of one. Difficulties in understanding, helping, and controlling one's own children can lead to abuse, bitterness, or break-up. Disparity between children's potential and parents' expectations can easily lead to alienation.

Southeast Asians also have their share of other generic problems, literally from the cradle to the grave. As is the case with many poor people, prenatal and neonatal care is not yet widely practiced. Many preventable diseases, particularly those associated with diet and lifestyle, still continue unabated and some such as heart disease and cancer are increasing.

As children grow older, many parents still lack adequate understanding of how the school system works in order to supervise and help their children. By the time their children reach the teenage years, many parents—and young people—have difficulty coping with the bewildering youth culture in this society and sometimes their reactions range from excessive strictness to virtual neglect.

On the other end of the age spectrum, the romanticized myth of the Asian "extended family" begins to break down as well. Older Southeast Asians, even when they live with their children, are increasingly being isolated: few can learn a new language, few can afford to drive, very few can find employment even if they are very motivated to work. During the daytime, when the adult children go to work and the grandchildren are at school, many elderly are virtual prisoners in their own home, unable even to answer the phone or the door. Where there are pre-school age grandchildren, often grandparents become built-in babysitters without pay. In the worst scenario, they may even be abused, mentally if not physically, and often neglected by their own children.

It follows that among the Southeast-Asian elderly population, depression is rampant, due in part to such external conditions and in part to their own sense of loss, of uselessness, of isolation, and frustration. Sadly, they are often given perfunctory respect and filial duty. But, throughout the country, there are fewer than half a dozen programs specifically designed to assist the Southeast-Asian elderly.

For women, the new-found freedom, educational opportunities, and economic potential—all liberating and empowering—can also become causes for family dysfunction and for personal dilemma. How would a Hmong girl, barely into puberty, resist the family pressures and traditions to be married, in order to finish high school? How to reconcile the need of a college graduate, who is still single, to live on her own, with her parents' wish for her to live at home until marriage? How would a successful career woman switch from her assertive, logical attitude at work to the deferential behavior expected of her at home? How would a high school girl handle dating, sex, contraception, or abortion when her parents still believe that their daughter should not date and still presume that she is both sexually ignorant and inactive?

Juveniles fare no better. Many are lost between the two worlds. At home and in the community, they no longer have the complete command of the native language, customs, or culture, and thus often are looked at as having lost their roots. At school and in society at large, they may be able to communicate but without fully understanding the social context, the cultural implications, or the peer dynamics. In effect, they are neither here nor there, while deep down they want to be in both places. The dropout rate is increasing steadily, and more and more tangle with the law, from truancy to drugs, from car theft to robbery, even murder. Even those who stay in school and are good students often find it a continuing personal trauma to maintain an apparent balance between the two worlds.

Making it even more difficult for newcomer youths to adjust are the *structural* changes in this country's economy. On the one hand, the United States lost over ten million manufacturing jobs in the two decades from 1970 to 1990, while on the other hand, most of the newly created jobs are either in the generally low-paying service industries or in the high end of technology. With a substantial increase in working-age immigrants and refugees who can hardly cope with language and cultural problems, and a growing native youth population who, by and large, are not adequately trained for a technological work force, the job competition is fierce and the prospect for the near future is even bleaker. Southeast Asian youths, like the majority of all youth in this country today, lack a marketable skill and face an insecure future with respect to being able to make a living; on top of all that, many of the newcomers cannot even overcome the language barrier that they must cross in order to be gainfully employed.

In this context, one must inevitably conclude that, despite the outward signs of primarily individual successes in academia, in business, and soon in politics as well, the Southeast-Asian community in the United States still has to overcome barrier after barrier, to resolve conflict after conflict, and to devise new strategies for this new environment.

## A Strategy for Accelerated and Balanced Integration

### The Context

After nearly twenty years of working in the United States with refugees and immigrants from Southeast Asia, I have reached the conclusion that it is possible for newcomers in the last part of the twentieth century to join the American mainstream much faster and much more effectively while still keeping a balanced identity that up to now has been ignored or discarded.

As one can readily see, this is a marked departure from the traditional "Americanization"—or what used to be erroneously called the "melting pot"—of immigrants and refugees, where normally the first generation stays out of the mainstream, labors hard, and invests in the second generation, who joins the professional ranks, and by the third generation, one becomes a monolingual, monocultural, homogenized "American."

It is now possible—and indeed indispensible—to, on the one hand, collapse the two-to-three generation process into one while, on the other hand, developing a new model of a truly pluralist "American," fit for the new age of economic and human cooperation. It is possible to expedite the integration process because circumstances have changed drastically in the last half of this century.

First and foremost among these changes are the achievements of the civil rights and related movements. Equal protection of the law and equal opportunity for all people regardless of race and sex open up whole new vistas that used to be off limits to newly arrived immigrants. Better housing, better employment, and better educational opportunities, in turn, promote a sense of belonging and dignity among the newcomers. The Voting Rights Act and the Civil Rights Act of the 1960s completed what the Emancipation Act started: making all Americans equal before the law. For refugees and immigrants, one more stepping stone is required.

The second major change is revision of the immigration law itself. The 1965 changes in the Immigration and Naturalization Act are still unrecognized as an important milestone in the development of American society. It abolished the racist Asian exclusion and the inherently self-perpetuating formula of admitting immigrants according to the existing percentage of each ethnic group in the country. It replaced those policies with the comparatively more equal admission quotas: a maximum of 20,000 people per country per year under a ceiling of 180,000 per year for the Western Hemisphere and another 180,000 per year for the rest of the world. Beginning in 1968, when this law took effect, the United States as a society underwent a radical change in its demographic composition. Only very preliminary data is beginning to trickle in, among which is indication of a faster integration of newcomers.

The third major change lies in the domestic and global economies. The United States lost its economic predominance abroad while at home the economy shifted noticeably from production to service industries and developing new technologies at breakneck speed. Newcomers, thus, are no longer confined to a few labor-intensive sectors; but, because of the changes and their own education, they find themselves excelling in technological fields. It does not take much skill to deduce that a first generation immigrant today who happens to be an engineer in Silicon Valley or a medical researcher would look at the United states—and at the same time be perceived by the rest of society—very differently from his or her counterpart of a couple of generations ago who toiled in fish houses, steel mills, or laundries. We are not assuming that these changes have been easy or consistent; rather, the changes have taken place in spite of racism, exploitation, and sexual harassment of the refugees. But, because of these major changes, Southeast Asians have more avenues within which to develop their potential.

It is also necessary for the United States to evolve into a truly pluralistic society, and in this context, recently arrived refugees and immigrants—who happen to be more brown-skinned than any other pigment, reflecting the world we live in—serve both as the catalyst and the vehicle toward this goal in the twenty-first century.

We cannot repress a sense of wonder about the profound human instinct for improvement as well as about the momentous events in the world since 1989. In just a few short years, many of the long-standing beliefs, orthodoxies, ideologies, and practices were simply turned on their heads. We witnessed the Soviet withdrawal from Afghanistan; the Vietnamese withdrawal from Cambodia; the United States cutting off the Nicaraguan contras, then invading Panama and crushing Iraq to impose its order; the euphoria of the Beijing 1989 spring followed by the June massacre and the aftermath of repression; the recognition of Tibet's struggle for independence; the Prague civilized revolution; the collapse of the Berlin wall and reunification of Germany; the bloody and swift retribution in Romania; the figurative resurrection of Nelson Mandela and the dismantlement of apartheid in South Africa; the demise of communism as an ideology and the collapse of the Soviet Union from its own weight, followed by chaos as the various republics try to pick up the pieces in their own ways; the Palestinian and Israeli recognition of each other as legitimate counterparts; the emergence of the United Nations as a potential world arbiter and peacekeeper; the almost universal acceptance of democracy; and so much more. The human race seems determined to redeem itself from the brink of self-annihilation and to realize, for the first time in recorded history, that planet Earth is a community from which we cannot run nor can anyone damage it with impunity.

The basic needs for human happiness and dignity can be reduced to two simple components: food and freedom. The common threads running through virtually all people's movements in the last half century, from the many struggles for independence in the third world to civil rights marches, from Tiananmen Square to Tibet, from Zimbabwe to Romania, from Pretoria to Prague, from Nicaragua to Sri Lanka, from the Baltic to Burma, from boat people to migrant workers, from Seoul to San Salvador, from Calcutta to Cuba, from the West Bank to East Timor, are either basic physical well-being or a sense of freedom, thus dignity, and often both.

Food means not just a full stomach but also a sense of security toward tomorrow, opportunities to improve one's economic situation, and a reasonable belief that one's children will live in a slightly better world. Freedom, likewise, prescribes not only individual liberty but also a democratic society, respect for human rights, and a process where citizens can effect changes. In a real sense, people no longer live by bread alone, they also want to determine their lives and, collectively with others, their futures.

In this context of global evolution and interdependence, no country can afford to be an island or can mandate deference from the rest of the world. Rather, we depend on each other for materials, for markets, for labor, for the environment, for peace, and for travel, among other things. Conversely, successes or disasters in any part of the world can be instantly felt on a global scale. Witness, for example, Chernobyl, the Brazilian rain forest, the ozone depletion, El Niño, Somalia, Tiananmen Square, the Berlin Wall.

The United States, consequently, has to learn to deal with the rest of the world not as a commander but as a partner, more powerful to be sure, but inherently equal. The popularity of the English language, rock music, and blue jeans notwithstanding, we as a country can no longer dictate the political regimes or the terms of trade as we used to do until very recently. Rather, we have to market our products, negotiate our terms like everyone else, and respect other people's self-determination. In other words, we have to persuade rather than prescribe, convince rather than conquer, and therefore, to be successful we must be able to communicate with our partners. This is precisely where the "melting pot" model of assimilation must be discarded and replaced by a balanced integration approach. This delicate balance functions at least at two levels: between the old and the American cultures and among the three key components of modern life: social, economic, and political.

## *The Experiment*

Certain portions of the Southeast Asian community, most notably in the San Francisco Bay Area, have deliberately adopted this model of accelerated and balanced integration. Field-tested for only about ten years, it is evidently still too early to render a verdict on its validity and usefulness. However, based on the early results, one may draw some preliminary conclusions. At the very least, this chapter can serve both as an interim report from the field by a community development practitioner as well as a restatement of the strategy. By necessity and in fairness to other practitioners who pursue alternative models, we must narrow the scope of this strategy to our working and ongoing experience at the Center for Southeast Asian Refugee Resettlement (CSEARR).

Started in 1975 and incorporated in San Francisco as a social service agency assisting newly arrived refugees, CSEARR has evolved over the years and expanded its services to meet the needs of a growing and diversified constituency. By 1985, CSEARR operated throughout the San Francisco Bay Area with offices in four adjacent counties, providing a nearly comprehensive spectrum of services, from greetings at airports when refugees first land, to making business loans to help start a business enterprise. In between, the Center teaches English, finds jobs, upgrades skills, translates, counsels, helps people become citizens, and generally troubleshoots on any issues involving refugees or Southeast Asians. It was established as a community-based organization (CBO), a nonprofit corporation, and it continues to be led, managed, and staffed predominantly by former Southeast-Asian refugees. In the early 1990s, the Center serves from 8,000 to 10,000 clients annually with a staff of thirty. Three-quarters of the staff come to this country as refugees; in this sense we spring forth from the community, we empathize with the people we serve, and we understand and anticipate the community needs.

As a community-based agency, CSEARR's mission, philosophy, and ultimate goal is to integrate and empower the Southeast-Asian community in the United States. The single guiding principle running through all of CSEARR's services and activities is the empowerment of the people it serves.

The Center teaches English so that newcomers can function in this society. It offers vocational training and employment services so that fellow refugees can get back on their feet financially. It provides a wide range of social services—from orientation to earthquake preparedness, from the reduction of smoking to AIDS prevention—so that its clients, young and old, male and female, can keep their bearings in this bewildering environment. It facilitates citizenship naturalization and voter registration so that its fellow citizens can begin to regain some control over their own lives. It provides business technical assistance and small business loans so that the pioneer entrepreneurs can lay a solid economic foundation for the community. At the same time, the Center also facilitates the maintenance of former languages and cultures so that these new Americans and their children retain their roots, their identity, and their dignity as complete human beings.

We want both integration and identity for several reasons. First and more practically, as an ethnic minority with distinct skin color and facial features, Southeast Asians cannot become white Anglo-Saxons as the "melting pot" would like. We can accommodate, adapt, and acculturate, but we can never assimilate. Second, the United States has changed and is well on its way to becoming a truly pluralistic society; thus the ability to retain one's culture and language is fast becoming a source of pride rather than a cause for embarrassment. Third, it is an advantage for the United States—economically, politically, and diplomatically—to have citizens who are multilingual and multicultural. Having statespersons, professionals, scientists, business people, artists, and even soldiers who are fluent not only in English but also in another language is a definite asset for this country in dealing with the rest of the world. And lastly, it is the right thing to do.

To reach this balance of integration and identity, we at CSEARR pursue a three-pronged strategy: social services, economic and community development, and political participation. Essentially a social service agency, we also know that the

Center is only as stable and effective as the community is influential, thus this strategy.

While social services are the fundamental requirement that every community has to provide to its members, those same services are effective and lasting only if buttressed by a certain amount of political and economic weight. On the other hand, pure economic or political power, without ties to community services, runs the risk of losing its proper perspective and often ends up chasing power for its own sake. And naturally, political power does not exist in a vacuum without economic power, either as cause or effect, or both.

Firmly rooted in this strategy, the Center has provided consistent quality and innovative social services to fellow Southeast Asians since 1975 and will continue to do so in the future. It has facilitated the establishment and development of hundreds of small businesses owned and operated by Southeast Asians. It has formed a revolving loan fund to help businesses that have no access to standard capital. It has encouraged community people to become citizens, to register to vote, to actually vote, and increasingly to run for offices as well. Concurrently, it has hosted candidates' forums without endorsements and used communications media to educate the community on issues of importance. These economic and nonpartisan political activities will continue in the foreseeable future.

But the Center should not, and cannot, stand still in time. By laws of nature, we all evolve, and the Southeast-Asian community is no exception. By 1994, two factors come into play and alter significantly the operation of the Center: a new generation has come of age and the United States no longer bans Vietnam as an enemy country.

The children who were born in the summer and fall of 1975 to parents who were the earliest refugees to this country are now going to college. Not only are they citizens, they have grown up all their lives in relative peace and stability, and have been educated completely in English. They have little experience of Vietnam, Cambodia, and Laos, but rather impressions gathered from family talks, school books, their peers, and the media. They are curious about their countries of origin; they want to know and understand them better; in many cases they also want to help; and almost universally, they want to be proud of their origins. To this generation, and by extension to most Southeast Asians born after 1960, the war is a distant occurrence that affected their lives through other people and circumstances rather than directly.

In February 1994 when the United States lifted the trade embargo imposed on Vietnam—first on North Vietnam in 1964 and against the whole unified country after 1975—this country in effect recognized for the first time that Vietnam is a sovereign country in the family of nations. Until this time, relationship between the two countries had always been abnormal. When the Vietnamese emperor first wrote to President Abraham Lincoln in the mid-nineteenth century and just before the French invasion of Indochina, his attempt was ignored. Toward the end of World

War II, the U.S. Intelligence Service used a faction among the Vietnamese freedom fighters, led by Ho Chi Minh, to gather intelligence on the Japanese in southern China and Indochina. But when the French insisted on resuming its colonial empire, Washington tipped the balance in favor of a European ally and at the expense of an Asian country about which it knew very little. After the Vietnamese defeated the French in 1954, cold war fever prompted the United States, once again, to make another wrong move; it propped up the anticommunist side in Vietnam as a proxy to stem the red tide. From that time on, South Vietnam was a puppet to be manipulated at will, while North Vietnam was the enemy.

The situation presents CSEARR with both a challenge and an opportunity. The distance in time from the Vietnam experience allows the Southeast-Asian community to take a fresher look at itself and perhaps organize itself more effectively; this same distance also weakens the links, and thereby identification, with the countries of origin. The recognition of Vietnam, Cambodia, and Laos as sovereign countries places the Southeast Asian issue on a different level; no longer is it strictly a refugee issue, no longer is it strictly a humanitarian endeavor to help these poor countries, and no longer can the United States manipulate or bomb these countries. Good, beneficial relations with Southeast Asia are in the U.S. national interest. Yet, even as the future beckons, one cannot ignore the past; and one reality is that adult refugees came to this country as a protest against the existing regimes in Southeast Asia. Many have mellowed, have accepted the changes, and even began looking forward to an improved homeland. Others, however, still carry open wounds from the war and its aftermath; in their eyes, the mere recognition of the regimes they fought so bitterly is an act of treason.

As a community-based agency, the Center for Southeast Asian Refugee Resettlement finds itself once again at a historical crossroad. But the choice is clear: it has to stay with the community in order to serve it well; it must meet the needs of the majority of its constituency without neglecting the minority; it must look forward without diminishing the collective heritage, and it must remain relevant to the future generations of Americans of Southeast-Asian descent. In short, the Center itself has to evolve, just like the community it serves.

As we prepare for a new millennium, no one among us is immune from the effects of the revolutionary changes taking place all around this planet, and few of us can remain unmoved by these events. It is hardly an overstatement any more to claim that all of us are taking some part in these momentous events and that we are, in effect, shaping a new human dynamic for the next century. These are heady days; a little scary, but full of hope.

It is in this context of global revolution that the very small Southeast-Asian community in the United States intends to make its modest contribution to human development by replacing the "melting pot" assimilation model with a new strategy of accelerated and balanced integration. It is applicable not only to ethnic minorities in the United States, but to all ethnic groups everywhere. Before 1990, such a strategy was deemed excessively optimistic, if not altogether unrealistic. In light of the ongoing fundamental changes in the way we think and behave, anyone who lives in only one culture and functions in only one environment will be a disadvantaged person. An accelerated and balanced integration—not just by the minority community but also by the majority population of society—has become the best vehicle to brave the new world. This is what community organizing is all about.

## *Endnote*

1. For the purpose of this chapter, "Southeast Asian" refers to refugees and immigrants from three countries only: Cambodia, Laos, and Vietnam. It is accurate when used in the context of the refugee status because the United States currently recognizes no refugees from any other Southeast-Asian country. The author concedes that the term is less accurate in a more general sense, though preferable to "Indochinese," a vestige from the French colonial days. The use of Southeast Asian is also a vehicle to unite and organize the three nationalities by emphasizing the common bonds and circumstances of people in similar situations but who had much to disagree about in their respective pasts.

# 12

*Community Development and Restoration: A Perspective*

ANTONIA PANTOJA AND WILHELMINA PERRY

Community work in the United States has been arbitrarily divided into two broad major areas: economic development and community development. These two areas of theory and practice are separated by the professions and disciplines. Policymakers, government agencies, and funding sources support the separation. In this artificial separation, economic development is viewed as a highly technical area dominated by the professions of business, economics, and planning. Experts in these areas, predominantly males, labor to create a community economic infrastructure of housing, physical facilities, and local economic ventures as well as the introduction of large outside industries that will create employment for residents of the targeted communities. This work is generally devoid of considerations of human development, community control, community education, and community ownership of the enterprises that create employment and create local wealth.

The separation is further sustained in communities because the human service and the social work professions work in services unrelated to the economic development activities. They create the social services, the human development, and community education programs, and the broad array of social welfare programs.

In the real world of community practice and in the world of academia, these two groups function with little or no contact with each other. The lack of an approach that is holistic, integrated, and culturally relevant has sustained the dependency of our communities and impeded the authentic processes of empowerment, community participation, community control, and the emergence of a local economic system that would provide local employment and develop local wealth.

This is not to argue naively that a holistic and integrated approach, in and of itself, will magically dismantle the institutionalization of neocolonialism but, without such an approach, we surely deny our communities the opportunities for meaningful engagement with the problems that they face.

If development work continues to be imposed and orchestrated from the outside or by the technical experts, there will be no sustained physical or human development. Economic analysis and understanding will escape the community residents, and human development efforts will continue to avoid the crucial need for the groups to attain their own economic empowerment.

In our work, as faculty practitioners and members of oppressed communities (African-American, Puerto-Rican, and women) we have been searching for ways to integrate theory and practice for community economic development. In our minds, the artificial separation must end. Economic development is central to the work of community development.

The values and the method that we use in our work have a philosophy that is developmental and nurturing. The knowledge base is holistic and does not fragment the human experience into separate distinct pieces. The method of work is nonaggressive. The acquisition of power is not a central objective, although power is recognized as an essential resource. Evaluation and corrective mechanisms are constants in our teaching and work processes.

This chapter is written for people who want to find a way to liberate their communities. We have used our teaching and practice to find a way to organize and test conceptual and practice models for restoring our communities to more holistic and productive functioning—communities that fulfill the needs of its members. Mythology aside, we do not live in an integrated society. We live in pluralistic communities within the larger white society. These communities are created both by chance, preference, and exclusion. They must be given the necessary resources and help to survive.

## What Is Community? Definitions

### Community as Geographic Locale: Vignette #1

*In early January 1985, we arrived at our farm in Cubuy. Living in the hills and on a farm was entirely foreign to both of us. We quickly learned that two women living alone would need some help with the heavy work. John*

*Luis, a young man in the area, was a member of a crew of handymen that helped us out. As custom requires, he became like a family member rather than simply a "stateside" handyman. He was unemployed and his prospects for a job were dismal. We began to informally involve him in sessions on entrepreneurship skills. Eventually, he asked whether his friends and family members could join him in these sessions. Before we could proceed to accept his suggestion, John Luis explained that we had to talk with his family and the parents of other youths who would be coming. We visited homes to introduce ourselves and explain the purpose of the youth sessions. Before long, the sessions expanded to formal Saturday morning meetings with eight of his relatives and friends.*

*Word spread around the small village that two "American" teachers from California had come to live in the area and that they were teaching the children. Within a week, John Luis brought a verbal invitation for us to present ourselves at a meeting of the local association. Not knowing what to expect, we arrived at the meeting fully equipped, carrying documentation as to who we were. We were seated in a small room opposite eight older gentlemen and one woman who never spoke throughout the meeting. The men were dressed in the true "jibaro" style. They wore sparkling clean and ironed "guayaberas." We introduced ourselves and they asked why we had come to their village. We spoke for several hours. At the end, fully satisfied, the association asked us to work with the entire community in solving its serious unemployment problem. We told the association that we needed a planning and action committee. They named a committee, immediately including some of those present and others whom they could notify. Our work began that night. Every Thursday evening we met to plan and create a model for action. As a result of our work, Producir, Inc., an economic and community development corporation, was legally incorporated in June 1986.*

The two barrios are connected by custom, history, language, church affiliation, and family relationships. In spite of hardships, people wish to remain in the area. Our distance from the municipality (thirty minutes by car) binds us together as residents to handle and solve problems that we must face together, such as electricity blackouts, the shutoff of water, lack of public transportation, difficult and ill-kept roads, flooding caused by continuous rain, and lack of all the basic services that one takes for granted in an urban area.

## Community of Interest: Vignette #2

*I can remember as a child attending a Black Holiness church with my dad. My dad was a deacon and the treasurer of the church. We were "Deacon Ward's daughters" and members of an extensive network of relationships.*

*Just as we had our identity and the accompanying expectations for conduct and behavior, the sisters, deacons, mothers, and ushers had their respective identities, and we all lived out a full set of behavior during the week and on Sundays. We performed a standard unchanging set of behavior at funerals, and we celebrated in song and worship the new members that joined the flock. I can remember longing to be "saved" and to have the opportunity to participate in these joyous activities. Those who violated the customs and rules were called "back sliders," and they were dealt with severely. However, punishment was always delivered with compassion and forgiveness. We knew of each other's problems and we cared for each other.*

*In my memories, the doctrines of the particular religious teachings have long disappeared. What I remember is the sense of belonging, identity, and community that was created in a small building on 141st Street in Harlem.*

A second type of community can be a group of people who have no physical location that they own or inhabit, but that are bound together by historical and/or contemporary circumstances; racial, religious, or national origins; and who share a common set of values, mutual expectations, and aspirations. In this typology of community there are many groups that we consider reflective of the cultural pluralism movement. Among these groups are communities of ethnic groupings, homosexuals, women, seniors, physically impaired, environmentalists, religious groups, etc.

Most of our work has been done in locality-based communities, and we will proceed from this information base. However, we maintain that our model of community development also has usefulness for emerging communities of special interests.

## *Community Origins and Functions: Vignette #3*

*A tragic and violent incident occurred in our community last year. Two young men from two large families were drinking in a newly opened discotheque and they became involved in a bad argument. Rumor had it that they were drunk or under the influence of drugs. Harsh words were exchanged and one of the men hit the other. A more serious fight was avoided by removing the contenders from the premises. The next weekend, members of both families were at the discotheque when it opened for business. The man who had struck the first blow the week before was about to apologize when his victim shot him. He also shot his brother who had come to his aid. Everyone ran out of the bar, including the two wounded men. One of them fell to the ground, the gunman jumped into his truck, ran over his two victims, killing them, and fled into the woods.*

*The next day, the news of the terrible incident was being discussed all over the close-knit community. All agreed that the discotheque was not a desirable addition to the community. Everyone agreed that the shooting was a terrible thing, but to have run over the wounded men was brutal and insane. A delegation of three neighbors, members of the Board of Producir, went to see the police officer on duty at the local station. The police officer's response was that the community was blowing the incident out of proportion and that the incident was the result of a feud between the two families. Police action would take place in due time. The officer told the delegation to stay out of the situation and leave matters to the police. By the following day, the community was boiling with discussion groups. Some urged speaking to the family of the victims. Members of the family wished to go after the killers and still others wanted to hold a community meeting to discuss the situation and to take some action before things got out of control. Everyone agreed that the discotheque must be removed.*

*Community leaders asked the president of the community development corporation to call a community meeting that Thursday. The meeting was announced at churches; notice was sent to parents with school children and announced by loudspeaker throughout the area. Preparations for the meeting started Monday. The announcements were made Tuesday. The family of the victims was invited. On Wednesday, a delegation asked the regional police to attend the meeting. The meeting packed the community center. Residents gave their condolences to the relatives of the victims. The regional police were represented by the area commander, the chief of the drug and vice squad, the captain of the township, and local officers. The mayor also came. The meeting covered an agenda designed by the residents, the "Asociación Cívico Social," and the Community Development Corporation.*

*The first order of business, after introducing the purpose of the community meeting, was to hand over to the grieving mother of the victims an amount of money collected in the community to help with the funeral and other needs of the family. Residents insisted that the police give assurances that the suspect would be apprehended and brought to trial. The brothers of the victims said that they would abide by the police handling of the matter. The assembly then discussed the matter of the discotheque. Both the police and the mayor said that the business was proper because it had its licenses and permits. The community was adamant. Outsiders from downtown established the discotheque, and were suspect. These outsiders could introduce illegal activities in the barrio which the community would find difficult to prevent. The business, located next to a church, violated the law by selling liquor, the residents said. They added that the business was bringing in women from the outside to work as waitresses and entertainers, that the law against serving minors was not observed, and that they were not convinced that drugs were not being sold in the establishment. The meeting concluded with everyone requesting that the law and other persua-*

*sive methods be used to close the discotheque. The discotheque never reopened. The murder suspect was apprehended, tried in court, and found guilty.*

Many traditional sociologists, writers, and social observers will say that communities no longer exist. They characterize communities as inventions of primitive and prehistoric people. We are even taught that a desire to belong to a community is an outdated need not entertained by sophisticated people who are socially or physically mobile. They arrived at this conclusion by noting the following conditions:

- Neighborhoods (geographic entities) are no longer intact because modern people come and go, meeting their needs in different institutions of the total society.
- The community functions of mutual support, social control, socialization, and defense that were once met in local neighborhoods are now met for all people by the state through commonly shared and supported government agencies.
- Work, as the basic economic function that once held people together, is now performed wherever it is best for the production process and the market, and companies no longer feel it is necessary to be located where the workers live.

These statements serve three purposes: (1) they postulate the idea that the human person is an island unto him or herself and that this condition of "aloneness" is the natural and preferred state; (2) they deny and negate the tenacity of the human community and the inventiveness of people to sustain themselves within social groupings that meet their needs; and (3) they promote the destructiveness of human communities by devaluing all forms that do not meet some traditional norm.

Why is it necessary to destroy the realities of communities and even to deny the concept of community? We think that by doing so a process is set in motion that separates the individual from his or her group and standards of behavior, expectations, and support systems. Each person is rendered vulnerable and weak, and each person becomes a potential employee left to negotiate his or her own "contracts" in the marketplace. Each person who is not a member of the dominant group of the society becomes a potential absorber of the products and behavior of an "idealized" dominant culture. The processes that are the prerequisites and reasons for destroying the community are also the foundations for securing our society's inequitable functioning.

In a political environment, where individuals are constantly being disconnected from their communities, the dominant group in our society retains control. No equally strong community group or coalition of smaller communities ever effectively challenges its power base.[1]

## Community: Model for Analysis

Over time, we have developed a model for analyzing community to provide an organized way of approaching community development work. We found it necessary to proceed in this way because we found in our work with learners that they held unexpressed ideas that communities were created by metaphysical processes, or they had never intellectually examined the origin of community. Their knowledge base of anthropology and sociology had been so completely fragmented or discarded that learners who were members of oppressed communities were not able to understand and accept that their people had originally made communities and had the power, capacities, and right to continuously search and recreate more perfect forms for their well-being and meeting their basic needs (see Figure 12.1 on page 224).

Once learners acquired an understanding and acceptance of the right and need for change, it became necessary to have a guide (road map) by which analysis and action could occur within some rational, orderly, and sequential series of steps by which community restoration/development could occur.

Using a multidisciplinary knowledge base for our work, we have organized a coherent explanation as to how and why the human group invented community. Based on a perspective of the human person that is multidimensional, the model helps the community worker to understand how people, who are the creators of communities, can reconstruct them again and again when changes are required and/or desired for the continuing survival of the group. Our working model relates each human need to a system of institutions that were invented by people to fulfill their needs in a collective human system, that is, the community.

In our model of community development/restoration (of which parts are presented in this chapter) the most crucial and essential function of community is the function of production, distribution, and consumption.[2] This function is performed by a series of institutions related to human work that form the economic system of a community. Without this function and the systems that perform it, the human group cannot adequately survive.

Other functions of community were invented by humans to satisfy other needs and to support the economic function. These functions include:

- *The socialization function,* to teach the members of the community the accumulated knowledge (the science and technology, the history of the group, the language to communicate, the norms, rules and customs).
- *The social control function,* to create rules, laws, accepted behavior, and the punishments or rewards for violating or accepting these standards and the institutions that would create, enforce, and reward.
- *The social placement function,* to institute associations, groupings, and ceremonies that would help each member of the group to accept it and find a position in it, and to be accepted and be given recognition by the group.

Dimensions:

Basic Needs:

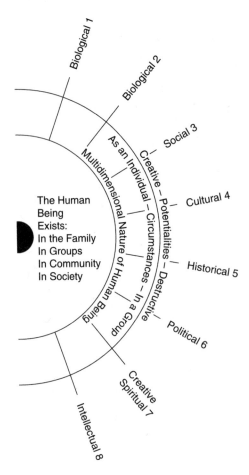

1. Food, water, shelter, clothing, medicine, exercise, rest, recreation, work tools, machines, sexual expression
2. Love, belonging, identity
3. To exist in groups and patterns of relationships, to locate oneself in relation to others, to form groups and associations, help from others in time of emergency
4. Express ideas in symbols (language, art); to celebrate life in ceremonies, rituals and festivals; to establish norms, values and customs
5 To tell and record the deeds of the group and of individuals, to study the past to evaluate the present events
6. To use power to control, to attack, to defend, to protect, to create order through rules, laws, organizing systems
7. To depict the past, the present and the future through pictorial forms, color, sound, words, acting, movement, to explain that which is not known
8. To find explanations, interconnecting the nature of things: environment, the elements, nature and natural phenomena; to develop knowledge to control the elements of nature; to investigate and experiment

**FIGURE 12.1 Nature of the Human Being: Her/His Dimensions and the Needs These Create**

- *The function of mutual support,* to develop an array of institutions and relationships that would ensure that each member of the group would be assisted and provided for in times and circumstances of emergency or extreme need.
- *The function of defense,* to create a manner through which the group and its members would be protected against attack and dangers from within the group and from outside the group.

- *The function of communication,* including mobility and expression, to create a common language and symbols (verbal, written, pictorial, and expression through sound), to create methods of moving in space, and methods of expression of ideas and expressions of the senses.

These functions and the institutions that perform them vary from one human community to another according to geographical, historical, cultural, and other circumstances that surround the particular group (see Table 12.1 on page 226).

## Communities Becoming Dysfunctional: Forces at Work

We do not believe that minority communities want to live in slums with dilapidated housing and drug-infested schools. People suffer these conditions because they become powerless and unable to correct the situations that destroy their well-being. We believe that our communities have been abandoned by the institutions to whom we have relinquished control for community services. Our children are not educated by the public schools. Our housing is inadequate or nonexistent. The police do not protect our neighborhoods. The churches in our neighborhoods preach and talk to one another. The public welfare services operate as instruments to define and promote morality and behavior. With all these circumstances, the tenacity and perseverance of the human community is clearly demonstrated in the retaining of their language, their families, their culture, the secure and enduring social affiliations, and mutual support systems.

We maintain that people who live in rural and urban communities function with kinship bonds, communication networks, and communal relationships. These are the functions that the larger society allows to exist or does not destroy in processes of institutional controls or cultural domination (internal neocolonialism). Dysfunctional internal processes are precipitated by the destruction of the "economizing function" that is primary and central to a community's stability. Once this function is destroyed, all other supportive functions become severely impaired or deteriorated. Without the right to work, to be productive, there can be no legitimate roles. Community members are rendered economically impotent and dependent with some subsequently internalizing this dependency and abandoning their rights and privileges to be in charge of their own communities.

Throughout history, all communities have developed the functions of community that we have discussed above. However, some communities have emphasized one function over another. We do not know why some communities expand, become aggressive, and use their power and technology to conquer and absorb others. It is as if the function of defense had been viciously twisted and turned into attack. Various explanations can be found in literature and in the writings of other disciplines. To our knowledge, there is no empirical data to explain these activities.

**TABLE 12.1   List of Human Needs and the Systems and Institutions That Function to Satisfy Them**

| Dimension | Need | Systems of Institutions | Functions |
|---|---|---|---|
| Biological | • Food<br>• Shelter<br>• Water<br>• Tools/Machines<br>• Clothing<br>• Medicine<br>• Rest & Recreation | • Economic Systems | Production<br>Distribution<br>Consumption<br>(Work—convert<br>resources into<br>goods & services) |
| Social<br>Psychological<br>Cultural | • Medicine<br>• Sexual expression for pleasure and recreation<br>• Patterns of relationships Language verbal & non-verbal | • Family System<br>• Education System<br>• Religious System<br>• Linguistic System | Socialization<br>Communication |
| Political | • Using controlling/destructive potentialities of power<br>• Need for protection from inside and outside forces that would destroy, capture assets, resources, people | • The State/Nation<br>• Government System<br>• Family System<br>• Religious System<br>• Judicial/Penal System<br>• Legislative System<br>• Police<br>• Military System<br>• Family System | Social Control<br>Defense |
| Historical<br>Cultural<br>Psychological | • Tell and retell events and acts of heroic figures<br>• Provide a way of locating oneself in a social context<br>• Need for identity and belonging | • Civic Participation System<br>• Historical Societies<br>• Museum Associations<br>• Clubs, Civic Organizations<br>• Social Organizations | Social Integration |
| Creative<br>Imaginative | • Record in symbolic and actual language life of group<br>• Need to explain that which is not immediately known<br>• Need to depict the world as it was, as it is, as it would be using common symbols and the senses | • Folk object festivals<br>• Art disciplines<br>• Religious institutions<br>• Philosophical schools of thinking | |
| Intellectual | • Desire to find explanations, relationships, connections, answers about nature of things, events, environment and its elements<br>• Use of knowledge to control the elements of nature | • Education System<br>• Scientific & Technological System<br>• Philosophical System | Socialization |
| Social<br>Psychological<br>Cultural | • Help to individual or group when established functions go wrong | • Social Welfare System<br>• Religious System<br>• Family System<br>• Friends<br>• Neighbors | Mutual Support |

Therefore, we use world history and analysis as the basic sources for our understanding.

Historically, some human communities have attacked other communities to use their economic productivity, their territory and natural resources, their scientific and technological knowledge, or the labor-power of their people. Over time, through aggressive activities of conquest and annexation, these communities become nations with great accumulated wealth, large landed territory, slaves, armies and low-paid workers. These nations acquire colonies to provide raw natural resources and to provide potential customers to purchase finished manufactured and processed goods and products. Members of the conquered and colonized communities have been brought into the metropolises of the great aggressive nation-empires to become part of the large numbers of unknowing and low-paid workers. These imported groups become the impoverished internal colonies that suffer great social problems.

Today and within the context of our national sphere, these destructive forces are institutionalized and sanctioned, not only through public policies, but through traditions, customs, and values taught in school to the general population. Minority group communities are denied their rights, access to information, and knowledge. They are denied access to protection of the law by denying them participation in the political processes that govern the country.

The dynamics and mechanisms of destruction are now less direct and obvious. Because they are covert, they are more difficult to identify. Their impact is so insidious that the victims are blamed for their own situation and, ultimately, they learn to blame themselves. We are at a time in the history of our minority communities when racial oppression, political and economic disenfranchisement, withdrawal of basic social supports and services, and internal crime threaten to destroy completely any solidifying ties that hold people together in the ghettos and barrios of the United States. The threat also applies to any solidarity that existed among different groups of disenfranchised and oppressed peoples. We know, however, that no matter how destroyed a community may appear to be, some members are willing to rebuild their lives and the life of their community to obtain a better situation for themselves and their families.

It is around these desires and expectations that community development and community restoration take root. In the United States during the 1960s and 1970s, as people grew in consciousness of the forces of destruction described above, they began to analyze how their communities become destroyed. It is within this analysis and learning that members acquired "conscientization" and that community building and development must take place.

The work of community development must begin with the worker and the community identifying:

- What functions of the community have been destroyed?
- Which are still functional and which are dysfunctional?
- What are the forces at work that destroy the community?
- What are the destructive forces emanating from the colonizing process?

- What are the destructive forces that are set in motion in the total society to keep colonized members of the community in a state of oppression?
- What are the forces that keep community members subjugated and colonized and in a state of subjugation and oppression?

Once these realities are understood, the rebuilding process can begin on solid ground.

## What Makes an Effective Community Development Worker? Vignette #4

*It is not my purpose to tell a story, but rather give you a slice of my life and the types of experiences that have shaped me as a community worker. I grew up in a barrio of Santurce called Barrio Obrero (the village of workers). This was a section of the new city of San Juan that had been built as a housing project for World War I veterans. Our family was well-known throughout the community because my grandfather, my uncle, my mother, and one aunt worked at the cigar factory at the entrance of Old San Juan. Grandfather knew all the other cigar makers who lived in Barrio Obrero and worked at the American Tobacco Company. When the idea to organize a union to secure better wages for the workers in the factory began to take root, my grandfather was a key person to hold meetings in that area. The contacts were made in the evening on Avenue A where there was a gathering place around a "friquitín" (a corner business where a woman fried codfish wrapped in dough, "bacalaítos," and plantain dough with stewed meat in the middle, "alcapurrias"). Men came to buy the fried products and take a shot of rum. They discussed politics standing around a homemade stove, a large can where wood would burn and a large iron cauldron with boiling oil fried the frituras. This was an excellent place to meet everyone if a meeting was called and to present and debate ideas. Meetings where more formal agendas were decided were called in a worker's house.*

*I was six years old, a very curious, introspective, and quiet child. My grandfather, Conrado, was a very dear person to me. I thought him to be handsome, distinguished, and very wise. Periodically the group of men organizing the union would meet in our humble house till late hours of the night. My grandmother would prepare a salad called "serenata," made of boiled potatoes cut in slices, raw onions, scales of dried codfish, slices of pepper, olives, oil, and vinegar. The men discussed mixing loud cursing phrases interspersed into their arguments for this or that point.*

*I had been put to bed to get me out of the way of adult business, but I would get up and sneak near the bedroom door so that I could peek at the group. The discussion would reach me in pieces, I would hear cursing, which would scare me, but I remained glued to the scene of the men around the table, with long spirals of gray smoke going up from their heads from the cigars they smoked. At that age, I did not know why they held the meetings, why they were angry, but one evening a group of men carried my grandfather in arms and everyone commented that the union breakers at the friquitín, where cigar workers gathered, had thrown boiling oil on his hands. Grandmother was very upset and I began to cry but then I stopped when I heard the men say that the nurse at the dispensary had said the hands were not badly burned. Since this incident, I concluded that organizing is done by and with working people; that organizing is a dangerous activity since people who do not want you to organize could attack you and hurt you. Although I never understood then the full meaning of the meetings in our house, later I learned that they met to ask for changes in their wages and in the conditions of their workplace. The owners retaliated employing people to hit the main organizers. The workers went on strike and were out many, many months. I heard adults in our house talk about the strike being a success. Since that strike, our family suffered from the deterioration and the extreme poverty that comes from unemployment of all the wage earners in a household. The workers won the strike, but the owners packed the machines and tools in crates and left Puerto Rico. The factory was closed.*

*This experience, early in my childhood, gave me an opportunity to suffer close to me injustice and to incorporate in myself what all adults, whom I respected, were saying about this event. My grandfather and his friends said: "Rather than share the wealth they were making from the skill of our hands, those bastards removed our source of honest work. They left us to starve with our successful strike. The sons of bitches. All we asked was a miserable increase to help us feed our families." I learned that life for those people, "like us," was hard and that we had to learn how to fight against "the sons of bitches" (words I was not supposed to use but which I repeated in my head in quiet murmurs). I also learned that to struggle against whatever evils will come, one had to join together with others who suffered also. I began my education early.*                                    *A. P.*

## *Vignette #5*

*I am the daughter of a union organizer. My father became the founding president of the first integrated union for employees of the Pennsylvania Railroad System. Talks of discrimination and the system's inequities were a constant part of our getting together at the dinner table. We were taught that strategies of picketing, demonstrations, and legal petitions were rightful actions to correct social injustices. Social change has always been something that I considered necessary to correct injustices that black people experienced. Change was a goal to make the larger society better, but changing ourselves was also a requirement to make ourselves more prepared for opportunities. My father, with his strong union background, taught us not to be afraid to fight for our rights and to never deny our racial heritage or our people.*

*Fiery and angry words at the dinner table were moderated in the outside world by a strong religious affiliation typical of most black families, with roots in the South. Religion contributed a mixture of forgiveness, peacefulness, and perseverance.*                                              *W. P.*

In our model of community development, there is no particular profession or discipline that has a monopoly on the capacity to prepare people for the work. A community development worker can be a priest, an artist, a human service professional, a social worker, a planner, or an environmentalist, among others, but all these persons must share a philosophy, a political perspective, knowledge, and methodology for working with people. We do not think that one can be fully prepared in a formal educational institution because we do not believe that the dominant society's institutions prepare people to value cultural differences—the ultimate desirability of a truly pluralistic society—nor are students taught to examine, analyze, and challenge the society's practices of inequality. We believe that education in a formal institution so partializes and fragments knowledge that it is impossible to acquire the necessary conceptual lenses to approach the holistic work that community development requires.

The worker, as a member of the community, must bring enormous energy and personal resources that can be sustained only if she or he has a deep and unswerving commitment to eliminating circumstances of economic oppression and social injustice. The decision to work in community brings one face to face with the inconsistencies of our country's professed values and democratic principles and the actual practices of institutionalized inequality and injustice. It is frequently impossible to institutionalize the desired changes or the gains accomplished. The business of oppression and racism does not go away, and social change efforts can often be characterized as "one step forward, two steps back, and so forth."

Ultimately, in community development work, it is the members of that community who will decide who is with them and who is not. They choose whom they will work with and whom they want to work with them. Community residents make these choices based on their gut reactions, their ideological views of people, and the demonstrated and informed results of their work together.

"Conscientization" is an important process in our model of work. It means that the community development workers must bring a political perspective, knowledge, and skill that community members may not initially possess. This being the case, the community development worker must face the task with willingness and conviction to allow her or his knowledge, access, influence, and resources to be used by and in behalf of the community. This permits that the work will proceed on relationships based on equal rights. The partnership will result in services, resources, knowledge, skills, and increased rights becoming available to community members. What characteristics make for an effective community development worker and how does effectiveness come about? Obviously there is no litmus test that can be applied. Table 12.2 on pages 223–233 illustrates the knowledge base, skills, characteristics, and values that we consider necessary for an effective community development worker.

## *What Is Community Development and Restoration?*[3]

New communities are constantly being created and existing communities are being adapted to survive in a changing, frequently hostile, environment. In the United States, people move in and out of several communities to meet multiple needs. Investments and affiliations vary, based on the needs being met, but most people still consider that they have a "home-base community." In fact, human beings have lived in communities throughout history because the human person cannot survive alone. We invented community because we need community.

Starting with every newborn infant and ending with the aged person and going through every age and stage of the group, people need each other to sustain activities that support life and ensure full development of the group and each of its members. Accumulated knowledge, from biology, sociology, psychology, history, the sciences of government and political relations and economics, to knowledge of art and religion attest to and explain the fact that the human species survives, even though more powerful and physically better-equipped forms of life have disappeared. This survival into full development can be traced to the human being's capacity to think (remember, analyze, synthesize, and integrate). Human groupings have used these capacities to provide for the basic needs of the group and its members using the human resources and resources of the environment in different ways according to the natural circumstances in which they find themselves. These differences are called culture.

In our community development restoration activities, we are intervening in an environment that has become destructive to people, and we are acting to influence, direct, and reshape energies, values, and work efforts toward a more desired functioning. We use community development/restoration with a specific meaning. It has philosophy, a definition of goals and products. It also has a methodology consistent with the philosophy and an evaluatory process from the beginning to the end.

We emphasize development to reinforce the participatory and educational goals involved in community work. Community development, as we define it, rests heavily on a series of developmental processes, but the tangible, concrete end-product goals are equally significant, and development/restoration cannot take place unless process and product goals are equally valued and operationalized. Community development requires timely realized products that have both short- and long-term accomplishments and impact. We are talking about products and outcomes that include worker/owner business ventures, cooperatives owned by the community

**TABLE 12.2  What Characteristics Make for an Effective Community Development Worker?**

| Basic Formal and Preparatory Experiences | Basic Prerequisites, Philosophical and Political World Views | Basic Characteristics and Skill Base | Knowledge Base |
|---|---|---|---|
| • No particular prior profession and/or educational experience is required.<br>• Positive experiences in which the person experiences her/himself as a member of a community.<br>• Direct experiences with discriminatory circumstances and/or practices of being excluded because of one's membership in a particular group.<br>• A member (by birth and/or acceptance) of the community in which work is to be undertaken.<br>• Sufficient skills in working with people who have gained knowledge, confidence in her/his interactional skills and her/his abilities to understand and influence others. | Believe that:<br>• The human person should be viewed as a multi-dimensional person with multiple needs emanating from this nature.<br>• People do not choose to live or survive alone.<br>• The human community is an invention of people to meet current and changing human needs.<br>• Culture groups differ in their environmental context and adaptation to environment, and it is around these adaptations and choices that cultures are made.<br>• Intolerance for injustice and commitment to equal opportunities and access. | • Planning and management skills.<br>• Communication skills.<br>• Problem-solving skills.<br>• Analytical and conceptual skills.<br>• Flexibility.<br>• Investigative and evaluative skills.<br>• Creativity and inventiveness.<br>• Curiosity and an exploratory approach to problem-solving.<br>• Self-confidence and integration as a person.<br>• Ability to recognize, mobilize, and integrate resources within a work effort.<br>• Ability to work, within time constraints, to realize product and process goals. | • A working conceptual base that allows for an acceptance and willingness to use knowledge holistically from these areas:<br>• Definitions, functions, and origins of community (Anthropology).<br>• Social systems functioning (organizational theory).<br>• Basics of economic anthropology.<br>• Political science (theories of community power, use of power in political arenas, origins, functions, processes of social policy, analyzing social and group interaction policy arenas).<br>• Social change theories, strategies, community organizing models (social work). |

**TABLE 12.2** *(Continued)*

| | | |
|---|---|---|
| • Sufficient skills in working with people to have understanding and appreciation of others, their personal differences, cultural context, and behaviors as members of groups and communities.<br>• Physical strength and endurance to work hard and long hours. | • Human persons cannot realize maximum productivity and fulfillment living alone and/or isolated from relationships with others.<br>• Human groups that identify themselves as communities have the right to define their needs and create/control the systems necessary to meet these needs.<br>• The human community is made dysfunctional when its needs are controlled from the outside.<br>• A community that may appear to be in the process of dysfunction has the desire and internal capabilities for restoration/redevelopment processes. | • Ability to learn, acquire new knowledge, integrate, change and adapt to new ideas and information.<br>• Specific skills as may be required by particular program activities such as fund-raising, entrepreneurial, business development.<br>• Patience and respect for a truly democratic way of working with others.<br>• One must become a continuous learner with an appreciation of the fact that learning can come from many sources. | • Leadership development theories.<br>• Perspectives on racism, feminism, and agism.<br>• Traditional and radical analysis of the development of U.S., particularly U.S. history as it relates to its colonies, internal and external.<br>• Definitions, manifestations, and uses of culture.<br>• Definitions and perspectives on cultural pluralism.<br>• Origins of language and relationship of language to culture.<br>• Comparative philosophies and definitions of the human person.<br>• Basic concepts and principles of logic and community.<br>• Sociology of knowledge.<br>• Perspectives on "creative education" and analytical thinking.<br>• Theories of role performance, social and group interaction. |

members, cultural activities, and celebrations reinforcing and securing the group's history and values, and social service delivery systems cooperatively or collectively owned by community members.

In our definition, community development/restoration is the work with people through which members of an economically dependent and politically disenfranchised community accept to work together with the following purposes:

1. To understand the forces and processes that have made them and keep them in their state of poverty and dependency.
2. To mobilize and organize their internal strength, as represented in political awareness, a plan of action based on information, knowledge, skills, and financial resources.
3. To eradicate from individuals and from group culture the mythology that makes them participants in their own dependency and powerlessness.
4. To act in restoring or developing new functions that a community performs for the well-being of its members—starting with the economizing function.

Development involves people working in a process of understanding, acquiring skills and knowledge, and learning how to use new information that can change the circumstances of their lives. By development, we mean:

- A process of education that allows people to analyze and understand forces that create and sustain the integrity and conditions of exclusion for persons such as themselves.
- A process of education by which people come to know they possess strength, knowledge, and skills; they can access, value, and utilize their individual and collective resources as they can be integrated into community development goals.
- A process of education in which people are learning how their activities, values, fears, and behaviors allow them to be victimized.
- A process by which community members learn to defend themselves against forces, inside and outside their community, that would deny them their rights, resources, and privileges.

## *What Is Community Restoration and Development? Major Processes*

We are presenting the model of practice included in this chapter as the guide for our current work. Through continuing practice and study, we expect to develop it to its fullest potential. The project and its work are done within the context of activities of a movement in which symbols, myth, campaign, and slogans are significant in involving people to secure their emotional investment as well as their commitments.

The model will be presented in three phases and our work in Producir, Inc., Cubuy and Lomas, Puerto Rico, will be used to demonstrate our philosophy, principles, and methods of work. The following illustration represents the community development model as it is operationalized in Producir, Inc. (See Figure 12.2 on page 238.) Each of the four organizational components was developed with the community functional areas in mind. While each organizational component may carry aspects of all seven functions, each has a primary function.

- Phase I: Contract-making between community development worker and community.
- Phase II: Development of political awareness and the decolonization process within the action planning body.
- Phase III: Activities of community development/community restoration within the total community. (See Table 12.3 on pages 236–237.)

## Phase I: Contract-Making

This phase involves the introduction of the community development worker to the community. We prefer that the worker be a member of the community where the work is to take place. In our case, we are residents. In the case of students of the Graduate School,[4] all learners were residents who had to receive approval and endorsement from a community agency for themselves and the basic idea for an educational plan.

The important consideration is that the community development worker must have an invitation and an endorsement for the work to be done. The worker must be accepted as a member of the community with a compatible base of experiences, values, and affiliations. As a member of the community, he or she must have the freedom to work with residents who may be challenging the legitimacy of the existing power arrangements. The worker's decision to work in community must be legitimized by (1) residents who suffer some problem that they wish to change and (2) a group that makes a commitment for comprehensive work that will require their time and energies.

Community development work cannot be undertaken by agencies controlled by outside entities or heavily funded by government. Examples of these are: agencies heavily staffed by professionals whose commitments and interests are outside the area; agencies whose missions are rooted in social welfare programs; and agencies whose personnel or past activities/accomplishments are questioned by residents.

Once a decision is made by a worker and a community group to begin working together, it is necessary to have direct and clear discussions about the mutual responsibilities and expectations. At this time, decisions are made regarding objectives, organizational base, legal considerations, funding sources, manner of working, representative nature for the working group, accountability, and communication with the community.

**TABLE 12.3  Major Phases in Community Development Work**

|  | Phase I | Phase II | Phase III |
|---|---|---|---|
| OBJECTIVE<br>A<br>N<br>D | Contract-Making<br>• Have worker and community introduction; establish agreements for work together; to form an action group (a committee or a corporation) | Developing Political Awareness<br>• Secure the organizing body<br>• Prepare a planning action committee for work to be undertaken<br>• Assess the scope and parameters of work and to make a plan of work | Community Development Activities<br>• Implement a plan of action with goals and products<br>• Organize and establish community participation beyond initial core group<br>• Add other resources to extend the core group activity<br>• Legitimize entity<br>• Provide services and activities<br>• Creation of new production and distribution ventures in cooperative modes<br>• Establish or reopen service, cultural, educational, artistic institutions<br>• Establish business entities through their delegates<br>• Community through multiple strategies of services, board membership, community activities, task groups |
| MAJOR EMPHASES | • Establish consent; roles of mutuality; defining work mission and goals; expectations for products and outcomes | • Legitimize activity in community<br>• Refine and initiate a plan of work |  |
| PARTICIPANTS | • Community<br>• Community development worker<br>• Community group to undertake project | • Resource development<br>• Collect information from inside/outside community<br>• Analysis of information circumstances re: community<br>• Community<br>• Community development worker<br>• Outside resources |  |
| MAJOR ACTIVITIES | • Community meetings for education and information |  |  |

**TABLE 12.3** (Continued)

| SOME BASIC PRODUCTS-OUTCOMES | • Identification and meeting with leadership<br>• Identifying members of a committee or corporation composed of community members<br>• Preparing profiles of community from census data<br>• Agreement to work together with a philosophy that works<br>• Clearly stated objectives and products to be pursued<br>• Statistical profile of community | • Legally established entity for sponsoring work<br><br>• Community meetings for education and information<br>• Data collection and analysis<br>• Resource development<br>• Communicating with community and establishing processes<br>• Augmenting initial core with personnel, others<br><br>• Assessment and analysis of functions of the community<br>• A model for work and action<br>• An action body informed and ready to involve others in implementing plan | • Community development worker<br>• Community sponsoring entity<br>• Other entities providing resources<br>• New businesses open and producing<br>• Services and activities<br>• Community meetings for education and information<br>• Board and sector planning committees, meetings, and projects<br>• Resource development<br>• Institution building and leadership development<br>• A number of cooperative and worker/owner businesses<br>• New buildings, housing, businesses, services, and recreation<br>• Specific products and goals as indicated in action plan<br>• Community mobilized and in action through multiple strategies to realize goals and objectives as planned |

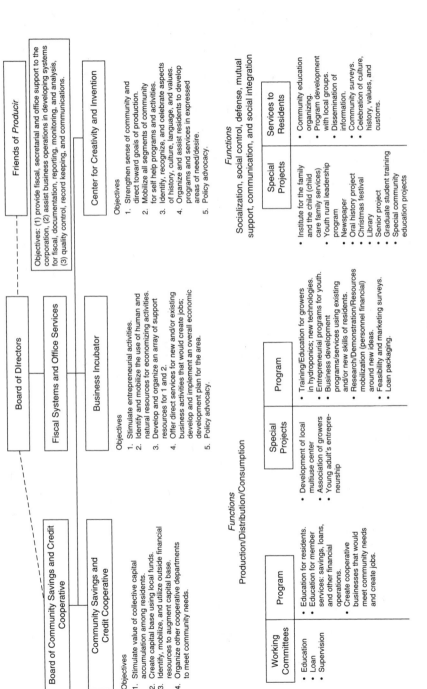

**Board of Community Savings and Credit Cooperative**

**Community Savings and Credit Cooperative**

Objectives
1. Stimulate value of collective capital accumulation among residents.
2. Create capital base using local funds.
3. Identify, mobilize, and utilize outside financial resources to augment capital base.
4. Organize other cooperative departments to meet community needs.

| Working Committees | Program |
|---|---|
| • Education<br>• Loan<br>• Supervision | • Education for residents.<br>• Education for member services: savings, loans, and other financial operations.<br>• Create cooperative businesses that would meet community needs and create jobs. |

**Board of Directors**

**Fiscal Systems and Office Services**

**Business Incubator**

Objectives
1. Stimulate entrepreneurial activities.
2. Identify and mobilize the use of human and natural resources for economizing activities.
3. Develop and organize an array of support resources for 1 and 2.
4. Offer direct services for new and/or existing business activities that would create jobs; develop and implement an overall economic development plan for the area.
5. Policy advocacy.

*Functions*
Production/Distribution/Consumption

| Special Projects | Program |
|---|---|
| • Development of local multiuse center<br>• Association of growers<br>• Young adult's entrepreneurship | • Training/Education for growers in hydroponics; new technologies.<br>• Entrepreneurial programs for youth.<br>• Business development programs/services using existing and/or new skills of residents.<br>• Research/Demonstration/Resources mobilization (personnel financial) around new ideas.<br>• Feasibility and marketing surveys.<br>• Loan packaging. |

**Friends of Producir**

Objectives: (1) provide fiscal, secretarial and office support to the corporation, (2) assist business operations in developing systems for fiscal, documentation, reporting, monitoring, and analysis, (3) quality control, record keeping, and communications.

**Center for Creativity and Invention**

Objectives
1. Strengthen sense of community and direct toward goals of production.
2. Mobilize all segments of community for self help programs and activities.
3. Identify, recognize, and celebrate aspects of history, culture, language, and values.
4. Organize and assist residents to develop programs and services in expressed areas of need/desire.
5. Policy advocacy.

*Functions*
Socialization, social control, defense, mutual support, communication, and social integration

| Special Projects | Services to Residents |
|---|---|
| • Institute for the family and the child (child care family services)<br>• Youth rural leadership program<br>• Newspaper<br>• Oral history project<br>• Christmas festival<br>• Library<br>• Senior project<br>• Graduate student training<br>• Special community education projects | • Community education organizing.<br>• Program development with local groups.<br>• Dissemination of information.<br>• Community surveys.<br>• Celebration of culture, history, values, and customs. |

**FIGURE 12.2 Community Development Model for Producir, Inc.**

238

## Phase II: Development of Political Awareness (Phases II and III May Occur Concurrently)

No work can be expected to be lasting or continued by community members unless they have grown in awareness and understanding, adopting additional skills of analyzing, planning, acting, and evaluating; secured a working relationship among themselves; tested themselves and grown in understanding, commitment, and operationalizing the mission, goals, and objectives for the work.

In the case of Producir, this phase took almost a year of weekly and ongoing meetings with a core group of ten persons selected by the local social and civic association, and it still continues with board members, personnel, and residents. Meetings were held with us and with others who handled information, content, or skill areas. During this time, the group was also engaged in activities such as writing bylaws and articles of incorporation; obtaining legal incorporation and tax-exempt status, developmental and organizational structure; acquiring an office; securing a first grant; program planning; visiting government agencies; gaining friends and supporters; fighting takeovers by a larger established entity; hiring personnel; establishing program and service priorities; and developing a process for expanding the planning/action base by adding members to the board.

The development of political awareness involves the acquisition of various types of information and content that are internalized and applied in concrete activities and for concrete goals:

- Information from residents through community surveys, available from census data, municipal data, other surveys, and local leadership, and information that allows them to analyze the situation of their community.
- A community profile of resources, institutions, services, businesses, leadership base, organization groups, needs, deficiencies, and discussions that allow for an understanding of the social stratifications within and outside the community.
- Governmental planning and economic policies regarding the area (intentions, projections, plans, uses) and beyond that have consequences for the area and allow for controls over residents.
- Basic content and conceptual lenses for the community development work (definitions, origins, nature of community, nature of social problems, nature of power, concepts of leadership, systems theory, social policy formulation, nature of human person, and belief systems about people).
- Basic skill learning—planning, fund-raising, data gathering, policy development and analysis, budgeting, grantsmanship, public presentation, analysis of information, and communication skills.
- The emphasis in this phase is always on the acquisition of information and skills; its analysis and decision-making regarding the use of the information for policy, programs, and activities, and decisions regarding the methods to be used. In this process, analysis of information and experiences is constant for

members to learn the difference between reality, gossip, and hearsay, individual experiences as contrasted with group experiences, prior indoctrinations in contrast to newly acquired information; and community development goals in contrast to the development of social service programs and activities.

This phase must culminate with the community development worker's engaging the core group in deciding whether they wish to continue in this activity. Do they have the disposition, interest, time, and energy? Can they hold themselves accountable to the community? Do they view themselves and their lives as intimately connected to the well-being of the community? Can they risk and/or protect the interest of their community?

## Phase III: Activities of Community Development and Community Restoration within the Total Community

This is the phase that has major characteristics of need assessment; augmenting the core base to include personnel and others; program planning/development; resource mobilization; setting in place the evaluating and feedback mechanism; securing the philosophy and methodology through the system; community organizing and educating for participation in the work; providing services and activities to residents; and legitimizing the entity and integrating new persons (personnel, consultants, residents, community groups).

In this model, Phase III is continuing and has no end as one usually sees in organizing models. Since the worker is a member of the community, there is no traditional exit process for her or him and there is no final transfer of power/control/authority from a professional worker to a community group. The central role of the worker is constantly shifting as new leadership constantly emerges through board membership, personnel, and neighborhood and/or community committees that assume different responsibilities for sustaining the philosophy and implementing the owner-worker work plans. New organizations, businesses, and worker-owner ventures and cooperatives are developed by residents. The board of the entity is expanding and changing with representation from various segments of the community. Because communities change, the activities of the work will change. Since the processes of destruction and deterioration are constants, the work of community development must be continuous.

## Endnotes

1. This point of view was developed in the 1950s, when progressive social scientists renewed the concept of community and analyzed the circumstances under which a community can be destroyed (Joyce Lardner, Charles Hampden-Turner, Robert Blauner, Thomas Gosset, Frantz Fanon, Albert Memmi, and others).

2. We wish to acknowledge the writings of Ronald Warren, *The Community in America;* Melville Herskovitz, *Economic Anthropology;* Frederick Engels, *The Origin of the Family, Private Property and the State,* with an Introduction by Eleanor Burke Leacock, among others, for assisting us in organizing our ideas on functions of community. These writings are listed in the references that follow.

3. We have added the concept restoration to community development to recognize that, even under the most destroyed circumstances, many functions continue to exist.

4. Doctor Pantoja and Doctor Perry established a Graduate School for Community Development, in San Diego, California, that existed from 1974 to 1983.

## *References*

Peter L. Berger and Thomas Lockman, *The Social Reconstruction of Reality* (Garden City, NY: Doubleday & Company, Inc., 1966).

Robert Blauner, *Racial Oppression in America* (New York: Harper and Row, 1982).

Frederick Engels, *The Origin of the Family, Private Property and the State,* Eleanor Burke Leacock, ed. (New York: International Publishers Co., Inc, 1972).

Paulo Freire, *Pedogogy of the Oppressed* (New York: Seabury Press, 1970).

Thomas S. Gossett, *RACE: The History of an Idea in America* (New York: Schocken Books, 1971).

Charles Hampden-Turner, *From Poverty to Dignity* (Garden City, NY: Anchor Books Paperback, Anchor Press/Doubleday, 1975).

Jacquetta Hawkes and Sir Leonard Woolley, *History of Mankind, Cultural and Scientific Development, Volume 1, Prehistory and the Beginnings of Civilization* (New York: Harper and Row, Publishers for UNESCO, 1963).

Melville J. Herskovitz, *Economic Anthropology, The Economic Life of Primitive Peoples* (New York: W.W. Norton and Company, Inc, 1952).

Inter-American Development Bank, *Community Development Theory and Practice* (Mexico City, Round Table, Inter-American Development Bank, 1966).

Thomas S. Kuhn, *The Structure of Scientific Revolutions,* 2nd ed. (Chicago: University of Chicago Press, 1970).

Joyce A. Lardner, *The Death of White Sociology* (New York: Vintage Books, A Division of Random House, 1972).

Albert Memmi, *The Colonizer and the Colonized* (Boston: Beacon Press, 1967).

Albert Memmi, *The Dominated Man* (Boston: Beacon Press, 1971).

Michael Novak, *The Rise of the Unmeltable Ethnics* (New York: Macmillan Company, 1972).

Jose Ortega y Gasset, *The Revolt of the Masses* (New York: W. W. Norton and Company Inc., 1957).

Antonia Pantoja, Wilhelmina Perry, and Barbara Blourock, "Towards the Development of Theory: Cultural Pluralism Redefined," *Journal of Sociology and Social Welfare,* 4 (September 1976), 125–146.

David Ricci, *Community Power and Democratic Theory* (New York: Random House, Inc., 1971).

Walter Rodney, *How Europe Underdeveloped Africa,* rev. ed. (Washington, D.C.: Howard University Press, 1981).

William K. Tabb, *The Political Economy of the Black Ghetto* (New York: W. W. Norton and Company, Inc., 1970).

Ronald L. Warren, *The Community in America,* 2nd ed. (Chicago: Rand McNally College Publishing Company, 1972).

Richard Weisskoff, *Factories and Food Stamps, The Puerto Rico Model of Development* (Baltimore: Johns Hopkins University Press, 1985).

These references are a partial listing of a collection of readings that we consider essential for developing a political and theoretical perspective for community development/restoration work.

# 13

*Epilogue:*
*Reaching toward*
*the Twenty-First*
*Century—Fraud in*
*the Inducement?*

*FELIX G. RIVERA AND JOHN L. ERLICH*

"As long as some citizens live in houses and others live on the streets, the Civil War is still going on, it's still to be fought," said African-American historian Barbara Fields in Ken Burns's documentary *The Civil War.* The struggles being waged by communities of color present us with some of the greatest challenges of the 1990s. When we look at the recent reversal of many of the modest gains made during the 1960s and early 1970s, the challenge to organizers is clear. The deep commitment required all too often leads to disenfranchisement, burnout, and a movement toward "safe" community organizing and less threatening social work practice in general. Like the homeless, who have too many problems—economic; drug or alcohol

243

related; other health problems, psychiatric and the like—for comfortable intervention, communities of color demand much more from us than we can comfortably
deliver.

## The Urban Centralization of Problems:
## Persisting Racial Inequality

Despite slow expansion in the suburbs, smaller towns, and rural areas, it is no
accident that the changing and emerging communities described by our authors are
largely an urban phenomenon. The inner cities within the inner cities continue to
offer shelter to new arrivals mainly because of housing costs, employment possibilities, and ethnic support structures. It is these neogemeinschaft pockets that have
been victimized by dramatically increasing poverty rates.[1] Census data demonstrates this pattern in urban ghettos and barrios.[2] There was a 59 percent rise in
poverty between 1969 and 1982, from 8 to 12.7 million. Poor inner-city African
Americans increased by 74 percent, from 3.1 million in 1969 to 5.4 million in 1982.

Those people of color who have managed to escape the inner cities since the
1960s have been more than replaced by a wide variety of immigrant and migrant
populations—refugees from China, Hong Kong, and Taiwan; those escaping political and economic oppression in South and Central America; Native Americans
seeking employment off reservations; and the like. This "crystallization" of the
underclass is supported by the secondary labor market and its underpaid service
occupations and other menial employment.[3] Massey has also shown that, indeed, a
majority of the most recent immigrants and refugees tend to come from Latin
America and Asian countries.[4] Direct connections between home countries and
inner cities are supported by bridges to family or group economic and social ties.

The economies of these Little Havanas, Manilas, and Hong Kongs help to
support the growth of inequality in the United States. Race is and continues to be
the main determinant of inequality. Whites continue to be overrepresented in white-
collar jobs. They are almost twice as likely as African Americans (1.71 times) and
Latinos (1.97 times) to hold these kinds of jobs. Forty-seven percent of African
Americans and 43 percent of Latinos work in the service sector, compared with only
27 percent of the white community.[5]

The research by Tienda also suggests the growing evidence of poverty among
people of color.[6] She identifies three general conditions for the exclusion of people
of color from the labor market: (1) limited access to education, (2) the role played
by ascription (discrediting by blaming) as a method of placement that triggers
racism and exclusion from participation in political, social, and economic systems,
and (3) uneven distribution of opportunities for social advancement.

Education continues to be both a strength and weakness for communities of
color. When compared to students from foreign countries, American students fair
poorly. Sociologist Rumbaut reported that American-born students spent less than

an hour on homework; foreign-born children spent nearly three hours daily. Third generation American children have an average grade point average of 2.11. In contrast, Vietnamese immigrants scored 2.42, underscoring the value and role played by cultural traditions that have been attacked by the assmilationists in this country (*Sacramento Bee,* February 24, 1994).

## Differences and Similarities

Differences in culture, language, economic, political, and social histories, and the disparate ways the communities of color see their agendas for the future present a picture of diversity. This section of the epilogue addresses the similarities and differences of the communities as presented by the authors. The information is not intended to be used to assure entry into communities or as "correct" organizing rhetoric. It is intended to serve as a place for *beginning* to understand communities of color from a social change perspective. It would be presumptuous to assume that a thorough understanding of any culture can be garnered from a single exposition or book chapter.

The editors have adopted Teresa A. Sullivan's multipurpose model of distinctive populations and subpopulations as a design for their discussion.[7] Sullivan identified minority status, race, time of arrival in the United States, language, and national origin as the most important variables affecting a group's identity with their attendant implications for community organizing.

**Race.** Although the concept of race is useful in the discussion of different skin characteristics (African-American, Asian, etc.), it does not endure in a more analytical look at these communities. For example, within the African-American communities are all gradations of skin tone, from the darkest to the lightest color differentiation. An outsider looking at that community could find no easy skin-color label. The African-American community does not have any unique surnames that can be used for purposes of identification. Many names that have descended through the years were given by masters during slavery. The phenomenon of taking Muslim names is an added variable that must be assessed, for it lends another important dimension to the identifiable characteristics of the group. The confusion this causes in those unaware may prove embarrassing, for there is a potential problem for mistaking one group for another by surname alone.

The issue of color as an indicator of race in the Asian community is further complicated by distinctive physiological characteristics. Again, the uninitiated may fail to distinguish between Japanese Americans, Chinese Americans, Pilipino Americans, Vietnamese, Cambodians, and Laotians. However, to members of those distinct culturally *different* groups, the uniquenesses are readily apparent. It is dangerous to think of the Asian community as monolithic. The chapter on the Southeast Asians, for example, addressed the problems faced by numerous ethnic enclaves within Vietnam, Cambodia and Laos. Add skin hue to the picture, and we can see that there are too many differences to permit an assessment by race alone.

Native Americans are also difficult to identify by racial characteristics alone. Some have been mistaken for Latinos, some for Asians, and some for whites. Most Native Americans have "white" names, unless they, like many African Americans, go back to their tribal or ancestral names.

The Latino community presents an even more complex phenomenon. Because of Spanish colonization, the slave trade from Africa, and the mingling of Indian and Moorish blood, racial characteristics are not easily discerned. Add to this confusion the immigration in the nineteenth and twentieth centuries of Europeans to Latin America and the problem becomes even more complicated. And if these racial characteristics were not confusing enough, we can add Asian racial features to many segments of the population. The Japanese Peruvian elected to the presidency of Peru, Alberto Fujimori, is an excellent example of this. Differences among the Latino population range from black to the fairest of individuals. Further complicating this reality is the use of surnames that may reflect Irish, German, Spanish, Italian, Chinese, or Japanese ancestry. The resulting racial mixture has led to some exotic names in an attempt to classify them, such as mulatto, mestizo, coyote, zambaiqo, lobno, chamiso, morisco, cafe con leche, castizo, etc.[8] In an attempt to unify the various Latin-American racial groups, Vasconcelos identifies Latin Americans as belonging to "La Raza Cósmica."[9] Thus, despite national differences, language and cultural ethos serve to bind Latin Americans into one cosmic identity. However, when asked who they are, they do not answer "Latino." Rather, their answers reflect their cultural nationalism. They say that they are "Cubano," "Chicano," "Salvadoreño," or Puerto Rican, even if they were born in New York or Los Angeles.

To summarize this section of the model, it is important for community organizers not to lump cultural and ethnic groups by skin color alone. There are more differences than similarities when we address the issue of race. All too often organizers work from a stereotype of what they have been socialized to believe is a "typical" individual of color. That stereotype would soon be challenged when they met an African Cuban American whose last name is O'Reardon!

**Language of Choice.** Another significant variable is language. This identifying characteristic was relatively simple until the heavy migrations from Southeast Asia began: communities of color generally spoke English or some variation, or else they spoke Spanish or some variation of it. However, as the model we presented in Chapter 1 indicates, the primary and secondary levels of intensity of contact make speaking in the communities' native language a must. The Southeast Asian community presents new and unique challenges to organizers; the many languages represented in this community are a challenge, even to individuals from that cultural group who have been somewhat removed from the community and have lost fluency in the language. As was also mentioned in chapter 1, organizers must be sensitive to the dialect or parallel language spoken in that inner city. Some of the nuances of language may be class-specific, thereby possibly offending someone from another class, or, what is accepted parlance in one community may be insulting or derogatory in another community with another group speaking the same language but coming from a different country. In sum, it behooves organizers to be aware of the language levels, nuances, idiomatic expressions and accepted slang. Organizers using the accepted mode of speaking will be welcomed allies.

**Time of Arrival in What Is Now the United States.** Time of entry into the United States is significant for both historical and strategic purposes. The implications of time of arrival are germane to issues of pride and self-esteem, citizenship, and of turf and proprietorship. Organizers need to understand the dynamics of time of arrival—both historical and contemporary—so as to better analyze the ethos and sense of community shared by specific communities of color and subgroups within that community.

Native Americans were in the United States long before the white man arrived with his "Manifest Destiny." The Indians lost everything, thereby making them total victims of an external oppressive force. The resultant loss of self-esteem is still experienced today as described in the chapter by Edwards and Egbert-Edwards. Organizers cannot join in the struggle with Native Americans without being sensitive to the issues surrounding their lands.

The Spanish influence on this country has also been significant. Mexicans living in the United States have felt a sense of proprietorship—many still believe that the white man is living illegally on their lands. The heavy influx of Latinos from Cuba and Central America in the last fifteen years has caused a backlash in the dominant society; border crossings have become armed camps, and the Immigration and Naturalization Service has taken on an air of control beyond the mandate of its office. The backlash has been responsible, in part, for the demise of bilingual programs and schools of ethnic studies across the country. Families have been split up by the new immigration laws.

The Cuban experience has been markedly different; being political refugees, they have been victimized by the earlier refugees to places like Dade County, Florida. The 1980 Mariel immigrants received harsh treatment at the hands of the non-Hispanic population as well as some of the conservative Cuban Americans. The fact that many of these new arrivals were Afro-Cuban, male, and young cannot be ignored, for it has played a significant role in the racism and xenophobia experienced by them.

The Puerto-Rican experience, as discussed by Morales in his chapter, is unique. Being part of a commonwealth has given Puerto Ricans citizenship, which permits them to move back and forth between the mainland and the island. Much of their rancor toward the United States has to do with what they see as preferential treatment toward many Cubans and Central Americans because their political refugee status has permitted these groups to obtain social services much more readily than the Puerto Ricans. Another difference is the fact that Puerto Ricans, while experiencing a Diaspora that began in the 1940s, are still being treated as second-class citizens decades after their arrival in the United States, while very recent arrivals have not had to put up with the intensity and length of discrimination suffered by them.

The Asian community's time of arrival in the United States also evokes strong feelings about preferential treatment of one group over another. The classic example, of course, was discussed by Murase in his chapter on the Japanese-American experience in this country. Although the Japanese made their presence known after the Chinese immigrated to the West Coast, it was the Japanese Americans who were put in concentration camps during World War II, not the Chinese. This has led to deep resentment within both communities. Similarly, the Vietnamese friends of the U.S. government were given preferential treatment in resettlement and social services, again causing resentment in other Asian communities. However, the boat people have been victims of gross racism, because they were not part of the preferred group and also because these newest arrivals were poor and therefore largely without connections.

The African-American experience has been well documented. African Americans arrived in this country in the 1600s and have been treated as second-class citizens ever since. Their struggles for liberation and self-esteem have been embittered when they see new arrivals being given preferential treatment. The reparation settlements for the Japanese-American community have come under attack by some African Americans; their position is that their having experienced slavery for hundreds of years also makes them eligible for some kind of reparation.

It must be repeated that organizers cannot get involved with a community without knowing its history within the United States and the implications of that history for organizing strategies. The similarities and differences of the various communities' experiences are deeply ingrained in the degrees of their wishing to belong to the mainstream. The longer a group has been present in this country, the more reliance organizers can place on broader values, a sense of place and history, and the roles these groups can and should play within that continuum. The more recent arrivals require more education about those values and systems, they require an understanding of the double oppression they frequently experience—from inside their communities and outside. The implication of not having citizenship is critical. Experience has shown that people without citizenship are much more reluctant to involve themselves in a public struggle; they are more accepting of the injustices around them. And if that group entered the United States without papers, then it is safe to assume that their fears, negative self-esteem, and unwillingness to involve themselves in a struggle for self-determination and social justice will be greater than those of the above-mentioned communities.

**National Origin.** National origin is an important variable because, as has been stated several times, organizers cannot lump all Asians, Latin Americans, or African

Americans into one monolithic group, assuming that their oppressions are generally similar. Each country has its unique culture, history, political ethos, art forms, and social makeup. One cannot assume that, for example, all Central Americans are the same. In comparing the neighboring countries of Costa Rica and Nicaragua, Harrison has pointed out a multitude of differences that one must recognize and respect.[10]

The many Asian communities' national origins have different languages, cultures and social systems. Some of the histories of these countries have been intertwined since World War II with distrust and even hatreds that have abated but little. Similarly, the Native-American nations share English as a common language, but their tribal customs, languages, and traditions are unique, and successful organizers must get to know these differences.

Citizenship has not helped the quality of life experienced by African Americans and Puerto Ricans, who are born citizens of the United States. Their continued oppression and exploitation have been well documented by Devore and Morales in their respective chapters. A brief observation is in order, however. Many individuals within these communities believe that programs benefiting other communities of color should be available to them; political refugee programs, for example.

**Minority Status.** The confusion between minority and ethnic status has not been resolved by social scientists, planners, or politicians. Traditional definitions of minorities as meaning "fewer than" is no longer valid in such large and diverse states as California, whose population will be over 50 percent people of color by the year 2000. Part of the problem with the term is that it has taken on a definition that is convenient for those interested in labeling communities of color as second-class citizens. To identify a group as belonging to an "ethnic" group means that the community has specific uniqueness—culturally and often linguistically—that remove from it the stigma of being "second class" and places it with many mainstream groups in the country. Thus, Italian, Irish, Jewish, and Polish neighborhoods are seen as "ethnic," while Chinese, Vietnamese, Nicaraguan, and other communities of color are perceived as "minority" neighborhoods. What distinguishes one from the other? What about African-American communities? Those communities of recent arrivals are more "ethnically pure" vis-à-vis the traditional variables of culture and language. Yet the role played by *color* and *racial* differences feeds into the racist views of people who have low toleration for diversity.

This racism and xenophobia continue to be manifested in the media. Thus during the Gulf war all individuals who looked "Arab-like" were accused of being Iraqis, and were victimized by these stereotypes. Foreign accents, unfortunately, are tolerated only if they are West European in origin.

Imagine the reactions of people of color experiencing the racism and xenophobia of the United States for the first time. Latinos, if they are Afro-Cuban, Afro–Puerto Rican, or Mexicans or Central Americans of Indian descent, will not have favorable experiences. Similarly, white Puerto Ricans or other Latinos, who have never perceived themselves as minorities within their countries, are shocked when they come to the United States and are victimized by a society intolerant of their accents. What is especially difficult for organizers to understand about the Latino experience, for example, is the awareness that, notwithstanding the similar experiences of racism and exploitation, not all Latinos identify as minorities. Some are given that status while others are not.[11]

Vietnamese, Cambodians, Chinese, and other Asian groups continue to be perceived as minorities rather than ethnic groups. Nevertheless, whatever the perceptions of the dominant society, white Americans treat groups that have been the majority in their countries (with some exceptions, such as ethnic subgroups within a country) as second-class citizens in the United States.

The implications of minority status perceptions require that organizers be sensitive to the ethos, and possible stigma, shared by the community, especially with recent arrivals. The education that must take place hinges on the notion that these communities must be made to feel like "subjects" rather than "objects," they must be helped to believe that they can effect meaningful changes in their lives and for their communities. They must be worked with to develop a sense of empowerment that leads to action.

## *An Agenda for the Late 1990s*

When asked, communities of color are clear on what they need: jobs, housing, economic revival of inner cities, better health systems, and education. What is less clear, however, are the strategies and tactics deemed most efficacious in achieving these goals.

Although the perceived needs of communities may be similar, some of their cultural and sociopolitical experiences have led to differences in the ways they have perceived their situations and ways to alleviate those problems. Political attitudes range from the extreme right to the extreme left. Some cultural nuances discourage public behavior, while other groups are hampered by the fact that so many of their communities are monolingual in languages other than English. Recent arrivals, especially the undocumented, are often reluctant to engage in self-help activities that may thrust them into the public arena. Further complications are presented by the generational differences found in these communities. With these caveats in mind, we will discuss strategies and tactics that seem the most viable

Based on the conditions described throughout this book, the editors have identified coalition-building, increasing the communities' power base through political and legislative reform, working toward ending racism in all its manifestations, and nurturing the growth of true cultural pluralism.

**Coalition Building.** It is clear that if disenfranchised communities are to be heard they need to join together, identifying common concerns and issues, and present a united front to the world outside. It is also clear that the communities need advocates, brokers, and leaders who are able to hold together diverse interests, agendas, and strategies for change.

The problem in coalition-building arises when we try to identify the cadre responsible for forming the coalition and issues of self-determination within communities and their impact on coalitions.

Historically, coalitions have had difficulty staying together, even when the group was homogeneous. Working with communities of color involves so many problems and so many generational, race, ethnic, and sociopolitical issues that keeping a coalition together seems almost impossible. Added to these problems are concerns over short- versus long-term issues.

Dluhy has identified some of the organizing principles of coalitions as consisting of the following: bread-and-butter, consciousness raising, networking, preassociation, prefederation, and presocial movement.[12] Depending on the rationale for forming the group, there are then structural, political, ideological, resource, staff, membership recruitment, and communications issues that need to be resolved. Thus, organizers interested in forming and working with coalitions must be aware of the dynamics and difficulties in working with them at the various task levels. Given the nature of fear and caution in many communities of color, the process is difficult.

To say that coalitions are best served with single, winnable, issues is too simple; the many concerns intrinsic to communities of color are such that, in our opinion isolating single issues around which to organize is too difficult. This may be the prudent way to organize, but experience has shown that when organizers are working with their communities, it is difficult to maintain a single focus at the expense of other concerns.

Should white people work with communities of color through coalitions? As has been pointed out in the introduction to the book, there have been instances in the history of social change where organizers from outside the community served specific and successful roles in bringing about meaningful change. What is different today, however, are the dynamics of the inner cities with their racial and ethnic representation. We have to fall back on our Organizer's Contact Intensity and Influence model from chapter 1. The organizer needs to determine the level of coalition-building at which he or she is functioning. Simply stated, it is foolish for an organizer not from the community—racially, linguistically, or culturally—to attempt to gain the confidence and trust of the community. The organizer will have that many strikes against her or him to start with. However, we are aware that there are always exceptions to the preference stated here. This is particularly the case in circumstances where the coalition includes white organizations or multicultural organizations (which include whites). In sum, the coalition-building task has to be undertaken within the unique context presented by the organizing challenge.

**Politics and Legislative Reform.** The 1990s present challenges to communities of color that are comparable to those of the civil rights work of the 1960s. The steady erosion of civil rights since Ronald Reagan became president has been swift and thorough. President George Bush's veto of the 1990 Civil Rights Act does not augur well for the years ahead. Moreover, the appointment of conservatives to the Supreme Court presents a challenge to communities of color for the next thirty years. Each community has its own agenda. That is understandable and to be encouraged. However, organizers working within these communities need to develop a shared vision of the struggles ahead and set limits to compromises that lead to partial victories. The unfulfilled Clinton agenda presents little new hope.

*Political actors must be careful not to let secondary issues, such as the filling of affirmative action quotas, deflect attention from the more fundamental issues of economic bifurcation and rising poverty among some minority groups.*[11]

Although there have been some isolated victories around the country, like the Japanese-American movement for reparations, the struggle for social justice is foundering because the onslaught of the conservative movement is so strong. Vu-Duc Vuong, author of the chapter on Southeast Asians, ran for the Board of Supervisors in San Francisco, California. Although he lost his bid for the seat, he helped raise the consciousness of the white community about the plight of Southeast Asians in the Bay Area. This was the first time a Southeast Asian had ever run for political office in San Francisco—that in itself was a small symbolic victory.

**Racism.** Communities of color must get together to fight for an end to racism. We are addressing the racism experienced by them from both outside the community and from other communities of color. Kenji Murase, in his chapter on Japanese Americans, warns against "exceptionalism," where the white community defines a particular community of color as a "model minority" because it embraces the values of the white middle class. What follows, of course, is the logical conclusion that the other communities of color are lacking, because they have a deficit that does not make them exceptional.

Finally, we caution against the malignancy of intracommunity racism. Several of our authors have addressed this sad dilemma. Organizers need to be prepared to deal with it, especially organizers from a different cultural and racial group who have gained the confidence of groups other than their own. Tienda notes:

*The looming question for the 1990s revolves around the course of political participation of minority groups, and the viability of rainbow coalitions to provide economic and social concessions to minority constituencies, as well as protecting the gains achieved during the 1960s and early 1970s. But, in defining and striving for collective economic and social goals through "rainbow" political strategies, it is important to recognize that growing divisions within and between groups, with their deep class and regional underpinnings, almost certainly will undermine the formulation of collective minority agendas designed to improve the economic position of all people of color.*

**Social Work.** How might social work respond more effectively to the challenges presented by communities of color and those wanting to work in them?

The trends that have clearly emerged in the 1990s point to what many consider a sellout of the original mandates of the profession. Specht has taken a critical position against those who, he believes, have made an about-face from the original mission of the profession.[13] Specht points out the surveys by the National Association of Social Workers showing that 75 to 80 percent of social workers in this country are committed to psychotherapy as a major form of intervention. Specht makes a passionate plea for social workers to get involved in building strong communities.

A research study published in *Social Work* underscores Specht's concerns. In answering the question "is social work racist?" McMahon and Allen-Meares point out the disturbing trends in the social work literature from the 1980s.[5]

*Social work, by adopting an individualistic approach, tends to blame the victim while ignoring the ecological perspective and person-in-environment configuration. It gives lip service to fighting conditions of poverty, institutional practices that perpetuate racism, and other conditions external to the individual.*

Writing about how social work deals with people of color, the authors state:

*the surveyed literature, by adopting a generally individualistic approach, ignores societal conditions and the ecological perspective. Taken as a whole, as a decade's reflection on social work practice with minorities, the literature can be categorized as naive and superficial. It can devalue minority values by urging or expecting minority clients to accept and assimilate the social and family values of the majority society.*

And

*Social workers, therefore, must be more than sensitive or aware; they must be antiracist if there is not going to be a breach between their ideals and reality. Being antiracist implies transformative action to remove the conditions that oppress people. There is no neutral position. Not to take a stand is a political statement in itself because it reinforces the present institutional racism. Antiracist social work means both helping people reflect on their situation so that they can understand the oppressive system they are in and working with them to change it. It means a shift in practice to social activism and social change by working for racial equality and social justice.*

Are schools of social work (and others who prepare students for the human services) responsible for offering training to those who want to work in these communities? The editors believe they are. Either they are, or the rhetoric of support for diversity, equality, and social justice needs to be made consistent with what is offered. Otherwise, to maintain the rhetoric without the community involvement is to perpetuate a fraud, a fraud borne of promises all too often in the past honored by avoiding and sidestepping issues that bring the academic program into conflict with universities, powerful welfare programs, institutions, or governmental bodies.

For social work—educational programs and local units of the National Association of Social Workers—this means actively and aggressively recruiting students of color, building appropriate support structures so that these students can be retained, and finding the scholarships, paid field work, and loan funding that will make it possible for these students to survive economically. Without a strong base of economic support, the commitment to diversity and community organization is mostly hot air. Indeed, social work's pretentious language without action to support it makes a mockery of what we say we believe, and undermines our recruitment of minority students who truly want to serve their communities.

At the same time, there is much that can be done to support research, especially ethnographically sound research, in communities of color. There is little reason why our assistance cannot be put at the service of ethnic enclaves as it has been put at the service of welfare departments, mental health agencies, and public schools.

The curricula of schools of social work can be greatly enriched by the documented experiences of both established and emerging communities of color. Indeed, this should be regarded as a marvelous opportunity for the growth and development of what we know about people of color, but in this case clearly adjusted to take account of local—state, city, and neighborhood—conditions.

The issue of multicultural education in schools of social work needs to be addressed. It is imperative that the curriculum be sensitive to the inclusion of materials on communities of color. Even though the Council on Social Work Education has an accreditation standard that requires such material in the curriculum, some schools of social work have made the material—watered down at best—an elective course. We believe that the material must be taught in a required course, but also that it be disseminated throughout the curriculum. In that way students will learn about communities of color from a total social work perspective, clearly needed in a society that is reluctant to pay attention to understanding and working with communities of color.

Given the limitations of the job market for organizers and community developers, academic programs need to reflect better not only full-time roles for organizers, but part-time (or "own time") opportunities as well. However, such efforts are no substitute or excuse for not vigorously seeking to develop employment opportunities for students of color (and white students) who want to help empower emerging and changing communities of color. An unscientific, but fairly comprehensive survey of a national sample of schools of social work suggests that such efforts on any major scale are virtually nonexistent. Surely, this arena has room for a great deal of work.

There is also a sense, as noted by a number of our authors, that many people of color continue to feel that their interests are the last attended to, regardless of the economic situation. As one young Latino put it, "Upturn or downturn, somehow it's never our turn." The political conservatism that has extended from the 1980s into the 1990s suggests an extension of a celebration of "diversity" with a lot of rhetoric, modest high-visibility programs (filled with "photo opportunities"), and very limited medium- and long-term financial commitments. Given the budgetary constraints that now appear likely to extend into the late 1990s, especially in light of deficit reduction and proposed health care and welfare reform, this resource problem is not going to take care of itself. It would appear, then, that one part of the social work commitment to the maintenance of efforts in minority communities will involve working with those communities (and other local organizations, like the Urban League) to secure public and private external funding.

Certainly there will be roles for white people in these funding efforts. There will be, just as certainly, roles for white people in a variety of activities described by the authors and the editors. However, white organizers must resist the tendency to slip, slide, or be pushed into inappropriate leadership roles, especially because they feel they can "do it better" or "do it more quickly." They must also resist the all-too-human temptation to allow their feelings to be hurt (and thus withdraw from the field of action) if they are regarded with suspicion or their commitment to a particular group of color seems denigrated. There are no "Friend of Minorities of Color" stripes to be won and then kept forever.

For organizers of color and white organizers, there will be no quick fix or easy answers. Coalitions may need to form, devolve, and come together again. But the rapid changes occurring in communities across the country demand sustained vigilance if anything approaching full advantage of the opportunities to back social work's rhetoric with action is to be taken.

## Conclusion

The chapters of this book may be regarded as a challenge, an agenda for community organizers with a commitment to working with communities of color. Issues and problems have been identified, along with change experiences and the strategies and tactics that may bring about meaningful change in the future.

Disenfranchised, abandoned, and underserved communities of color need organizers with an abiding commitment to helping these communities establish and re-establish dignity and opportunity. In this area of developing information super-highways, perhaps what is most urgently needed is a new vision, or a series of new visions. If empowerment is to have any real meaning beyond posturing, communities of color must be supported in building and controlling their own visions of the future and be aided in the difficult struggle to realize those visions. But the challenge that this represents should not be regarded as merely a local or regional phenomenon. As many of our authors have pointed out, the role and power of America in the world will be influenced by the nation's treatment of communities of color. These larger connections must not be neglected in a world where ancestral homes of people of color are becoming increasingly close to our everyday lives. This continuity can be actively supported to sustain a sense of pride and belonging, or neglected and further contribute to a sense of discrimination and loss. If the promise of diversity is ever to become a reality, it must embrace a future where participation in social change can lead toward empowerment and power, justice and self-respect.

## *Endnotes*

1. U.S. Bureau of the Census, *Current Population Reports,* Series P-60, "Characteristics of the Population Below the Poverty Level, 1982" (Washington, D.C.: Government Printing Office, 1984).

2. Rivera, F. G., and Erlich, J. L., "Neogemeinschaft Minority Communities: Implications for Community Organization in the United States," *Community Development Journal,* 16 (October 1981): 189–200.

3. Wilson, William J., *The Truly Disadvantaged* (Chicago: University of Chicago Press, 1987).

4. Massey, D. S., "Dimensions of the New Immigration to the United States and the Prospects for Assimilation," *Annual Review of Sociology,* 7 (1981): 57–85.

5. McMahon, Anthony, and Allen-Meares, Paula, "Is Social Work Racist? A Content Analysis of Recent Literature," *Social Work,* 37, no. 6 (November 1992): 533–539.

6. Tienda, Marta, "Race, Ethnicity and the Portrait on Inequality: Approaching the 1990s," *Sociological Spectrum,* 9 (1989): 23–52.

7. Sullivan, Teresa A. "A Democratic Portrait," in Pastora San Juan Cafferty and William C. McCready (eds.), *Hispanics in the United States: A New Social Agenda* (New Brunswick, NJ: Transaction Books, 1965).

8. Morner, Magnus, *La Mezcla de Razas en la Historia de America Latina* (Buenos Aires: Paidos, 1969). Translated by Jorge Piatigorsky as *Race Mixture in the History of Latin America* (London: Little Brown & Co).

9. Vasconcelos, Jose, *La Raza Cosmica,* 4th ed. (Mexico: Espasa-Calpe Mexicana, S. A., 1976).

10. Harrison, Lawrence E., *Underdevelopment Is a State of Mind* (Cambridge: Center for International Affairs, Harvard University & University Press of America, 1985).

11. Meenaghan, Thomas, "Macro Practice: Current Trends and Issues," in National Association of Social Workers *Encyclopedia of Social Work,* 18th ed. (Silver Spring, MD: NASW, 1987), 85.

12. Dluhy, J. Milan, with the assistance of Sanford L. Kravitz, *Building Coalitions in the Human Services* (Newbury Park, Sage Publications, 1990), 25.

13. Specht, Harry, *Unfaithful Angeles: How Social Work Abandoned Its Mission* (New York: Free Press, 1994).

---

# Examples from Training Manual, Center for Third World Organizing (Oakland, California)

**Organizing: What It Is and What It Isn't
(from: Center for Community Change—Rachel Sierra)**

| What It Is | What It Isn't |
|---|---|
| 1. A process, a way of getting to a goal. | 1. A goal by itself. E.g., building the organization for the sake of numbers, instead of as the structure which allows action on issues. |
| 2. Gets affected people together to decide on a course of action. | 2. One person deciding on an issue. E.g., Organizer or Board person would decide that "we need to work on nursing homes." They would give petitions to rest of Board and Staff. |
| 3. Allows people to act collectively in order to build/maximize the experience of collective power. | 3. Doesn't allow one or two people to assume all leadership and decision-making roles. E.g., countless CBOs that have fallen apart when the director leaves. |

4. Works toward a goal consistent with vision.

4. Not based solely on potential for victory. E.g., if we're working toward justice, two dozen stop signs ain't gonna do it.

5. Building on past victories and strategies. For example, PCMs naturally move to unemployment and jobs as the priority after workforce.

5. Jumping from issue to victory to the next issue promising victory.

6. Reflects ongoing efforts to broaden base and develop leadership.

6. Satisfied with 4 or 5 people who will work now and forever (Amen).

7. Acknowledges the need to sustain victory with deeper (or other) work.

7. Over with "the victory." E.g., fight for a rehab program and then go home. City develops a homeowner rehab program when it was renters that fought for the victory!

8. Allows people to develop a sense of power and control over their lives so they quit assuming a posture that they're asking for a favor. Experience of power, coupled with vision, allows people to feel "we have a right to . . ." E.g., No to Workfare! Yes to Fair Work.

8. Just changing someone's mind about "their" money. E.g., people should move away from "begging" for CDBG funds. CDBG is poor people's money.

## Campaigns

**Definition.** Organizing campaigns are large-scale activities focusing on a specific issue. In a campaign, organizations define and fight around issues to benefit both individual people and the organization.

### Reasons to Do a Campaign

1. Common experience for all members.
2. Direct action lets members confront the people who make decisions about their lives and take new roles by disrupting the system.
3. Concrete framework gives members real experience to base their analysis on.
4. Leadership development happens as members take on new roles.

5. Good campaigns can win changes that make a real difference to the individuals in your organization and their communities.

## *Characteristics of a Campaign*

1. Clear time frame:

   - We know about how long this campaign will take.
   - We have goals and set times to evaluate how we're doing.
   - Short campaigns give a sense of immediate power, but false expectations for how quickly things work.
   - Long campaigns can cause burnout, but also win bigger things and give more opportunities for leadership.

2. Clear target or enemy:

   - We focus on someone who has the power to give us what we want or can pressure the people who do.
   - Our target may change through the campaign, but it is always a specific person, not a vague institution.

3. Clear issues:

   - Our campaign issue automatically leads people to think of the solution. If the problem is unemployment, we may say the issue is that new jobs don't go to neighborhood people, the demand = 100 jobs to local workers in the latest redevelopment project.

4. Clear constituency:

   - People want to be part of your organization, making decisions, doing day-to-day work. Example: If you do a campaign on bilingual education, your constituency is likely to be recent immigrants with children in the school system.

5. Opportunities for confronting power and dramatizing the issue:

   - Campaigns should let members come face to face against powerful people as a group, rather than taking individual routes through the proper channels. Exaggerate the issue to bring attention to and educate people about your side, and to drag the terrain of battle away from your opposition.

## *Who Goes Where? Identifying Constituents and Allies Exercise*

Your organization, People Fighting for Our Neighborhoods, has built a reputation by working on neighborhood problems in the poorest part of a small city, such as traffic, clean up of empty lots, etc. You have one full-time organizer, 100 dues-paying members, and a solid core of 10–12 members. The core members have experience in dealing with the city structure. Most of your members are African-American, but there are also many Spanish-speaking and Asian immigrant peoples living in the community.

At your last membership meeting, the leaders decided that the organization is ready to take on some larger issues to tie all the individual neighborhoods together. They have identified problems in the local public elementary schools that affect children in all of the neighborhood—the classes are overcrowded, children are often forced to go to school in other neighborhoods, while 90 percent of the students are of color, only 5 percent of the teachers are, and 50 percent of students drop out before the tenth grade. There are no bilingual classes in the system. Your group is committed to being a neighborhood based organization controlled by people who live on the southside and are most affected by policies applying to that area.

This is a list of people who are possible constituents and allies of your organization:

> Families who live in the southside (African and African-American, Latino, Asian)
> Vietnamese Fisherman's Association
> Cape Verdean Family Services Clinic
> Cambodian New Generation
> Latino Rights Project
> School principals
> Teachers union
> Service Employees International Union, Local 212 (representing janitors, secretaries)
> Social workers
> School board members
> Single people who live in the neighborhoods
> Senior Citizens United
> Ministerial Alliance

Which of these people do you want to join your organization and why? How will you reach them?

Which would make good allies? What might be the self-interest of those individuals or organizations?

## Defining and Choosing an Issue

I. The purpose of this session is:

1. to teach the difference between a problem and an issue.
2. to show that organizing is systematic and that are ways to figure things out that can be relied on to produce consistently good answers.

**Issue:** La Fiesta supermarket in Watts wants a license to begin sale of liquor at the market

**Pro:** Owner wants to sell liquor to increase profits.

**Con:** Community groups opposed because of increased problems from liquor sales (crime, drugs, etc.).

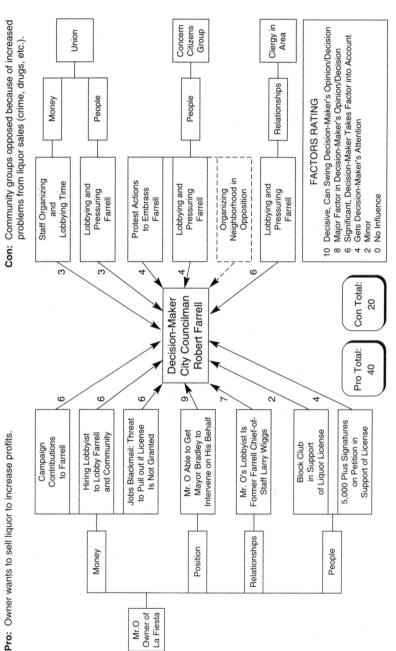

FACTORS RATING

10 Decisive, Can Swing Decision-Maker's Opinion/Decision
8 Major Factor in Decision-Maker's Opinion/Decision
6 Significant, Decision-Maker Takes Factor into Account
4 Gets Decision-Maker's Attention
2 Minor
0 No Influence

Con Total: 20

Pro Total: 40

**Sample "Tactical" Power Analysis**

263

**3.** to develop a check list of what makes a good issue.

**4.** to discourage subjective methods of choosing an issue such as "work on the worst problem first" or "help the poorest people first."

**5.** to show that there is a relationship between the issue chosen and the kind of organization that develops as a result of working on that issue.

**6.** to show participants a method of choosing an issue that they can then take and use within their own organizations.

**II.** Outline

There is an important difference between a problem and an issue. In this session we will draw that distinction, and then develop a check list for what makes a good organizing issue. Following that, we will put the information to work by doing an exercise that will look at different issues.

**III.** Issues vs. Problems

All of us hear about problems. Rising tuition is a problem, war is a problem, unemployment is a problem, racism is a problem. We don't organize on problems. We organize on issues. An issue is a root cause of a problem. Root causes will help organizations define the demands and goals of the campaign.

Not all issues work for all organizations. Some are objectively better than others. What are some criteria that an issue must meet to be good for an organization? Here is a list of some criteria that will help your group in making a smart decision. A good issue must:

**1.** Conform to three basic principles of organizing:

- Win real victories that improve people's lives.
- Make people aware of their power.
- Alter the relations of power by building staffed, permanent, and strong organizations.

**2.** Be winnable. How do you know? Experience. Who won it elsewhere? Have you a plan for winning? What will it cost the other side if you win? Do you have the resources (people and money)?

**3.** Be easy to understand. Test leaflet one paragraph.

**4.** Be widely and deeply felt. Are your members excited/concerned about this issue? Do they feel it is important? Are they willing to do something about it? Is the public interested/sympathetic?

**5.** Have a clear target. More than one if possible. A target is a person who can give you what you want. A target is always a person. It is never a board, an elected body, etc. Personalize the target. There are two types: Primary and Secondary. A primary target is the person who can give you what you want. A secondary target is a person who can put pressure on the primary.

**6.** Timeline a clear time frame. Beginning, middle, and end. Internal and external time frame. Is this the right time to do this?

**7.** Be able to raise money.

**8.** Be nondivisive, at least within your membership.

**9.** Build leadership and membership. Will people join your organization to work on this issue? Will the issue give opportunities for leaders to develop their skills? One that wouldn't is an issue that must be won in court. The lawyer becomes the leader. Other people learn to depend on lawyers.

**10.** Set up for next issue. Will this issue lead to next issue? Will it build for your organization a working knowledge and reputation for working on this issue that will help with the next one?

## What Organizations Get from Action

- Actions Bring Results:

  When effective, a strategy undertaken by a citizen group can force the existing structure to undergo enormous changes. Sometimes change is slow and imperceptible, and many groups disintegrate because results are too long in coming. But action makes a push on the system and forces an immediate reaction, which often serves as a weathervane (as the song says): to see which way the wind blows.

- Actions Bring Others into the Organization:

  Action draws attention to an issue: it makes some people aware (or reminded) of the problem; it gets many people stirred up; it shows people that you're a group that's making itself heard. Action, then, brings people into the organization at three levels:

  **1.** *Membership increases.* When Sam Lovejoy toppled the tower membership increased in the AEC from roughly 30 people to over 100: the community development projects in New York City have resulted in vastly increased participation in community projects.

  **2.** *Support increases.* In a town vote, nearly half the county opposed the nuclear power plant.

  **3.** *Coalitions are built.* The Jacksonville Coalition had to enlist the aid of other groups in the community before it won its case; the AEC got the help of "less radical" energy concerngroups—ecology and conservation groups within the system—thereby improving credibility in the community.

- Action Affects Power Relationships:

  Most people are powerless because of the manipulative power of a few. Effective action can redistribute that power to citizens. It can give people control over production, housing, economic development, jobs, utility rates and the media.

- Action Can Cause Broader Changes in the Community:

  First, it *raises the consciousness of the public:* the entire community is affected when one portion of the system is altered or challenged. The changes brought about in TV programming in Jacksonville no doubt affected everyone who watched the station. The model of self-sufficiency and economic independence which the New York City neighborhood provides other low income neighborhoods cannot help but influence and pave the way for future endeavors.

Secondly, it *can build a movement:* the AEC has not only delayed the Montague nuclear power plant so far, it has also helped thousands of people explore alternative sources of energy and self-sufficient life-styles. Over 2,000 people rallied to stop the Seabrook nuclear power plant; the occupation attracted support and created movements throughout the country.

Finally, it *can provide incentive for other groups:* it's always good for morale for anyone working for social change to read about another community organization's victory or success. Sometimes it can energize and inspire members of a dragging organization to keep going. A success for one can be considered a success for all, especially if the organizer seizes the opportunity.

| | |
|---|---|
| DOORKNOCKING: | Doorknocking is a give-and-take process of LISTENING ("The kids haven't anywhere to play" may mean the issue is a park), PERSUADING ("Of course, one person alone can't fight these big utilities, but if we have a group . . . "), and ASKING ("Will you join? Will you come to the first meeting?"). Much must be accomplished in the span of only several minutes. (*Community Organizing Handbook #1,* published by The Institute, 1976) |

## *DOORKNOCKING SEQUENCE*

**1.** Getting in the door . . .

- Introduce yourself and the organization and explain why you're at their door.
- Ask to come in to talk to them about problems in their neighborhood.

**2.** Breaking the ice . . .

- After sitting down, repeat your name and organization.
- Get their name, confirm address, get phone #, write it down.
- Glance around. Ask or acknowledge something you observe.
- Ask them how long they've lived in the area/if they know their neighbors.

**3.** What makes them tick . . .

- Ask what they think are the major problems in their neighborhood.

- Ask if they would like to do something about these problems.
- Explain that the organization brings people together to work on issues such as those the members decide is a priority.

**4.** Ask a person to join . . .

- Explain the issue that members are working on. Ask if they support the issue.
- Explain what membership means. Use props (i.e., membership card).
- Ask the person if he/she would like to join others in their neighborhood in fighting these issues. Name other people on the block who joined.
- Ask him/her to become a member. Collect dues. Issue card.

**5.** Increase the commitment . . .

- Invite him/her to the next meeting or action.
- Ask for names of neighbors who may also want to join.
- Ask him/her to do something for the organization (doorknock neighbors, host housemeeting, volunteer in office).
- Congratulate, thank, flatter, acknowledge.

## *Tips . . . What If . . .*

| | |
|---|---|
| The television is on . . . | Ask to turn it off or down |
| A person is silent . . . | Ask open-ended questions that require more than yes/no answers |
| A person is too busy to talk to you . . . | tell him/her you will not take up a lot of time (5 min.) or . . . ask when is a better time to come back |
| They ask a question you don't know the answer to . . . | Be honest, say you don't know, and tell them you will find out and let them know (call them back or visit them again!) |
| Don't hear no . . . | Hesitation does not mean NO, give more information or ask more questions |
| Get a yes or a no . . . | Ask for membership in different ways so that they get a clear yes or no |
| What to take . . . | Flyers, doorknocking cards, membership cards, pencil, pen |
| Be yourself . . . | Keep an open mind, be friendly, be honest, make eye contact, HAVE FUN!! |

## *House Meetings: Description*

A house meeting is a small gathering of friends who meet at the home of someone they know and trust.

The purpose of the house meeting is to discuss issues of concern and develop specific ways to work together, as a group, to address these issues.

House meetings are an effective way to bring new members into a community group. They provide a personal and comfortable environment where people can get to know each other, learn about community issues, become familiar with your group.

Because they are small gatherings, they provide an opportunity for people to listen to each other, ask questions, share ideas, and become informed. In the process, people can discuss ways to get involved in the organization that are best suited to their skills and interests.

A house meeting involves a host or hostess, a leader from your organization and some guests.

A host/hostess plans the house meeting with an organization leader. They pick a time and date for the meeting, decide who to invite, and plan what will happen. The host/hostess then invites the guests. Five (guests) is a good number.

The house meeting itself should last an hour and a half, at most. During the meeting, the host/hostess and organization leader work together to make the guests feel comfortable, lead the discussion, present the issues of concern, and generate interest in the group.

The goal of each house meeting is for the guests to become informed and involved. Each guest should leave with some specific thing to do.

At the end of the meeting, guests should be left with some written information such as factsheets, membership applications, or "things to do" lists.

The host/hostess should follow up on the meeting by checking back with the guests to get their reactions and encourage their involvement. The organization leader should follow up with the host/hostess to evaluate the house meeting and discuss ways for the guests to become active members in the group.

A successful house meeting will inspire guests to join your group and sponsor their own house meeting. Since your organization may begin growing at a fast pace, a house meeting coordinator should be selected so that someone is responsible for keeping track of each house meeting and new members.